"The man who writes about himself and his own time is the only man who writes about all people and all time."

George Bernard Shaw

To "love at first sight," and to my wife,
Lisa, who proved it can happen.

Contents

Chapter 1	The Enchanter Beckons	1
Chapter 2	The Ideal Boat	32
Chapter 3	Let The Adventure Begin	47
Chapter 4	Winter In The Caribbean	59
Chapter 5	Three Hurricanes	78
Chapter 6	India And Nepal	91
Chapter 7	Solo Voyage And Shipwreck	102
Chapter 8	Karakoram Expedition	112
Chapter 9	Second Marriage	127
Chapter 10	Near-Miss In Mid-Atlantic	136
Chapter 11	A Mistral And The French Canals	153
Chapter 12	Tonga Kilamanjaro And Obergurgl	177
Chapter 13	Panama Canal And Ecuador	198
Chapter 14	Corsica	210
Chapter 15	India, James Bay And Greece	226
Chapter 16	Thirteen Years As A Vagabond	241
Afterthoughts		251

CHAPTER ONE

THE ENCHANTER BECKONS

There is a violent snowstorm raging in the Laurentian hills of Québec, where I am now living in this beautifully appointed country house, near the picturesque ski village of Saint Sauveur. I am nestled in a high wingback chair in front of a roaring log fire burning in the fieldstone fireplace. It's snowing so hard I can barely see the lake, which is only a few metres in front of my window. There is something intrinsically comforting about being so warm and protected from the elements while outside nature is storming so inhospitably. It puts me in a contemplative mood.

I have rented this house for the winter and it is perfectly suited to my present circumstances. I feel like a Turkish pasha indulged by all this comfort, all these bedrooms with connecting bathrooms, this delightful wood-paneled study with built-in bookshelves and a wall of windows facing the lake. The dining room, also paneled, has an indoor barbeque grill, and the kitchen would make Julia Child feel right at home. There is a sauna for *après ski* use, but I'm not much of a sauna person. I make myself an espresso with my Italian coffee maker, one of the few possessions I brought with me when I moved here from the farm, and sit down at my desk. Today, I will put the finishing touches to a very important letter, which will completely change the direction of my life.

I am a forty-two-year-old airline captain at the top of my game. I came to Montréal seventeen years ago to join Air Canada and, if I continue with this job and stay healthy, I can look forward to another eighteen years before compulsory retirement at age sixty. It's a balanced equation, and although my high-salaried years are mostly ahead of me, I am smack in the middle of my chosen career. I came to Air Canada from the Royal Canadian Navy, where I had been flying anti-submarine aircraft off the flight deck of the aircraft carrier *Bonaventure*. Former naval pilots will tell you that once you have flown off the deck of an aircraft carrier at night, in bad weather with rough seas, nothing else in life can seriously challenge you. I came to my airline job thinking I knew everything there was to know about flying: then really began to learn the skills of the profession from the highly competent captains with whom I flew as their first officer. Most of these captains had been bomber pilots in World War Two and could have flown the box the aircraft came in. Flying is not only about hand/eye coordination. All airline pilots can fly the aircraft well. Rather, it's about experience and judgment: what to do when unusual circumstances are encountered for the first time, how to make the right command decisions which will lead to the most satisfactory outcome. After several years of such tutelage, I was ready to become a captain myself.

Being a captain for a major air carrier like Air Canada is a dream job. Most pilots have to be dragged from their cockpits when they reach mandatory retirement age. Another thing about airline pilots: they love their job so much (don't tell airline management) that they would probably continue without pay if that were the only way to fly. Also, contrary to popular belief, captains work in a totally stress-free environment, as they are given full discretion to match their full responsibility. This means that if they don't like any situation for any reason, they have absolute authority to correct it. All airline pilots will take the safest and surest path away from a potential problem and will never be asked to justify their decision. Any captain who feels stressed is in the wrong job and does not understand the concept of unchallenged discretion. I am often asked how pilots handle the huge responsibility for the lives of so many passengers. The answer is that pilots operate their aircraft in exactly the same professionally competent manner whether the flight is full or empty. It makes absolutely no difference how many people are sitting behind you.

The snowstorm seems to be easing a little at the moment, and the wind is abating. If you're an opera fan like me, the weather has changed from the stormy opening act of Otello to the cotton-wool snowflakes in the third act of La Bohème. I can just make out the silhouette of the boathouse down by the lake. I throw another log on the fire and stoke the coals. It's almost time for afternoon tea. Tomorrow, I am going with friends to the mountain resort of Mont Tremblant for a day's skiing. My next flight is not for three days, when I'm scheduled to fly from Montréal to New York and back; then return to New York for an overnight stay in Manhattan at the Roosevelt Hotel. I will try to get tickets for the musical, Cats, which has recently opened on Broadway.

Above my writing desk hangs a framed quotation, which I also brought with me from the farm when I moved to this house a few weeks ago. I have forgotten where or when I first came across it, but the text has haunted me ever since that fateful day and has become my mantra. It reads:

"What if the spell of a place falls upon a youthful heart, and the bright horizon calls? Many a thing will keep until the world's work is done, and youth is only a memory. When the old enchanter came to my door, laden with dreams, I reached out with both hands for I knew that he would not be lured with the gold that I might later offer, when age had come upon me."

I scan this gem of wisdom one more time, knowing the reasoning is absolutely irrefutable, and remain convinced that the time has come for me to follow the call of the "bright horizon" and realize those dreams before it really is too late.

I finish my letter of resignation to Air Canada with absolute confidence and conviction. I will quit this job in eight months, on the first of September 1984, and seek my fortune wherever destiny leads me. One thing is certain: if I don't leave now and grasp the dreams the "old enchanter" is promising, I will never forgive myself later in life.

I feel as if I'm riding in the first class section of a very fast, luxurious express train, a hybrid of the Orient Express and the Japanese bullet train. I am surrounded by all the comforts anyone could wish for and can see for miles ahead because the track is dead straight. The train is heading at full speed, non-stop, to my retirement age of sixty. I know that I must somehow find a way to jump off before it's too late, and before my short allotted time on this earth has expired. If I happen to meet my fellow passengers - my airline pilot colleagues - in eighteen years when we are all in our sixties, and their train has reached its destination without me, I have no idea what I'll be able to recount about my life. But if I stay on this train, my life story will be the same as theirs, and a pretty predictable one.

I don't remember when the dream to take off on a sailing adventure began to take form in my consciousness, but the seed was probably sown when I was a small boy growing up on the Cornish coast of southwest England. My parents had rented a house on the beach in the pretty seaside village of Harlyn Bay, near Padstow. The house was furnished and included a huge library stocked with a treasure trove of interesting children's books. I remember reading all of Arthur Ransome's adventure books and also Kenneth Graham's *"The Wind in the Willows,"* which forged an indelible impression. In the first chapter, Ratty, the sage boatman, tells his new friend, the timid mole, as they row down the river together:

"Believe me, my young friend, there is nothing - absolutely nothing - half so much worth doing as simply messing around in boats."

The water rat, daydreaming as he spoke, inadvertently rammed his boat into the riverbank. Undaunted, he continued his monologue about boats:

"In or out of 'em it doesn't matter. Nothing seems to really matter that's the charm of it. Whether you get away or whether you don't; whether you arrive at your destination or whether you reach somewhere else, or whether you never get there at all, you're always busy, and you've never done anything in particular; and when you've done it there's always something else to do."

Quite a metaphor for an adventurous life, and a very compelling road map for a nine year old who was trying to grasp the meaning of his existence. Now, at the age of forty-two, I am ready to adopt the water rat's philosophy. Part of my new life will certainly be spent "messing around in boats."

It has finally stopped snowing, and it's time to put the kettle on for afternoon tea. I admit that I don't follow the English tea rituals too rigidly. Warming up the teapot beforehand and putting milk in the cup before pouring the tea don't seem to matter, but I do like my "cuppa" in the afternoon accompanied by something sweet. The day would be incomplete without it. I always use three tea bags, make sure the kettle is on a rolling boil before pouring the water into the teapot, and let the tea steep for a minimum of five minutes before serving it with milk. My dear father goes crazy if the teapot is not pre-warmed and he goes ballistic if the milk is not put into the cup first. I have often threatened to conduct a blind taste test with him to see if he really can tell the difference, but have always demurred as a dutiful son should.

Twenty-five years ago when he drove me to Union Station in Ottawa, my father imparted one last piece of advice, which I suspect is another reason I'm moving on from Air Canada. I was leaving home to become a naval officer and was on my way by train to the Royal Canadian Naval College, *HMCS Venture*, in Victoria. His parting words on the platform were: "Malcolm, as you go through life, never refuse an invitation." I have always done my utmost to follow this wise counsel both with reference to social occasions and as it applies more generally to life's serendipitous opportunities. It has never failed me. I suppose he was telling me: "Whenever you have the chance to try something new or different, grab it." Now I have the opportunity of a lifetime, and there's no way I'm going to let it slip through my fingers.

I have decided to submit my resignation when I go to the airport for my next flight, but I do feel as if I am committing treason. My fellow pilots love their way of life so much: they will never understand my motives for leaving. However, there is a big disconnect in the way most airline pilots view themselves and their work. They rarely admit that their flights can often be boring and repetitive. Sitting for long hours at thirty-five thousand feet, while waiting to land at the final destination, is not too exhilarating. I suspect most pilots have a blind spot on this issue, no doubt caused by the over-riding positive factors of high salaries, agreeable working conditions, lots of time off, and a genuine love of flying. Many pilots have other jobs and hobbies to keep themselves busy when they are not flying. As for me, I have been a full-time farmer for the past seven years, growing cereal crops, raising sheep and cattle, managing my forest, and making maple syrup.

For obvious reasons, it is not a great idea for airline pilots to be overly creative while at the controls. An engine failure during takeoff or any other emergency requires an instinctive, disciplined and highly professional reaction. It is not the time to experiment with a new-fangled procedure to see if it works. Pilots do exercise their creative talents in their spare time, but it can be very difficult to turn on the artistic tap for short periods and then resume the strict, highly-programmed mindset needed for the next flight. After eighteen years as an airline pilot, I am keen to develop my creative side and discover my true potential.

Finally and most crucially, I believe that the most important thing in life is how we manage the preciously small amount of time we are allotted. As soon as we are old enough to reason, we know that our time on earth is finite. Most of us suppress this unpleasant idea when we are growing up, but sooner or later the realization that we are not immortal slowly comes into focus. I am convinced that if I want to spend part of my life adventuring and exploring this magnificent planet, I can't afford to wait until I'm sixty to begin. Either I take the time to do it in this life, or gamble that there will be another one.

As if to prove that point, after two days skiing at Mont Tremblant and a small dinner party here at my house last night, it's already time to go back to work. The snow has been cleared from the country roads in my area, making it an easy drive to the Dorval airport. My flight to New York leaves at eleven in the morning, and I have to be in the briefing room one hour before the scheduled departure time. Airline pilots follow three sets of regulations: Federal Ministry of Transport rules, those imposed by the employer as a condition of employment, and those negotiated by the pilots' union. Federal rules trump all others. Air Canada pays me to be in the briefing room one hour before the flight and expects me to be on board my aircraft thirty minutes before departure.

Today, I am at the airport earlier than usual to drop off my letter of resignation. It's addressed to Captain Charles Simpson, Vice President of Flight Operations. Charlie is a good leader who is well-liked and respected by his pilots. He started his administrative career as President of the Canadian Airline Pilots Association, where he did such a good job that Air Canada management offered him his present executive position. I know him well, as I used to fly with him as his first officer years ago when he was a new DC9 captain. I remember him attending at least one of my infamous, annual rum punch and steel band masquerade parties, which I used to throw to celebrate the opening of the summer sailing season in Montréal. I don't think he'll be completely surprised by my letter, which I submit to his secretary.

In the briefing room, I meet my first officer, who will be with me for the entire two-day cycle. Each month, first officers select the flights they wish to operate after the captains have made their choices. In this way, personality conflicts are avoided and cockpit harmony is ensured. We will be flying the Douglas DC9, a medium range, twin-engine jet that is the sports car of the fleet and a very enjoyable aircraft to fly. For safety reasons, airline pilots are not permitted to fly different types of aircraft. They choose the type that they wish to fly according to their seniority. In fact everything is decided by seniority: the work schedule, type of aircraft, vacations, and also rank (captain or first officer). When pilots join an airline, they get a seniority number depending on their ranking in the initial training course. This number gets smaller as pilots retire off the top of the list, and gets padded from the bottom when new pilots are hired. It's a great system, which, unlike the military model, allows pilots to get on with the job of flying without having to worry about promotion, career building or someone unfairly usurping their position.

Once a pilot has successfully bid to fly a different airplane type, he or she must take an intensive ground school course followed by simulator training, flight training, and then pass a Ministry of Transport flight test in order to have his or her Airline Transport License endorsed for that aircraft. This sequence is followed with inflight checking by supervisory staff before the pilot becomes fully qualified on type. Captains and first officers complete exactly the same training and are equally qualified as far as the license endorsement is concerned. Experience and seniority determine rank. When a first officer has enough seniority, he may elect to bid as a captain. If successful, he must complete a rigorous captain's training program, followed by one hundred flying hours under supervision; then pass a final route check before commanding his own ship.

The ship analogy is quite appropriate, as the maritime lexicon was transferred intact from marine to aviation use when airplanes were invented. In fact, many of the original passenger aircraft were flying boats. Hence, airplanes have rudders, galleys, bulkheads and port and starboard sides with red and green navigation lights. Unlike most other professionals, all airline pilots are constantly retested to validate their competency. Every year, Air Canada pilots are tested four times in the simulator, at least once aboard the aircraft, and must pass two medical examinations - so their jobs are on the line seven times. A pity that this is not the case for doctors, dentists, lawyers, politicians, bureaucrats, judges and financial planners, who are rarely retested. Most airline pilots choose to protect themselves from health problems by purchasing expensive "loss of license" medical insurance policies.

In the flight planning room, the Air Canada flight dispatch team is ready to brief us. This group of highly-qualified, licensed professionals has already done the preparatory work for my flights to New York and back. The flight plans are computer-generated and contain data such as route to be taken, requested altitudes, estimated flight time, fuel required and alternate airports. They are extremely accurate and detailed. The captain is ultimately responsible for accepting, rejecting, or making any changes he wants to the flight plan. I can predict, given the weather forecast calls for fog, that we will probably be delayed in a holding pattern over New York, so I load on some extra fuel for this eventuality. Interestingly, airliners are not routinely filled up with maximum fuel before each flight, but carry just enough fuel for the intended trip, plus fuel to get to an alternate airport, plus an ample safety reserve. This is because the more an aircraft weighs, the more fuel it requires to reach destination, so it costs the airline money to carry unnecessary fuel. Of course, safety is never compromised, and sometimes, when the captain requires a full fuel load, cargo or even passengers might have to be off-loaded to meet the certified maximum takeoff weight of the aircraft. Today, I don't like the dispatcher's choice of Philadelphia as our planned alternate airport. If LaGuardia airport closes due to fog, most of the other aircraft heading there will also be diverted to Philadelphia, causing a huge backlog and chaos on the ground. I have changed the alternate airport to Montréal, so we can come back here with very little inconvenience to the passengers if LaGuardia closes. Another advantage of this strategy is that we can turn around at any time while *en route* if the weather goes below landing limits in New York before we arrive. An airport can only be legally designated as an alternate on the flight plan if the weather forecast there meets strict government minimums. In other words, the forecast must be, without any doubt, good enough to guarantee a safe landing. The flight dispatcher gives my first officer and me a comprehensive weather briefing and reviews the latest *Notices to Airmen* appropriate to our flight. These information bulletins cover everything from radio frequency changes, to airport construction details, to deficiencies of airport equipment. I sign the amended flight plan, which the dispatcher will transmit to Air Traffic Control (ATC) while we are walking to our departure gate. During the flight, we will monitor two radio frequencies simultaneously: one with Air Canada and the other with ATC. The flight dispatcher will follow our progress all the way to destination and will inform me immediately of any changes pertinent to my flight.

Uninitiated passengers can be overwhelmed when they look in the cockpit door and glimpse the vast array of switches, levers, instruments, and lights. However, it is not as complicated as it appears. If your car had two engines, you would need twice as many engine instruments and controls: starters, engine warning lights, oil pressure gauges, rpm indicators, water temperature gauges, alternator lights, etc. Now imagine how cluttered and complicated your dashboard would look with all those extras. Keep this in mind as I walk you through and demystify a typical aircraft cockpit.

To begin, the cluster of instruments, which pilots use to fly in cloud without external reference, is duplicated: one set in front of each pilot. These show, at a glance, the aircraft attitude in relation to the horizon, the airspeed, rates of climb or descent, altitude and compass heading. Incorporated in this grouping of instruments are navigational radio indicators, which allow pilots to navigate and to carry out instrument approaches. Fighter pilots telling tall tales around the bar have been known to boast: "There I was, upside down at forty thousand feet with nothing on the clock but the maker's name," when referring to their airspeed instrument.

Next, there are the engine parameter instruments, usually located in the middle of the front panel between the pilots. These tell you everything about the engines: power settings and rpm, fuel flow, fuel used and remaining, temperatures and pressures, electrical, hydraulic and pneumatic indications. These may look complicated, but there is much duplication, especially in four-engine aircraft where you need four separate instruments for every parameter. The DC9 has two main propulsion jet engines and one smaller one called the auxiliary power unit, located in the tail cone, which supplies the air conditioning and electric power when parked at the gate and provides air pressure to start the main engines. Adding to the cockpit kaleidoscope are lots of switches, lights, levers, and gauges that may not be needed at all during a given flight, but are required only for certain eventualities or emergencies. Examples would be engine fire extinguishers or the switches that activate the airframe de-icing system. Others are used only once during a flight (engine start switches) while many would be self-evident even to non pilots: autopilot, flight attendant call button, "no smoking" and "fasten seatbelt" light switches, outside air temperature gauge, clocks, intercom system, a myriad of different light switches and many rows of circuit breakers or fuses.

To manoeuver the aircraft in-flight, each pilot has a control column in front of him as well as two rudder pedals on the floor. Deflecting the top of the rudder pedals forward activates the main wheel brakes. Nose wheels do not have brakes. On a floor console between the pilots, there are engine throttle levers with attached reverse thrust levers, selectors for the landing gear, flaps, speed brakes, fuel shut-off levers to shut down the engines, and aircraft flight control surface trim wheels. Add some radios for communication and navigation, a transponder so air traffic control can identify the aircraft, weather radar for detecting thunderstorms and you have the total package. In the DC9 cockpit, there is a multi-message information panel covering all aircraft systems, which gives the pilots an instant snapshot of what's happening to their aircraft: green lights for routine information, amber for caution and red for serious problems. That's all there is to an aircraft cockpit, and with every technological advance, they are becoming less complicated. Pilots have to be good drivers and excellent multi-taskers. They need to have a thorough understanding of their aircraft's systems, but they do not have to be rocket scientists, aviation mechanics, or intellectuals.

At the departure gate, the first officer and I meet our flight attendants and give them a briefing on the flight. I explain that we might be delayed due to fog in New York, but apart from that, the flight will be routine and smooth at cruise altitude for their cabin service. Passengers often ask me about turbulence and the effect it has on airplanes. It is one of the most disturbing concerns for anxious flyers. I explain that even though aircraft can sometimes get tossed around making things very uncomfortable in the cabin, there is no danger to the airframe or to passengers wearing seatbelts. Turbulence in clear air is usually associated with wind and is often encountered when flying close to the jet stream. Naturally, airline companies try to take advantage of this fast-moving, high-altitude wind to shorten flight times, but it's usually difficult to get the wind advantage without encountering some turbulence caused by wind sheer. If your flight is forecast to be considerably under schedule, you can probably count on some bumpiness. Strong winds at lower altitudes close to the ground can create mechanical turbulence, especially over rough terrain. This will usually be encountered during the final approach just before landing and for a few minutes after takeoff. High winds, as well as updrafts and downdrafts associated with thunderstorm activity, can cause very severe turbulence. These storm clouds are easily detected on the aircraft's weather radar, and pilots will always take measures to avoid them. The rule is: don't land or takeoff during a thunderstorm and avoid them at all costs when *en route*. Finally, like boats, aircraft produce wake turbulence which, although it dissipates quickly, can be significant, especially if a small aircraft crosses the wake of a much bigger one. Let me spoil many people's scary flying anecdotes by pointing out that there is no such thing as an "air pocket." Air is a homogeneous compound made up mostly of nitrogen and oxygen atoms and, like water, cannot have pockets. Abrupt changes in altitude are caused by updrafts and downdrafts or by wind sheer.

Back to our New York flight, the fuel company has received our fuel requirements from flight dispatch and has started pumping the requested amount into a series of inter-connected tanks located in the wings. Jet engines burn a type of kerosene, not the more flammable gasoline. After inspecting the passenger cabin, we take our seats in the cockpit. The captain always sits on the left side of a conventional aircraft (on the right in helicopters), and this is reflected in the cockpit design. For instance, in the DC9, the nose-wheel steering and parking brake are only accessible from the captain's side. I check the aircraft maintenance logbook and read the recent history of this airplane as documented by previous captains and maintenance chiefs. The last captain to fly this aircraft wrote that he had experienced a slight vibration in the nose wheel during takeoff. Maintenance experts have examined the nose wheel, made some adjustments, and indicated in the logbook that it is safe to proceed. Nothing is left to chance in the airline industry. Every important system is duplicated, designed to be fail-safe and constantly monitored. Any maintenance work must be inspected and signed off in the logbook by a supervisor who is then legally responsible for the repair.

When a new aircraft type is certified to fly commercially, the Ministry of Transport, in cooperation with the manufacturer, issues a *Minimum Equipment List*. As the name implies, no aircraft can be dispatched on a flight with passengers unless all of the equipment specified on this list is functioning properly. However, the captain still has the discretion to refuse an aircraft for any reason and insist that the problem be fixed, even though the item is not on the *Minimum Equipment List*. A good example of this happened to me last summer in Edmonton. A captain flew a DC9 from Vancouver with an unserviceable weather radar, which is not on the *Minimum Equipment List*. He did not need the radar, as the weather for his flight was excellent. By the time my flight, with the same aircraft, was due to depart, there were thunderstorms forecast *en route,* so naturally I insisted the radar be fixed before takeoff. During the extensive flight-testing leading to government certification, the manufacturer decides how an aircraft should be operated, then issues a detailed operating manual. This manual includes emergency procedures as well as normal operating protocols. Captains are responsible for operating their aircraft "by the book" thus ensuring seamless crew cooperation between pilots who may have never met each other before their flight. The in-charge flight attendant has brought us coffee, and we settle down to our cockpit drills. We check every system, test every light, and verify all switch positions. We do this together, backing each other up to avoid errors. We start by adjusting our oxygen masks and smoke goggles before stowing them on a quick release mechanism. We check all of the warning bells and buzzers, including the engine fire warning systems. We set the cabin pressurization controller to our flight planned altitude, so as the aircraft climbs to thirty-three thousand feet, the cabin will simultaneously climb to about five thousand feet. The altitude inside the passenger cabin is not kept at sea level because the pressure differential required to do that would stress the aircraft structure. After takeoff, cabin compressors start to pump outside air into the cabin and manage to maintain a sea level cabin pressure until the aircraft altitude is about twenty thousand feet. The final cabin pressure varies by aircraft type. In the DC9, the cabin altitude is about five thousand feet when the aircraft is actually flying at thirty-three thousand feet. All of this is controlled automatically and is monitored by the pilots, who have a manual back up in case of a malfunction.

Anyone who has flown commercially has endured *ad nauseum* the oxygen mask demonstration. I have never experienced a situation when these masks actually deployed, but let's examine a hypothetical situation where a DC9 at thirty-three thousand feet blows out a window. The cabin altitude would rapidly increase from five thousand feet to thirty-three thousand feet as pressurized cabin air escaped through the hole. The passenger oxygen masks would deploy automatically. The pilots would don their oxygen masks, which have an independent oxygen supply and initiate a rapid emergency descent, reaching a safe-to-breathe altitude in a few minutes. Pilots practice this procedure frequently in the flight simulator, but I have never heard of it actually happening.

After completing our cockpit checks, we review some emergency drills together. This is always done before the first flight of the day and at any other time the pilot team changes. My first officer and I review our respective duties for an engine failure during takeoff, a rapid depressurization, and an engine fire at cruise altitude. The captain decides which of the many emergency procedures to practice.

Our passengers are now boarding, and the first officer is copying our ATC clearance to New York, while I listen attentively to the instructions. All clearances are read back, word for word, to the controller to verify absolute correctness. There can be no misunderstanding as to the assigned route or altitude. Now that we have our ATC clearance, we set up our navigation instruments and altitude warning alarms, as we will do at all times throughout the flight whenever we receive a new clearance. If there is ever the slightest misunderstanding about a clearance, we will immediately resolve it by asking ATC to clarify. I will be doing the flying on the first flight leg of the day, and my first officer will back me up and handle the radio communications. The captain is always completely responsible for all aspects of the flight even when the first officer is flying. Most captains share the flying duties with their first officers, although there is no rule to that effect at Air Canada. Remember, the first officer is a potential captain and has the same qualification on his license. When I first started with Air Canada, I flew with a senior captain who had been a bomber pilot during World War Two. He used to joke, "I always let the first officer fly the first leg. If he does a good job, I make him do all the flying. There's no way any damn first officer is going to show me up." I suppose whenever two people are doing the same job, there is bound to be some healthy competition.

In those days, the captain's word was law, and first officers were reluctant to question this authority. However, after several incidents, including a fatal DC8 crash in Toronto in the late Sixties, a philosophy of closer crew co-operation and shared responsibility was introduced and enforced by the entire airline industry. The new policy is proving to be much safer. Now, first officers are encouraged to speak up immediately and to question the captain if they don't feel comfortable with any aspect of the flight.

We review the noise abatement regulations for our assigned takeoff runway. These procedures reduce, as much as possible, the impact of engine noise on people living close to the end of the runway. In North America, new airports are usually built in wide-open spaces, so at first, no noise abatement regulations are required. However, the airport soon attracts industry, hotels, housing and complaints about noise, necessitating the introduction of noise abatement procedures and curfews.

I have now established communications with the ground crew responsible for our push back and departure. The first officer has copied our load information from Air Canada and verified the passenger count with the in-charge flight attendant, so now we can calculate the takeoff data. The speed at which I must rotate the aircraft into the flying attitude and the runway distance required for takeoff are different for each flight. The main variable is the aircraft weight, but air temperature, airport altitude, wind and other parameters have to be factored in. After doing the calculations, we set our airspeed instrument reminder indicators for the takeoff speeds. The other critical speed is the one pilots call V1 (vee one). This is the go/no go speed. If there is any problem before reaching V1 speed, I will abort the takeoff and stop the airplane on the runway. After V1 speed, I will continue with the takeoff and deal with the emergency in the air. If an emergency occurs before V1 speed when the first officer is flying, I will assume control and stop the aircraft on the runway.

The worst-case scenario would be an engine failure during rotation on a hot, windless day with a fully-loaded aircraft. This is a perfectly manageable emergency often practiced in the simulator. The takeoff would be safely continued with the remaining engine(s). Then, weather permitting, the pilots would fly the aircraft back and execute a safe landing. If the weather was below landing limits, the captain would proceed to the planned takeoff alternate airport and land there. Fuel dumping is sometimes necessary to prevent structural damage to the airframe and landing gear because an aircraft's maximum allowable takeoff weight is often higher than the maximum allowable landing weight. In an extreme emergency, the captain could elect to land without dumping fuel. He has full discretion to do so, and probably would cause no harm to the aircraft although a complete inspection for structural damage would be required before the next flight.

Today, the Montréal weather is fine: sunny, clear skies and a light southwesterly wind. All the cargo is loaded, we have our customs and immigration papers and the doors are closed. We are ready for push back. Jet engines cannot be reversed, so a tractor using a bar attached to the nose wheel will push us back. The term "reverse thrust" is not accurate. When reverse thrust is selected, normal engine thrust is mechanically deflected forward. Typically it's used to help slow the aircraft after landing, or during a rapid emergency descent (after loss of cabin pressure) to get the aircraft down to a safe altitude more quickly. We get clearance to pushback from Dorval ground control, complete the pre-start checklist, and I tell the tractor driver on the intercom, "brakes released, ready for pushback." To avoid miscommunications pilots say "brakes set" and "brakes released" instead of "on" and "off," which sound similar. After pushback, I start the two main engines, shut down the auxiliary engine, say good-bye to the tractor driver and salute my ground crew. We are on our way to New York. From now on, we will be in constant radio communication with ATC, starting with Dorval ground, then the control tower, departure, Montréal centre, Boston centre, New York centre, arrival, tower, and finally the ground controller at LaGuardia. Each sector has its own jurisdiction and discrete radio frequency, and we will be handed over seamlessly from one to the other. Pilots joke that they would rather do their job with controllers' salaries than work as a controller earning the much higher pilots' salaries. Controllers do have a stressful occupation although, if they cause an accident, they can still drive home at the end of their shift.

It's a beautiful day for flying, and we have been cleared for takeoff by Dorval tower. We complete the before-takeoff checklist as I steer the airplane onto the runway using the nose wheel and increase the throttles to takeoff power. We monitor all instruments very carefully during the takeoff, watching for the slightest abnormality. At V1 speed, I take my right hand off the throttles to indicate that we are past the no-go point. When we reach the pre-calculated rotation speed, I ease back on the control column and lift the aircraft smoothly into the air. We are airborne. It's always a thrill.

If I am going to miss anything after I leave Air Canada, it will be the bird's eye view of the natural wonders of our world, which pilots get to enjoy every working day from their cockpit seats. Whether it is flying over the Grand Canyon, the Pyramids, the Rocky Mountains or the autumn colours of Cape Breton, it's always an amazing privilege. From now on, I'll be observing the magnificence of nature from a more grounded perspective: the deck of a sailing boat or a Himalayan mountaintop. I have accumulated twelve thousand hours of naval and airline flying; that should be enough for one lifetime by anyone's measure of time management.

Now that I have submitted my resignation, the flight seems even more routine and repetitive than usual, and the urgency to embark upon new challenges is heightened. In operating this flight, we'll be following exactly the same procedures as our fellow pilots do on long overseas trips. The only difference is that we have an hour between takeoff and landing, while they have to wait up to ten or more hours before parking their aircraft at the arrival gate. This is the main reason I have chosen to finish my career as a DC9 captain, rather than using my seniority to fly long haul aircraft. My favourite flight is the late night Montréal to Québec City run, which takes about half an hour in the air.

For many years, I did fly overseas flights as a first officer. When I started this job, it was a thrill to be in Paris, Moscow, Los Angeles or Trinidad a couple of days each week. I would choose my flights to have five-day skiing layovers in Switzerland, opera layovers in Vienna or Christmas with my family in London, but the long hours and the effects of jet lag eventually wore me down. When Air Canada first got the Boeing 747 jumbo, there were too many seats for the market demand, so the upper deck was converted into a discotheque for first class passengers. A flight attendant in lounging pajamas served champagne and huge bowls of Beluga caviar with all the trimmings. I often took this flight from Montréal to Paris as a passenger when my work schedule had me picking up a flight in Europe. At the time, I thought this a marvelous way to spend my life, but no longer.

Climbing through ten thousand feet, we check the cabin pressure, increase airspeed and retract the landing lights. A few years ago, someone had the bright idea (no pun intended) of leaving the powerful landing lights on at all times when below ten thousand feet. Below nine thousand five hundred feet in clear weather, the same airspace is available for uncontrolled aircraft to use, so pilots are responsible for maintaining separation visually. Leaving the landing lights on in the lower altitudes makes airplanes much more visible, and is now an internationally accepted procedure.

We climb up to our assigned cruising altitude over beautiful Lake Champlain, the birthplace of the United States Navy, where

Benedict Arnold fought the British fleet at the battle of Valcour Bay. I know the lake well, having cruised every corner of it during the last ten summers. I crane my neck to identify the sheltered bay on North Hero Island, Vermont, where I keep my boat in the summer. The lake is partially ice-covered now, but is perfectly warm for swimming in August. This October, if all goes according to plan, I will take departure at the south end of the lake, navigate the Champlain Canal to the Hudson River, continue down to New York and set sail for Bermuda and the West Indies. I can hardly wait.

I am jolted back to reality by the voice of an air traffic controller assigning us a holding pattern. The fog is lifting at LaGuardia airport and delays are minimal. I slow the aircraft to holding speed, enter the racetrack pattern and advise the passengers what we are doing. All airline pilots are excellent drivers, but some lack the public relations skills to match. My attitude has always been that the passengers, having paid for the service we are providing, deserve to be kept informed. Air Canada's supervisory pilots are making an effort to raise their pilots' people skills to the level of their flying skills. After three circuits in the hold, New York approach radar gives us a heading and altitude for our approach to LaGuardia airport.

I always enjoy flying into this airport, as the procedures can sometimes have unusual variations. The airfield has two fairly short runways, borders the East River, and is surrounded by densely-populated areas. The airspace is squeezed by the control zones of JFK Airport, Newark Airport, and Floyd Bennett Naval Air Station, so while the controllers are excellent, the operation is tight. The frequency of landings and takeoffs is high, there is very little space on the ground, and limited gate availability. Four-engine aircraft are not permitted here. All of this means that we must sharpen our cockpit discipline, be extra vigilant, and be alert for last minute instructions.

Last summer, when operating a similar flight into New York on a clear, sunny, and unusually quiet Sunday afternoon, the obviously bored approach controller asked, "How well do you know the New York area, captain?" "Try me," I replied and he issued the following highly unorthodox visual clearance: "Air Canada 720, you are cleared to proceed from your present position directly to the Verrazano Narrows bridge; then directly to the Statue of Liberty; then directly to the George Washington bridge; then a right turn for an ILS approach to runway thirteen at LaGuardia. Maintain three thousand feet until over the George Washington Bridge and contact LaGuardia tower on final approach." I was bemused by this most unusual clearance, but readily accepted it. I knew the area very well, having sailed in and out of New York harbour many times. My first officer was a little perplexed, but I reassured him and suggested he sit back and enjoy the beautiful Manhattan skyline. This experience is a good example of what can happen in "anything goes" New York, that most wonderful and exciting city.

Today, we are cleared for an ILS approach to runway twenty-two (twenty-two being the first two digits of the runway's compass heading, 220 degrees magnetic). During this approach, I will be flying two sets of radio beams simultaneously: one lines me up with the runway's axis and the other guides me down an appropriate glide slope. This very accurate system allows me to descend on instruments until the aircraft is two hundred feet above the ground. Upon reaching that altitude, if I don't see the runway, I will carry out the missed approach procedure and proceed to the alternate airport. Today, I see the runway as we are descending through six hundred feet and line the aircraft up visually for the landing.

Pilots usually land the aircraft manually. The technique is to stop the aircraft's rate of descent and level off a few inches above the runway surface, then slowly reduce the engine power to idle, allowing the aircraft to lose speed and settle gently onto the runway. When the main wheels start rotating, the ground spoilers pop up automatically on top of the wings and neutralize all lift. After touchdown, the pilot not flying applies reverse thrust to help brake the aircraft. While soft landings are preferable for passenger comfort and pilot ego, they are not always attempted on short runways because sometimes pilots must set the aircraft down promptly to avoid gliding over the full length of the landing surface. In the gate area, there is a set of line-up lights and a horizontal barber pole. I line up the aircraft using the lights, and stop when the barber pole gently touches the windshield. We have arrived.

This is the work environment I'll be leaving behind when I stop flying for a living. If I had decided to continue flying for Air Canada for another eighteen years, I would have been obliged to retire without having done much else with my life. Of course, there will be new technological innovations, more modern airplanes, different routes, and some interesting personal relationships, but I am sure the "old enchanter" would be unhappy with me if I ignore his present offer. More importantly, if I pass up this chance, I am sure that I will never forgive myself later in life.

I join the first officer and our three flight attendants for lunch in the airport restaurant before checking the new flight plan and reviewing the Montréal weather for our return flight. With any luck, we'll be back in New York this evening in time for me to get a cancelled ticket for Cats. The Broadway show, which has just won a Tony award for best musical, is sold out for the next six months, but there are almost always last-minute cancellations. Tonight, I intend to be the first in line at the theatre box office.

This evening, when I got to the Winter Garden theatre where Cats is playing, there were already four people waiting for cancelled tickets, and soon afterwards the queue was around the block. The four girls ahead of me were Northwest Airlines flight attendants on a layover. I informed them with much bravado that they were in luck to be ahead of me, as I never failed to get seats on these occasions. Half an hour before show time, a man showed up with two unneeded tickets, which promoted me to third in line. Fifteen minutes before show time, the theatre manager announced that it was very unlikely there would be any more tickets and he encouraged everyone in line to see another show. Nobody budged. At eight o'clock, when I heard the orchestra playing the overture, I knew that our cause was futile and invited the two flight attendants for a consolation dinner at near-by Rosie O'Grady's restaurant. As we were dispersing, the manager came rushing out of the theatre shouting, "Who are the next three in line?" After quickly paying the cashier, we followed him into the theatre, were ushered hastily down the side aisle of the orchestra section, dodged a couple of Jellicle cats, and were led through a door leading backstage. Here, we were given three seats in the wings, usually reserved for theatre critics. By the final curtain, I had become completely infatuated with the entire magical experience and was on first name terms with Grizabella, the Glamour Cat. I was on such a high that I couldn't sleep for two days and still have no meaningful answer to the question: "How did you enjoy the show?"

Back in Montréal, the spring skiing is excellent. When I ski at Mont St. Sauveur, I wonder who is running the airline, as most of Air Canada's Montréal-based flight crews seem to be on the ski slopes. Many pilots and flight attendants live in the beautiful Laurentian hills and most of them ski. I'm taking full advantage of everything this area has to offer, as this will be my last winter in Canada.

I was right about my boss, Charlie Simpson. He was not surprised by my resignation. He asked if I would like to take an open-ended leave of absence instead of resigning, but I declined his thoughtful gesture. I feel that I must jump into the deep end and not simply test the waters. He also offered to qualify me on a more modern aircraft, so that I could fall back on a high-paying contract job with a Pacific Rim airline if I ever changed my mind and wanted to get back into the flying game. When Charlie realized that I was totally committed to my plan, he authorized a financial severance package, which amounted to a half-year's salary, tax-free. I must emphasize that this was an amazing goodwill gesture, as Air Canada was not obliged in any way to offer me this money. Throughout my airline career, I had volunteered for a program offering public relations visits by Air Canada captains to VIPs, heads of industry, and other valued customers. This may have been one reason for Charlie's generosity. The contingencies of the seniority system mean that my resignation is irrevocable as far as Air Canada is concerned. There is no turning back. It has been accepted as of the first of September this year, which means that with holiday credits, my last flight will be at the end of July.

In the meantime, there are a couple of complications to be worked out before I can set sail. First of all, I have been separated from my wife, Ginette, since last September, and we have not yet agreed on a divorce settlement. The other major problem is our 150-acre farm in Sainte Justine, Québec. Soon it will be time to till the land and seed a hundred acres of cereal crops. I am no longer staying at the farmhouse because Ginette is still living there, and we can't agree on how to proceed. The irony of this situation is not lost on me, as it was Ginette's idea to buy the farm in the first place. It was supposed to be part of our master plan.

Here's how it happened. Ten years ago in 1974, the possibility that I might leave Air Canada to pursue a more adventurous life took root. Realizing that many men have had similar dreams fizzle out, I decided to test the idea as soon as possible. That way I could either continue to plan for it, or abandon the whole notion. I thought that with the right strategy, I had a good chance of success. I was a former naval officer, had sailed since childhood, had owned and raced several large boats, had skippered my father's boat during Cowes Week races in England, and had often crewed aboard a friend's Dutch-built sloop in the Bahamas. If genes had anything to do with it, my maternal grandmother's maiden name was Drake, and one of my cousins has traced our family tree back to Sir Francis himself. I was also single. My plan was to stay single, buy the ideal boat, and test the dream before quitting my job.

When I was growing up in the Fifties, everyone's expectations of life were simple. You were supposed to get the best education your abilities and resources could achieve, secure the best job your education would permit, find the right partner, get married, have children and live happily ever after. My expectations were no different, but I was a late bloomer, so the marriage part didn't happen. Whereas some of my classmates married their high school sweethearts immediately after graduation from Naval College, and others followed suit shortly after we had joined our naval air squadrons, I didn't come close to getting hitched. I had girlfriends, but none with whom I wanted to spend the rest of my life.

Circumstances played their part. I was often out of the country, either flying aboard the aircraft carrier *Bonaventure*, or on leave in Europe with my family. When the aircraft carrier was at home base in Halifax, Nova Scotia, I would often appropriate an aircraft on weekends for a training flight to Montréal, Toronto, New York or Boston and explore those cities. Before I knew it, my naval career was over and I found myself in Montréal as a twenty-five-year-old, single airline pilot. I had not followed the expectations of my generation, and now society's rules were changing. It was 1966. More women were opting for full-time careers. The feminist movement was well underway, especially in Québec, and the birth control pill was liberating women and men alike. Air Canada was obliged by law to change its discriminatory policy of hiring female flight attendants on short-term contracts. The girls were not allowed to marry (although some did secretly), could not stay for a full career and did not qualify for in-charge positions. Only men were hired as pursers for full careers as in-charge flight attendants.

All of this was changing. It became apparent that I now had two distinct choices, both of which were exciting to contemplate. One was to continue along the conventional path, find the right girl (I was certainly well-placed for that), and raise children; the other was to stay single, not have children and pursue an adventurous lifestyle. To my parents' chagrin, I chose the latter, but it didn't quite unfold as I had planned.

I met Ginette by the hotel swimming pool, while on holiday in Barbados. She was attractive, intelligent and one of life's winners. She was leaving for Martinique the next day, so I invited her for dinner that evening. We exchanged addresses and agreed to meet later in Montréal. Coincidentally, she also worked for Air Canada as a flight attendant, but we had never flown together because management had singled her out early in her career to work in their training department as an instructor. We eventually met in Montréal several months later and started seeing each other. That led to a ten-year relationship: world travel, some open ocean sailing, seven years of hard work on our farm, many enjoyable holidays with friends and family - and some philosophical and cultural differences and problems. She was French Canadian, and many members of her family did not speak English, so my French really improved. Thanks to them, I had the privilege of becoming fully bilingual and, more importantly, bicultural during our time together. However, whoever coined the saying, "Marry the girl next door," probably knew what he was talking about.

At the beginning of our relationship, I was very involved with finding my ideal boat. The search took me to all the major boat shows: London, Paris, New York and Miami. For her part, Ginette couldn't understand how anyone in their right mind would pay considerably more money for a thirty-five foot sailing boat than they would for a beautiful three-bedroom country house in a charming Québec ski village. For that matter, neither could my bankers, but I convinced them to lend me the money by involving them vicariously in my dream. After I had ordered my boat from the reputable Hallberg-Rassy company in Sweden, Ginette and I went skiing in the French Alps to celebrate. Then, while waiting for a promised July delivery date, we chartered a boat in the Cyclades Islands of Greece. I fell in love with that country and added the idea of eventually sailing my own boat there to my wish list. By the time that I had taken delivery of my new boat, sailed her to Bermuda for the first winter, brought her back to Lake Champlain for the following summer, and sailed her down to the Bahamas for the second winter, Ginette had become part of the dream. However, in return for such a commitment, she made it quite clear to me that we should get married, although we did agree not to have children.

I had often wondered whether a couple's relationship to each other changed after marriage, or whether it was the attitude of friends and family towards the newly-weds that changed. To satisfy my curiosity, Ginette suggested we fly off to Bermuda for a civil marriage ceremony without telling anyone. I had spent the previous winter in Bermuda on my boat, commuting by air for my Air Canada job and had met many Bermuda "Onions" as the locals are affectionately called. Bermudian law required us to announce our intended marriage in the local newspapers before the ceremony, so eventually our friends there found out about the marriage, foiled our secret plans and organized a surprise wedding reception. Nevertheless, our conspiracy did work outside Bermuda, and nobody else found out about the wedding. I don't think we proved anything particularly earth-shattering by marrying this way, although we did upset our families and friends in Canada. Eventually, we told Ginette's parents, and the news of our marriage slowly leaked out to the rest of our world.

I was now a captain, eight years away from my planned departure date from Air Canada, and Ginette was restless. I was quite content living in our small but comfortable rented country house on an island near Montréal, sailing on Lake Champlain in the summer, taking our boat to the Bahamas each winter, flying, and generally enjoying life. Ginette had left her teaching job, was now working as a flight attendant again, but not enjoying it very much and was contemplating quitting Air Canada to go back to university. One day, she cleverly convinced me with my own argument that we would be wasting our precious time by continuing with the *status quo* for the next eight years while waiting to depart on the boat. She suggested we should do something more worthwhile, educational and productive with the time remaining. I could not disagree with her reasoning, so after much soul searching, we decided to buy some land and become farmers. I soon became quite excited by the project. I had previously completed some forestry courses at Macdonald College in Montréal, so the prospect of having my own forest to manage was compelling.

That, in a nutshell, leads us to where we are today. The eight years have passed. We have cultivated our 150 acres with reasonable success, and the time has come to move on with the sailing dream. The problem is that Ginette has become attached to our beautiful farm with its rural environment and is not ready to sell and move on. She left Air Canada a few years ago, went back to university for a fine arts degree and is very much part of the local community. There is also another very important obstacle making our situation impossible to resolve - except by divorce.

Shortly after settling into the farming life and wanting to share our considerable blessings, we offered our 1840s vintage farm house as a temporary emergency shelter for children who had no place to go after being banished from their foster homes. Ginette, with my blessing, decided to let one young boy stay with us on a more permanent basis. For several years, we did everything in our power to help him, but in spite of all our efforts, we were unable to effect any change. I was convinced that it was time to admit defeat. However, Ginette insisted on clinging to her mission, precipitating a total impasse.

Last September, we separated, and I agreed that the best arrangement would be for me to move out and leave them on the farm. In any case, I was going quit my career and sail away to the West Indies the following autumn.

So here I am in April with many things to settle before my departure date. I will commute daily to the farm from my rented house until the crops are seeded, and if we can't settle matters before I set sail in October, Ginette can contract out the harvest work, and we will try to resolve our affairs at a later date. After the crops are in the ground, I will move onto my boat for the summer and commute to the airport from Lake Champlain until I finish with Air Canada in July. I will continue to support my wife until the divorce is settled and the farm is sold.

A word of advice to anyone who has separated from their spouse for reasons of incompatibility, but is not yet involved in a triangle relationship: keep it that way until your divorce is final. The alternative scenario complicates things immeasurably by introducing emotions of jealousy and vindictiveness, which can seriously cloud and complicate the divorce proceedings. I speak from experience. I should have known better, but naïvely thought that, since I was separated and soon to be divorced, I was free to pursue other liaisons. Ginette thought otherwise. I had been faithful to her during our marriage, but now I wanted to move on. After seven years of backbreaking work on the farm and not much play, I rediscovered Montréal's restaurants, discos, nightlife, and the pleasures of being with a beautiful woman who found me attractive and who enjoyed my company.

I will call this woman Floria Tosca after Puccini's heroine, because she is insanely jealous and has already surgically removed Ginette's head from all the photos in my album. When she found out that her last boyfriend had been unfaithful, she snipped off a symbolic six inches from the sleeves of every business suit in his considerable corporate lawyer's wardrobe. I am enjoying this relationship very much and know that I will have a hard time ending it. Describing this short period between my separation and my leaving Montréal for the West Indies would easily fill another book, but I'd have to write it as fiction because nobody would believe my story. Mid-life crisis? I don't think so, but if I live to the age of eighty-four, these events will turn out to have occurred precisely in the middle of my lifespan.

CHAPTER TWO

THE IDEAL BOAT

There are just two months to go before my last flight, and I am living aboard my boat on Lake Champlain. The farm crops are seeded, but no divorce settlement is in sight. With a sigh of relief, I have ended my seven-year farming career, by far the hardest physical work I have ever done in my life. Ginette has agreed to find a farm contractor to bring in the harvest next autumn, and we will try to settle our affairs later. My boat is moored in a sheltered, almost land-locked, bay on North Hero Island, Vermont in front of a lakefront property which I bought for this purpose years ago. I am commuting to Montréal to operate my flights and am a source of great amusement to the American customs officers at the border when I return late at night in my pilot's uniform.

My boat's name is *Muscade*, which means nutmeg in French. When I was trying to choose a name, just before taking delivery in July 1974, I was hoping to find something appropriately bilingual, but failed to come up with anything suitable, so I settled for *Muscade*. For me, nutmeg evokes the spice islands of the West Indies, a rum punch during carnival in Trinidad, and it is an ingredient in many epicurean delicacies. In any event, a boat, like a child, soon grows into her name and takes on her own personality. Before I bought *Muscade*, I did considerable research. I was looking for the ideal vessel for my purposes: able to cross oceans safely, comfortable enough for a couple to live aboard full time, and spacious enough for two guests for limited periods. She had to be very strongly built with a full keel. I insisted on a diesel engine and a sloop rig (one mast). A Royal Ocean Cruising Club member's survey had recently concluded that the optimum boat for a couple wanting to do long-term ocean cruising was thirty-six feet long, five feet deep and eleven feet wide. I also had budget considerations.

I found a boat which met all of my criteria at the Vancouver boat show and knew immediately that she was the one for me. Built in Sweden by the respected Hallberg-Rassy company, she was perfectly suited to my requirements, but the price was much higher than my budget allowed. Thirty-five feet long, four and a half feet deep, and eleven feet wide, she had a full keel, was sloop-rigged and very strongly built out of fiberglass. The interior was like a wooden boat, beautifully finished in solid mahogany and teak, all authenticated with a Master Carpenter's Certificate. The centre cockpit was protected from the elements by a rigid, safety-glass spray dodger, which could be completely enclosed in bad weather. Behind the cockpit, with its own entrance, was a private double cabin for guests. The engine was huge for the size of boat: a four-cylinder, seventy-five horsepower Volvo Penta diesel. The marketing catch phrase on the sales brochure boasted: "Built to prevail in the North Atlantic," which turned out to be absolutely true.

Unfortunately, I couldn't afford to buy this boat. However, I knew that without Canadian import taxes, it would be thirty per cent cheaper in the United States, so as soon as I got back to Montréal, I phoned Eastland Yachts, the American dealer in Connecticut. I was in luck, as Jim Eastland was selling his last year's demonstrator boat at a discount price that I could just squeeze into my budget. I told Jim that I would arrange to fly down to Florida to inspect the yacht. A few weeks later in Pompano Beach, I took her for a sail and knew I had found my boat. As soon as I was back on the dock, I phoned Jim Eastland in Connecticut to confirm my purchase. He was surprised to hear from me. He had forgotten about my planned visit and had already sold the boat to another customer. Needless to say, I was completely shattered, and he was highly embarrassed.

Being a man of integrity, Jim felt honour-bound to sell me a brand new boat for the same price he had quoted for the demonstrator, so *Muscade* started out as a lucky boat on a lucky roll that was to last for over thirty years. It was also a good break for Jim's relatively new company because two of my friends bought similar boats from him at full price, and for years afterwards, I helped to promote his reputation as a fair dealer. In July 1974, I took delivery of *Muscade* in Essex, Connecticut. I had my boat, and now it was time to test the dream before committing to a drastic lifestyle change.

The maiden voyage from Essex involved sailing south-west down Long Island Sound, entering the East River to pass down the east side of Manhattan Island, rounding downtown New York at the Battery, sailing north up the Hudson river to Albany and taking the Champlain canal to Lake Champlain. Ginette and I, along with two friends, completed the trip in five days. It was fairly uneventful, except for one bizarre experience on the third day.

It was a spectacularly beautiful, warm, misty July morning as we left our overnight anchorage at Nyack, New York and motored northward on the Hudson. My friend, Jean Milette, and I were enjoying coffee and toast in the cockpit, while marveling at the green lushness of the towering riverbanks gliding slowly by on either side of us and reflected in the mirror of calm water. The stillness was surreal and a total contrast to the previous day when we had circumnavigated New York City with its ceaseless, intimidating buzz and busy interweaving of ferries, tug boats and other harbour traffic. The morning was so beautiful that we decided to wake our girlfriends so they could enjoy the scenery, but before they made it up on deck our tranquility was shattered.

As we rounded a bend in the river, the massive Bear Mountain Bridge came into view a mile ahead, and we could see the rotating lights of several emergency vehicles on the span, a hundred and fifty feet above us. When we got close to the bridge, a state trooper hailed us with a megaphone and asked if we would help them to recover the body of a recent suicide victim before it sank. We agreed to their request, and they directed us towards the partially- submerged body that was drifting up river on the tide. I brought *Muscade* alongside the dead man, attached a rope to his belt, and tied the other end to a deck cleat. At that moment, the girls appeared on deck, wondering what all the fuss was about.

I was in shock. I had never seen a dead person before, let alone recovered a still-warm body. I will never forget the forlorn look of total desperation on that old man's face and I still wonder about the circumstances which led him to take his own life. A police launch soon arrived on the scene. One of the police crewmen grabbed the rope from us and, after a quick wave of thanks, took off at full speed, dragging the body in the boat's wake. All in a day's work for them, I supposed. Two days later, *Muscade* was in lake Champlain, her summer home and the training area where I would get to know my new boat and prepare her for the next test, an ocean passage to Bermuda in November.

Sailing from New York to Bermuda in November can be a tricky proposition. It's the tail end of hurricane season and the beginning of the winter storm period, when low-pressure systems come barreling off Cape Hatteras with little warning. The other major factor is the Gulf Stream, a fast-moving body of warm water straddling the route, which must be crossed and where fog banks often occur at this time of the year. If strong winds blow against the flow of this current, abnormally large waves can form. In addition, magnetic anomalies on the route have been known to distort boats' compasses. Finally, there is a submerged barrier reef stretching for miles north of Bermuda, which can be encountered before the island itself is sighted. No wonder somebody invented the myth of the Bermuda triangle, and that it is almost impossible to insure small boats navigating in that area. Not that it mattered to me, as I had already decided not to insure Muscade.

I calculated the odds as insurance actuaries do and concluded that the risk was manageable. I was not expecting visiting friends and crewmembers to sue me. A small boat moving at six miles an hour cannot do much damage, so I was not concerned about hitting anything. In the event of a catastrophic loss at sea, I would probably be lost with the boat, so I would not be around to collect the money needed to replace it. For all other eventualities, I was prepared to accept the risk and insure the boat myself, as many cruising sailors do. Thus, insurance becomes a philosophical issue: once the idea of not having insurance is taken into account, the need for it disappears. Besides, insurance is more than just a contract on a piece of paper. Cruising sailors insure their vessels in other ways by keeping their boats in good condition, by changing the rigging when necessary, by ensuring the anchor gear is adequate, and by maintaining the engine. This is the best type of insurance, which becomes even more important when you don't have a traditional insurance policy.

My strategy for this voyage is to wait in New York for a perfect weather window before departing; then proceed to Bermuda as quickly as possible to avoid being overtaken by storms coming from the west. This will mean using the engine when there is insufficient wind to maintain a reasonable speed under sail. For planning purposes, it should be a six-day open ocean trip. My crew for the voyage consists of my father and two other friends, all good sailors. Ginette wanted to come and was disappointed when I insisted on having the most experienced crew possible for my first ocean trip in an unproven boat. In early November, my crew assembled at a marina on the south shore of Long Island. We didn't have to wait long before the weather forecast was ideal for our departure.

However, there was one problem to resolve before getting underway. My father was a senior executive with the Decca Navigation Company in London. His President could not believe that my total inventory of navigation equipment consisted of a compass, a towed spinner log to measure distance, and a cheap plastic sextant. He obviously had little faith in my navigational abilities and was concerned about the adverse publicity to his company if one of his executives got lost at sea. He had generously offered me the full range of Decca's navigation products, but I turned him down, as this equipment was designed for ships, was too bulky and consumed too much electrical power to be practical on a small boat. In any case, Bermuda is just out of range of the continental-based, Loran navigation system, so astro-navigation is the only method of determining the boat's position at the most critical part of the trip, just before landfall. Under pressure from Dad's boss, I relented and let Decca's engineers install a prototype Loran navigation system, which they were developing for the U.S. Navy. I made it clear that they were not to drill any holes in the cabinetry and made arrangements to leave the equipment with their agent in Bermuda. Actually, I never used the equipment at sea because it was designed to be continuously powered, and *Muscade* didn't have enough battery capacity. It worked fine at the dock in New York and the plastic sextant did the rest.

Before departing, I briefed my crew on emergency procedures, the most important one being the man overboard drill. I reminded them that if anyone falls overboard, the chances of recovery were not good. Staying on board was by far the best option, which meant wearing a harness with a lifeline securely attached to the boat. I made the wearing of harnesses obligatory at night, even in calm conditions, and at all times during bad weather. The main difficulty locating someone in the water is the lack of a point of reference. All waves look alike. I told my crew that they must assess the situation at the time the emergency occurs and act accordingly. Fixed drills don't work, as every case is different. The only reference at sea is the boat's compass, so an accurate heading must be steered and exact time noted, while the alarm is sounded. Then, when all hands are on deck and ready to help, the boat can be turned back on the reciprocal heading until the outbound time is equaled. The victim could have fallen after being hit by something, might be injured, or unconscious. To make matters worse, it is extremely difficult to hoist a waterlogged person back on board even in calm seas. I had equipped *Muscade* with all the usual lights, buoys and flags to mark the position of the accident, but that equipment works only in good weather. It is useless in storm conditions.

As it turned out, the trip took only four days and nineteen hours, which is race-winning time for my size of boat. I now realize that I pushed everything much too hard, putting unnecessary strain on the boat and on my crew. After years of competition, I still had a racing mentality, which doesn't allow for smooth, comfortable ocean passages. Racing involves fighting against nature to achieve the maximum speed and efficiency with little regard for sea conditions or wind strength. This often means carrying too much sail, ignoring the uncomfortable pounding of boat against wave, and being oblivious to crew comfort. On the other hand, ocean cruising is all about good management: departing with a good forecast, adjusting the sails to keep the boat comfortable with minimum angle of heel, never pounding the boat into wind, bearing off and reducing the sail area at night so the crew can get some sleep and providing good hot meals and hot drinks in all weathers. That is to say, generally striving for the well-being of boat and crew. These are all good lessons for future voyages.

We left New York in calm winds under engine power, crossed the predicted fog bank as we entered the Gulf Stream, and had brisk winds from there all the way to Bermuda. The most tedious part was having to manually steer the boat, as *Muscade* has neither electric autopilot nor wind-assisted mechanical self-steering. This meant that two of us had to be on watch at all times: one to steer and one to adjust the sails as conditions changed, although the person not steering could cat-nap under the shelter of the spray dodger. I was very pleased with the boat's performance and seaworthiness, but she still had not been tested in a major storm. That was to come soon enough.

One of the first people I met in Bermuda was lay preacher Tom Casey, when he was attempting to bring his small, rather fragile boat alongside *Muscade* in St George's harbour, the day after our arrival. His two young crewmembers seemed shell-shocked and unable to complete even the simple tasks of attaching a couple of fenders and securing their boat alongside *Muscade* at the customs jetty. I soon found out why. They had taken two weeks to sail what should have been a one-week trip from Florida, had encountered a storm and were obviously very grateful to have survived the ordeal. Tom told me that his mission had started with a dream, in which God had instructed him to buy a sailing boat and sail it to Israel. He had just completed the first leg of a potentially long and arduous voyage. His boat's mast sported the biggest Israeli flag I had ever seen, so I secretly hoped, for his sake, that it would be torn to shreds before he reached the Mediterranean, where he would have to transit the coastal waters of the mostly Muslim North African countries. Luckily, he couldn't continue his mission because his crew had high-tailed it back to the States, and his boat needed some repairs and modifications after the rough trip from Florida. He made himself quite at home in St George's, was adopted by some of the local church authorities and seemed in no hurry to leave. I convinced him that June was the only safe month to attempt the next leg of the voyage to the Azores islands. Whenever Ginette and I were in St George's that winter, we would look for Tom's boat and invite him for a home-cooked meal aboard *Muscade*. One afternoon, I took him sailing and gave him some badly needed navigation lessons, showing him how to fix his position with a sextant. I have no idea how he got to Bermuda from Florida in the first place. Maybe he used "cargo navigation," where you call up passing ships on the radio to ask for a position.

Fortunately for Tom, before setting sail for Israel the following June, he had another spiritual visitation. God told him to forget about going to Israel and to sail back to Florida instead, which he was more than relieved to do. Two days west of Bermuda on his way home, he was hit by a huge storm, which forced him to remove all the sails, batten down the hatches and tie himself in his bunk until the gale subsided. His small boat was thrown around by wind and waves for several days, and everything down below was smashed, including his sextant, the only means of navigation. When the storm abated, the boat itself was relatively undamaged, and the compass appeared to be working, so Tom figured if he headed west, he would eventually reach some place on the east coast of North America. He reset his sails and settled down for what would probably be at least a week of sailing. A few hours later, a miracle happened, "land ho!" He saw land dead ahead. Unbelievably, during the storm, Tom's boat had been carried back around Bermuda by wind and current, miraculously missing all the reefs, and had ended up a few miles east of the island. Almost enough to make me take up religion, and certainly proof that Poseidon cares for all sailors, not just his favorite Odysseus. Once again, Tom put into St George's harbour for repairs, and, eventually, I got a postcard from him reporting his safe arrival in Florida.

Another character I met during that Bermuda winter was the incredible British sailor (the total antithesis of Tom Casey), Paul Johnson. Paul had spent his whole life in a marine environment. Born to eccentric English parents, he lived full-time on their boat during his childhood and went on to study naval architecture. He then built his first boat, a sixteen-foot sloop, and sailed it to the Canary Islands. There, he met a group of like-minded sailors, including the famous Frenchman, Bernard Moitessier. When his friends decided to cross over to the West Indies for the winter, Paul followed them and unwittingly set the record for the smallest boat to have crossed the Atlantic Ocean. He then sailed to Florida, where he built his latest thirty-foot boat, *Venus*, out of pitch pine salvaged from a demolished church (now that's what I call good boat insurance). This amazing boat had no engine, no cockpit and no lifelines. Paul figured that engines fail, cockpits were unsafe because they fill with water, and lifelines give a sense of false security. *Venus* never took on a drop of water below decks, and her bilges were as dry as a bone. I have seen Paul bring his boat alongside *Muscade* when there was no perceptible wind. The only other person to have accomplished this feat did so two thousand years ago on the Sea of Galilee. The oceans of the world were Paul's playground, and he thought nothing of single-handing *Venus* anywhere at any time. Unsurprisingly, he almost always had a very attractive female crewmember with him.

When I met Paul, he was building a forty-two foot version of *Venus* out of fiberglass for his Bermudian architect friend, John Frith, with the understanding that he would then build another one for himself as part of the bargain. His new boat was also christened *Venus* and actually had an engine. John Frith named his identical boat, *Moon*. Years later, both boats were anchored in St Bart's harbour where the singer, Jimmy Buffet, owned a bar. One day, Buffet ran into Paul's son, Magnus, and John's son, Mishka, on the beach. When he asked them their names and where they came from, they gave him great material for his hit song: "Mishka and Magnus from the Moon and Venus."

I found a permanent mooring for the winter at the legendary Bert Darrell's boatyard in Hamilton harbour and enjoyed reciprocal privileges at the Royal Bermuda Yacht Club through my membership in the Royal Anglesey Yacht Club in Wales. In those days, the Royal Bermuda clubhouse had a sign at the front entrance: "Ladies will please enter by the side door." This appalled Ginette, and I am pleased to report that she and all our other female guests that winter totally ignored this anachronistic vestige of Victorian life by always marching defiantly through the main entrance, to the dismay of the local male "Onions."

Any time that winter when I was not flying for Air Canada, I lived aboard *Muscade* in Bermuda, a welcome change from frigid Montréal and a delicious taste of winters to come. Bermuda's climate is only semi-tropical, but it is very pleasant for sailing with good winds most of the time and mild temperatures. There is not a great variety of cruising, but the trip from Hamilton to St George's and back was always enjoyable, and there were lots of good overnight anchorages in Hamilton Sound. Ashore, there were certainly enough English pubs and good eateries to keep us happy. Ginette and I invited many guests from Canada to join us, and often kept company with Charlie Poirier, the Canadian Naval Liaison Officer in Bermuda. Charlie and I had flown on the same naval air squadron (VS880), before I left the navy to join Air Canada.

Winter passed quickly, and soon it was time to head back to Lake Champlain for the summer. Local sailors had warned me not to attempt the crossing back to New York before the end of May, but I knew better. I wanted to have the boat back on Lake Champlain for a full summer, so stupidly I ignored their advice. I planned to pick my weather window carefully and leave at the beginning of May. This time, I was confident enough to have Ginette come along on the trip, and Peter Waddell, who had done the outbound trip with me, completed our crew of three. On the morning of our departure, Charlie Poirier came down to the harbour in St George's to see us off. He had just picked up a five-day marine weather forecast from the U.S. Navy Weather Office. With his usual wry sense of humour, he said, "Forget it, you're not going anywhere with this forecast," then smiled and handed me a perfect five-day prognosis for the voyage. As things turned out, his joke fell flat.

On a small boat at sea, it is often difficult to receive marine weather forecasts on high-frequency radio, so the barometer becomes the primary instrument for weather forecasting. On *Muscade*, we record this pressure every time the watch changes. Peter and I were both airline pilots with extensive weather forecasting knowledge, so on the third day out from Bermuda we knew that we were in for a major storm. We observed a rapidly falling barometer, an ominous change of wind direction and storm clouds, which confirmed our worst fears. Even when expected, conditions at sea can change with astonishing speed.

The storm hit us with full fury on our third night. I was up on the foredeck changing the foresail down to a smaller storm jib, having already reduced the mainsail to the size of a handkerchief, when a huge gust hit us, and a breaking wave threw the stern of the boat to one side. Peter could not hold *Muscade* on course, and the wind got behind the mainsail and whipped it across to the other side, snapping the horseshoe fitting holding the boom in place. Luckily for me, the boom did not break away from the mast: otherwise, I would have been speared. After an hour of sheer terror, gale force winds and twenty-foot waves, we finally wrestled the boat under control as I lowered and lashed the main sail and hove-to with the emergency tiller lashed down and a tiny storm sail keeping us steady. There was nothing else to do but keep a lookout for ships and ride out the storm inside the boat with the hatches closed. Several times during that terrible night, *Muscade* was picked up by a breaking wave and thrown into the trough between waves with an ear-shattering crash. It was an endless, sleepless nightmare, but when dawn broke, we were still alive and the boat was dry and apparently undamaged, although the storm was still raging.

All that day and the following night, we remained hove-to with sixty-knot winds blowing against the Gulf Stream, creating huge waves. When a storm arrives quickly, it often abates just as rapidly when the low-pressure area moves away. This can lead to a situation where the wind goes calm, but the sea remains highly agitated. A small sailing vessel relies on wind pressure filling the sails for stability, so these conditions are far from desirable. We were left to cope with just this problem for two days after the storm had passed. Our elation at having survived the ordeal soon gave way to frustration as we motored through perturbed seas with the boat rolling from side to side, the boom banging back and forth, and the sails slatting. Challenges on this trip continued to test our resolve.

For the next three days, we coaxed *Muscade* towards our destination: sailing when there was some wind, motor-sailing when the wind was against us, and motoring during calm spells. We had motored so much that I was concerned about running out of fuel. Accurate fuel tank measurement is a problem on sailing boats, so whenever the engine is in use, I carefully record the running time and engine rpm, which gives me very precise fuel consumption data. I decided that I would stop using the engine when we were down to ten gallons of fuel remaining in the tanks. At that point, we would just have to sail for as long as it took to get within easy motoring range of New York harbour, where we could refuel. As it happened, when the boat was thirty miles from New York, I calculated that we had more than ten gallons of diesel fuel left, which was more than enough to make it into the harbour, or so I thought.

We had just finished afternoon tea on day seven when the engine stopped abruptly. I suspected that air had leaked into the fuel delivery system, so I bled the fuel lines and restarted. After a couple of minutes, the engine died again. I manually sounded the fuel tank. It was empty. As I was to discover later, a ten-gallon calculation error had been made in the list of boat specifications when the fuel capacity was converted from litres to US gallons. Almost at once, Neptune came to our rescue by providing a good sailing breeze, and we hoisted full sail. As *Muscade* was a sailing vessel, this was not an emergency, so I did not inform the Coast Guard. We decided to continue sailing into New York harbour during the night and anchor off a fuelling station, just inside East Rockaway inlet. As darkness fell, we were about twenty miles south of the harbour entrance and barely making headway in very light winds. To preserve the boat's batteries, I only switched on the navigation lights when we had conflicting ship traffic. Our main concern was how to avoid the constant stream of ships entering this busy harbour, as our ability to maneuver was extremely limited. Theoretically, sailing boats have right of way over powered vessels, but no prudent sailor would ever dare press that advantage. Often, ships just don't see small boats. During that endless night, when ships came too close for comfort, we shone a powerful searchlight on the sails to make ourselves more visible and had a red flare loaded into the signal pistol as a last resort.

It was another sleepless night with several close calls, but by dawn we had managed to nurse *Muscade* to East Rockaway inlet on Long Island, just north of the main New York harbour entrance. I had calculated the tidal currents for our arrival time at this entrance and knew they would be quite strong, so I had both anchors cleared away, ready to slip quickly. As we entered the inlet, a stronger-than-predicted current picked us up and swept us, out of control, towards a bascule bridge. There were big signs on both sides of the channel, "Danger Cable Crossing Do Not Anchor."

My choice was to risk snagging a cable with our anchors or lose the mast and maybe the boat when we were swept under the low bridge. I signaled to Peter to let our anchors go, crossed my fingers and hoped for the best. Fortunately, both anchors held without snagging a cable. We had arrived in New York.

Needless to say, I was not pleased with my performance on this voyage. It was clear that I still had a lot more to learn about ocean cruising before I could set off again with any confidence. I should have heeded the advice of the Bermudians and waited until June to depart. Sailing westwards means going towards the source of storm activity, so a much longer weather window is essential. When I knew the storm was coming, I should have prepared the boat much sooner and certainly before it got dark. From now on, I will always carry spare containers of diesel fuel and will purchase a portable generator to recharge the batteries, so the lights can be kept on if the engine is unserviceable. On the other hand, I was very pleased with how *Muscade* rode out the storm and now have full confidence in the seaworthiness of my boat. Extracts from the log confirm that we ate gourmet meals and, apart from the first night of the storm, the crew was reasonably happy. Ginette spent the worst two days of the gale closeted in the aft cabin, but was not spooked by the experience and was ready for another trip. Peter was invaluable and very good company. I did not force the boat and kept things as comfortable as possible. The trip took eight days to complete, double the time of the outbound passage.

The famous Welsh ocean sailor and yarn spinner par excellence, Tristan Jones, who has single-handed the Atlantic nine times and logged more than seventy-five thousand miles under sail, was once asked how he decided when to start reefing the sails (reducing sail area) in strengthening winds. His answer was, "As soon as the vaguest idea that the wind is too strong enters my mind, I start reefing." I plan to adopt Tristan's rule for all my future ocean voyages.

CHAPTER THREE

LET THE ADVENTURE BEGIN

My big day has finally arrived. *Muscade* and I are sailing southwards on Lake Champlain, bound for the West Indies. The dream has become a reality: eight years of planning have come to fruition, and I am ecstatic. Forty-three years old and as free as a bird and well clear of "the system." I shall never have to sell my time for money again unless I so choose. I have reached out to the "old enchanter" with both hands and eagerly await the adventures he might offer. I particularly wanted to be alone on this first leg of the voyage, so I would be at ease to really savour and appreciate the new reality of my life without distraction. I will meet my crew for the first leg of the trip in New York City, then change crews in Bermuda after the hurricane season for the voyage to Antigua.

As I sail down the lake, I am in a reflective mood and am trying hard to grasp that this adventure is actually happening. The anticipation of what the future might offer is almost overwhelming the quiet beauty of the moment. As *Muscade's* bow cuts through the crystal clear, Homeric "wine dark" waters of the lake, I wonder if we will some day sail together in the wake of Ulysses. The deep blue colour of the water in late afternoon contrasts starkly with the vivid crimson, gold, and green hues of the sugar maples in full autumn glory rising high up the mountains on both sides: Adirondacks to starboard and Green Mountains of Vermont to port. I find that my memory cannot hold the beauty of the fall colours from one year to the next, so every year I am astonished and surprised by nature's magnificent show. An appreciation for the wonders, integrity and equilibrium of nature has always been a huge source of strength and inspiration for me. In fact, it is my only religion.

Just before sunset, I anchor in a sheltered cove for the night and prepare a celebratory dinner. My Vermont neighbour stocked the boat with fresh vegetables from her garden this morning and gave me two-dozen eggs from her own chickens, so I will whip up a mushroom omelet with fresh vegetables and salad. I enjoy cooking and always take time to prepare a nutritious meal and set a proper table, even when dining alone. *Muscade* is fully provisioned with enough non-perishable food supplies for the voyage, as well as everything else I will need to be self-sufficient at sea: tools for every eventuality, repair kits, and spare parts. I carry lots of extra drinking water in case the water tanks become contaminated, and spare containers of diesel fuel after the New York harbour fiasco nine years ago.

I am also well stocked with sustenance for the mind: my onboard library will easily get me through the first winter. I plan to re-read a lot of the classics and to study some philosophy: Greek, Existential, and some of the more modern scholars like Bertrand Russell. I am reminded of Plato and Thomas Aquinas, who both considered the contemplative life to be the highest form of human activity. I am not willing to go quite that far, but will include contemplation, study, and some writing in the mix with high adventure. My selection of reference books includes a very colourful edition of *"Birds of the West Indies"* by ornithologist James Bond. The author Ian Fleming also had this book, staring at him from his kitchen bookshelf, and that inspiration is now literary history.

I have few pre-conceived ideas and no specific goals in mind for my new life, but will try to be spontaneous, leaving myself free to accept opportunities as they present themselves. This is precisely why I left my career with Air Canada. I do accept that it would be impossible to have this wide-open, blank-page approach towards the rest of my life, without having first shed the responsibilities and preoccupations of work, family life, community involvement, and social obligation. I am also quite aware that freedom by itself is not worth anything. I will have to tread the fine line between being free to accept new adventures and actually making a commitment to embark upon them. The Tchaikovsky opera Eugene Onegin comes to mind. The eponymous hero, a Russian aristocrat, finds conventional life a total bore, scorns his society, but doesn't find any worthwhile alternative to fill the void. Sadly, he ends up envying the mundane lives of his bourgeois friends, something I hope will not happen to me.

Some of my friends and former co-workers believe that it takes courage to abandon the conventions and norms of our society to try something different. I do not agree. I think it a far more daunting proposition to lock into the *status quo* of any job for an entire lifetime. I would add that, with the possible exception of sincere vocations in the arts, music, theatre, and perhaps some religious or charitable callings, most occupations lose their allure and eventually become routine and boring. People stay in their chosen furrow because it is comfortable and because humans have a built-in resistance to change. According to some psychologists, we have less tolerance for loss than we have satisfaction for gain, which tends to reinforce the path of least resistance. Our workplace system has been designed to discourage mobility by inventing seniority systems, trade unions, non-transferrable pension plans, and loyalty benefits such as the ubiquitous gold watch. Being reasonably content with one's life should not be an excuse for complacency. It should not preclude the possibility of being far happier doing something else. "Nothing ventured, nothing gained."

In some respects, I feel that I have cheated by waiting until I was financially independent before leaving my secure job. I have huge respect for artists, authors, composers and other free-thinking individuals who have extricated themselves from traditional lifestyles with no guaranteed means of financial support. These people, to be true to their convictions, struggle and fend for themselves on a daily basis in order to follow their chosen paths. In reality, they are the true adventurers. I am also acutely aware that if everyone chose to do what I am doing, our society would be chaotic, so I'm leveraging the system for my own benefit.

In contrast to these adventurous souls, my departure from "the system" was grounded on a solid foundation. When I joined Air Canada, it was still a Crown Corporation, so I was able to buy back my navy time for pension eligibility. This meant that when I began my airline job, I already had seven years' accrued service, and could retire after serving eighteen years with Air Canada. Twenty-five years is the magic number. I started Naval College at age eighteen and am now forty-three and retired. My pension is greatly reduced, as I quit eighteen years early, but I have an investment portfolio to augment my pension, a severance package, and hopefully half the farm equity will accrue to me when I reach a divorce settlement with Ginette. I have more than enough income to support myself in a very comfortable manner. When curious strangers ask about my financial status, as they often do, I reply somewhat facetiously: "I'm independently poor."

Another incredible benefit makes me in effect a rich man. Twenty-five years service is also the qualifying minimum number for lifetime airline travel privileges. This means I can travel at considerably reduced rates on any airline in the world and have a card identifying me as a former airline captain, which allows me to travel in the cockpit jump seat if the flight is full. The world is mine to explore, and I feel extremely lucky.

During dinner in this secluded Lake Champlain anchorage on the first night of my new life, I digest all of the above thoughts, along with my delicious dinner and a glass of excellent Oregon pinot noir. I permit myself a glass or two when the boat is safely anchored or docked, but never drink alcohol when underway.

My immediate goal is to get *Muscade* safely down to the island of Antigua in the West Indies and to spend next winter exploring the Caribbean. I plan a slow meander down to New York City, staying each night in one of the many quaint and sleepy villages on the Hudson River, using the time to complete a long list of final preparations, maintenance checks and last-minute jobs. I will have to lower the mast in order to pass under the bridges and navigate the locks on the Champlain canal system, so I will have a chance to inspect all the rigging. I replaced the standing rigging last summer and also fitted a self-steering wind vane, so now the person on watch will no longer have to steer the boat. This will be a huge advantage, and will allow me to single-hand *Muscade* on ocean trips. I have christened the Hydovane self-steering system "Heidi." She is a wonderful crewmember who will steer the boat indefinitely even in storm conditions, doesn't need sleep, care, or feeding and never gets seasick. Since the disastrous trip back from Bermuda ten years ago, I have gained much more ocean sailing experience (three round trips from Lake Champlain to the Bahamas) and now feel fully confident in my abilities as a skipper. *Muscade* has proven herself a serious and sea-kindly, ocean-going boat, and I am as familiar with most of her idiosyncrasies as she is with mine. More importantly, I have continued to nurture an enormous respect for the sea and remain humbled by the boundless forces of nature.

    Yacht delivery skippers and seasoned sailors all agree that the best way to go from the east coast of North America to the West Indies is via Bermuda. In spite of this truism, most cruising couples, leaving the north-eastern ports of North America for the first time bound for the West Indies, follow the American east coast down to Florida, then attempt to sail against the strong prevailing winds and currents to the Antilles. This choice of route leads to a soul-destroying voyage, and most couples eventually give up, falling back on the cruising grounds of the Bahamas, Florida Keys and Cuba instead. Their perfectly understandable reason for choosing the coast-crawl route is that first-timers are thereby not obliged to venture offshore. By following the intra-coastal waterway, they can stay within a reasonable distance of shelter, so the coastal route seems to makes the most sense - until they get to Florida and face an uphill slog to the West Indies.

    Seen scribbled on the wall of the "gents," in a London pub, "Professor Tolkien is Hobbit forming," and underneath in different hand-writing and much cleverer, "Now you're Tolkien." I have never been in a Hobbit's cave, but imagine that this place is exactly what it must be like. I am down below in the windowless main cabin of Paul Johnson's new *Venus*, anchored in St George's harbour, Bermuda. It is late in the evening. We have just finished an excellent dinner and Paul is now annotating my nautical charts of the West Indies with notes on everything from secure anchorages, to where to buy fruit and vegetables, to where to catch fish and find lobsters. He knows every nook, cranny, rock, and shoal and is kindly passing on this knowledge to me. This is often the way it works among the cruising crowd, who swap little gems of information as well as charts and cruising guides. As I say my good-byes and thanks to Paul, I know that our paths will almost certainly cross again in some exotic anchorage, now that I've adopted his bohemian way of life.

The trip from New York to Bermuda was a delight. I have decided that, if you can sleep well on the first night at sea, it bodes well for the rest of the voyage and probably means that you are as well prepared as you can be. I believe that, with the exception of Paul Johnson and a few others like him, one has to be a masochist to really enjoy an ocean passage in a small boat. Of course, there are many beautiful moments and marvelous sights to behold, but it is basically an uncomfortable way to get your boat from one fabulous cruising ground to another. There is always a feeling of accomplishment after a well-planned and well-executed offshore trip, but nevertheless I still see it as a means to an end. It could be that, because I have never attempted a really long passage, I am always anticipating the arrival before settling into the rhythm of the journey. Seasoned ocean sailors say that long passages can be euphoric, even to the extent that you don't want to arrive because that would break the spell, and shatter the illusion that you are living in a beautiful world of your own. I will reserve judgment until I have some longer voyages under my keel.

The over-riding improvement during the trip from New York was not having to endure the boring routine of steering the boat. "Heidi" held a steady course, allowing us to keep solo watches and to read and relax under the shelter of the spray dodger while on duty. The visible horizon on a small boat like *Muscade* is less than ten miles, so anytime a ship is sighted, there is always potential for an encounter, as that ship has already penetrated the ten-mile circle. I tell my watch-keepers to scan the entire horizon at least every fifteen minutes, which is the length of time one could go from nothing in sight to a collision. I also tell them to make sure they look behind the boat, as this is the most neglected quarter and probably the most likely place for surprises.

During my pre-voyage briefing, one of my crew thought I

was exaggerating the risk of collision, arguing that ships use their radar for anti-collision purposes. A day out of Bermuda, I came up on deck to take over the watch from this same person. It was a beautiful, clear, sunny, tropical morning with a fair wind blowing, and *Muscade* was gamboling along like a racehorse on the home stretch. As I stepped up into the cockpit carrying two mugs of freshly brewed coffee, I spied a ship a couple of miles astern bearing down on a collision course. I could even read the ship's name, *Oleander*, on her bow, so I called her up on the radio and identified myself. The bridge crew had not yet spotted us, and when I asked the officer-of-the-watch if we showed up on his radar, he said that it was not being used. His answer constituted both an inexpensive lesson for my crewman and a reassurance for me as navigator that we were right on track for Bermuda, as *Oleander* was an island supply vessel, heading to the same destination. In bad weather or reduced visibility, ships' officers do monitor their radar carefully, although small yachts - even steel ones - do not make good radar targets and can often be missed in the sea clutter on the screen caused by large waves. Most small boats, including *Muscade*, carry radar reflectors high on the mast, which may increase the chances of being detected.

After a lovely holiday with the vivacious Tosca in Bermuda, it was time to head south to Antigua for the winter. In theory, hurricane season was over although historically, there have been hurricanes in every month of the year except February. My crew of three airline captains, two of them former naval officers, joined ship at the R.B.Y.C. in Hamilton. I was definitely over-crewed, considering "Heidi" would be doing most of the steering. Our sail plan on this trip is to head southeast from Bermuda staying well east of the rhumb line, so that when we encounter the northeast trade winds and westerly-setting equatorial current, there will be room to comfortably bear off towards Antigua. Usually, on this route, one can expect to encounter the doldrums, an area of calm winds and flat seas. I plan to motor through this area until encountering the trade winds.

The day after my crew arrived, we set sail with good winds and an excellent weather forecast. Eight days later, we negotiated the narrow entrance to English Harbour, Antigua. *Muscade* had arrived in paradise. The trip was picture-perfect and a real pleasure cruise for me, as my competent crew did all the work. We only had three sextants, including my brand new Weems and Plath state-of-the-art model, so I delegated the navigation duties to the others, who were keen to hone their skills. We did have to motor through the doldrums for two days, but the rest of the time had great sailing winds. As cook, I provided delicious meals and kept my crew happy. It was a huge thrill for me to sail my own boat into Admiral Nelson's famous dockyard, the haven which gave the British a strategic advantage over the French by allowing them to keep their fleet well-protected during hurricane season. The inner harbour is completely sheltered from any wave action and is surrounded by high hills, which block the wind, making it a perfect "hurricane hole." I intend to base *Muscade* here for my first winter in the West Indies and explore all the islands from Guadeloupe north.

Several weeks have passed since I arrived in Antigua. My crew has long since departed and Tosca, who came for a week's holiday, left yesterday for Montréal and work. *Muscade* is anchored in front of the Admiral's Inn, inside the sheltered inner harbour of Nelson's Dockyard. I'm sitting in the cockpit in the shade of my sun awning, enjoying a delicious breakfast of excellent croissants from the dockyard bakery and a cup of strong coffee. The trade wind is caressing my body and keeping the temperature delightfully cool. The water surrounding *Muscade* is a translucent aquamarine colour. Squadrons of pelicans in formation are diving beside the boat fishing for their breakfast. The more elegant and graceful frigate birds are eying their prey, while soaring at a higher altitude. I really am in paradise and am starting to accept the idea that quitting Air Canada was a good decision after all.

However, I am becoming aware that there will be a lot of aloneness in my new lifestyle, and that is, on the whole, all right with me, as I am quite happy keeping my own company. Being by myself gives me time for contemplation, reading, writing, or just taking care of some of the jobs on the long maintenance list that never seems to get shorter. However, this morning is different. I am melancholy and feel isolated from friends and family. There will obviously be a substantial transition period as I adapt to my new circumstances and relearn how best to structure my time. Communication with the outside world is limited to ordinary mail, which takes forever. To make a telephone call, I have to take a bus to the capital, St. Johns, reserve the call at the Cable and Wireless Company office and wait for a connection. This can only be done during office hours, and success is far from guaranteed.

A couple of matters are weighing on my mind. The first concerns my pending divorce from Ginette. I met with a lawyer before leaving Canada and commissioned her to start legal proceedings. I would like proceed as amicably as possible, but suspect that Ginette is still holding out for reconciliation whereas I see divorce as the only solution. When things are eventually settled, Ginette will be able to stay on her bucolic farm, and I will be free to pursue my dreams without having to work the land during the summer months. I am hoping that, given enough time, we will resolve our differences by ending the marriage, the way most estranged couples usually do.

Next there is my relationship with the charming Tosca. The timing of our meeting could not have been worse. Not only does our affair heighten emotions, making the divorce process more difficult, but to continue our relationship would demand impossible sacrifices for both of us. We will continue together as long as it works out with her working as a flight attendant based in

Montréal, and me travelling the world. We will meet wherever and whenever we can.

A gregarious single-hander meets more people than cruising couples do because couples are happily doing things together, while singles are looking for company. When a lone sailor anchors his boat in a sheltered bay for the night, he is likely to be invited aboard other yachts for a drink or dinner. Yachts fly the flag of their country of registry on the stern, always a good starting point for an invitation. In the short time that I have been here in Antigua, I have met lots of people, so there is no lack of social opportunity. I like entertaining and am very comfortable inviting new friends aboard *Muscade*. However, I don't quite fit into any of the various categories of sailors found "messing around in boats" in the West Indies. I'm too young for the retired crowd, too rich for the charter boat crews, too poor for the owners of the crewed super yachts and too permanent for the couples who have taken a sabbatical year to sail. My closest allies are the sabbatical crowd and the rich owners.

Even though a rum-and-coke is the drink of choice for former naval pilots - to say nothing of yachtsmen sailing in the Caribbean - I am resolved not to fall into what I perceive to be a rum trap. Rum is so inexpensive here, that it is easy to consume far too much of it. One is likely to be invited aboard a neighbour's boat for a "rum" instead of a "drink," which assumes you won't ask for a beer or a glass of wine. It's much easier for me to protect my liver by fibbing that I don't drink rum.

I have decided to spend the time until I leave for Christmas circumnavigating the island of Antigua and exploring all the many bays, anchorages and small adjacent islands. At the same time, I can brush up on the reef-navigating skills that I learned during many winters sailing in the Bahamas. This technique entails taking a boat into uncharted waters, using only visual reference to the sea bottom. Sand has a different look from coral or weeds, and a good navigator can accurately judge the water depth by the colour. Most of the charts of this area were surveyed during Admiral Nelson's time and are not necessarily reliable today, so the visual method is the one sure way to proceed. This navigation skill requires good light and no glare from the sun. Grey-tinted, polarized sunglasses are a big help. Ideally, the sun should be high in the sky and astern of the boat. When one is planning a trip to an unfamiliar area, the arrival time is critical. Arriving too late can mean that bad light makes it dangerous to attempt an entry into the anchorage. Depth sounders measure the depth of water under the keel and can confirm that the crunch you just felt was indeed the bottom.

CHAPTER FOUR

WINTER IN THE CARIBBEAN

The first full calendar year of my new alternative lifestyle started, appropriately enough, in New York City, the home of the free-spirited. Tosca had a New Year's Eve layover, so I flew down on her flight. After a champagne dinner, we wandered with the crowd down to Times Square for the festivities. I had spent a very agreeable Christmas at her house in the Laurentian hills, a holiday which included some good skiing at Mont Tremblant. I saw many old friends from Air Canada on the slopes and in the *après ski* haunts. Most of the pilots thought that I was crazy to have abandoned my career and believed that I would surely live to regret the decision. The flight attendants said that I had absolutely done the right thing and was fortunate to have escaped "the rat race."

During my last year as an Air Canada captain, some of my fellow pilots refused to believe that I was actually going to leave the airline, so I would bet them a bottle of champagne that my intentions were sincere. Many took me up on the wager, but not one single pilot paid up. Airline pilots have a reputation for being cheap - just ask any flight attendant. This is probably because they get paid large salaries, but don't qualify for any tax breaks, so are stingy with the disposable income remaining after taxes. This trait, coupled with the fact that they are accustomed to staying in luxury hotels while on the job and can fly around the world on holidays for practically nothing, adds to their reluctance to spend a buck. When I first joined the airline, and before realizing that I was not obliged to accompany my captains on layovers, I found myself on many occasions being dragged through the narrow back streets of various European cities to their favourite haunts, where the food was cheap and cheerful. I soon learned to go out with the flight attendants, who appreciated the good things in life and who were quite happy to spend their expense money on a decent meal and a good bottle of wine.

To avoid income tax, a group of airline pilots in the USA started their own church and then donated their entire salaries to the institution without incurring income tax. Their church, in turn, paid them their money back as an allowance: unfortunately for them, the American I.R.S. soon put a stop to their scheme.

My dear father was also distressed that I had thrown away my high-paying career. I suppose that parents always worry about how their children are going to navigate life's obstacles, no matter what age they happen to be. When I decided to leave the navy, Dad called in all the big guns to convince me otherwise. At a black-tie dinner of the Anchorite's Society in London, I found myself sitting next to Sir Peter Hill-Norton, the First Sea Lord, who tried all evening to persuade me that my future was in the navy. Sir Peter was a friend and neighbour of my parents. I didn't have the heart to tell him that I had already accepted a training course date with Air Canada. Later, my father was very pleased when I became an airline captain, but couldn't believe that I was resigning from that job as well.

In spite of the negative sentiments from my pilot colleagues, I was really excited about my upcoming winter in the West Indies and took the first available flight back to Antigua. On arrival, I found *Muscade* just as I had left her, anchored in the inner harbour of Nelson's dockyard with her stern tied into the roots of mangrove trees for extra protection. After extricating her from the anchorage, I sailed around the island to Crabb's Marina, where I hauled the boat and painted the bottom with anti-fouling paint. This highly toxic paint prevents coral, barnacles, and weed from growing on the hull and is usually effective for about a year. Without this paint, the hull would soon become encrusted and the boat impossible to sail. *Muscade* is now ready for the winter. I have pre-arranged a reasonable compromise between having friends aboard and having time for myself. My invited guests will join me on specific dates in either Antigua or Guadeloupe. I will try this system for my first winter and refine it next year, if necessary.

I had some time before my first guest was due to arrive, so I decided to sail to Guadeloupe, the French island to the south of Antigua. This involved a forty-five mile single-handed passage, which would be good training for the future. A voyage between any of the main islands of the Caribbean chain is an open ocean experience, albeit a short one. The northeast trade winds blow from Africa right across into Central America, so the sailing is boisterous. In the winter months, winds are often twenty knots or more, and waves four to six feet high. Before setting sail from Antigua, while still in the calm comfort of my sheltered anchorage, I prepared the boat for the seven-hour trip to Guadeloupe. I lashed the inflatable dinghy on the bow of the boat, then secured drinking water, emergency equipment and a hand-held radio in the life raft. Everything down below was stowed away or secured and all hatches were closed tightly. I am a very cautious sailor, so I always close the shut-off valves for sink, shower, and toilet drains, leaving only the engine-cooling water intake open. This precaution reduces the possibility of leaks, and makes it easier to find the problem if the boat does start taking on water. I reefed the mainsail to suit the anticipated wind strength, as it is far easier to hoist more sail at sea if the wind abates than it is to shorten sail in strengthening winds. Finally, I put on my safety harness and secured it to the steel wires that go around the deck on both sides of the boat. I was well aware that, if I fell overboard while "Heidi" was steering, I would be dragged in the boat's wake and would not be able to get back aboard. Unsurprisingly, one develops an intense sense of self-preservation when sailing alone.

The West Indies chain of islands is a sailing paradise because the islands are oriented north/south and the prevailing trade winds are from the east. This means that the wind is almost always on the beam, or ninety degrees to the direction the boat is travelling, which is the best and most efficient point of sail. It also means that all of the bays and anchorages on the west side of the islands are perfectly sheltered from the wind. There are two complications to mar this otherwise perfect world. The first is the equatorial current, which flows from northeast to southwest and accelerates by venturi effect when squeezed between the islands. Because this current pushes the boat towards the west, the boat's heading when going north or south between the islands has to be adjusted into wind to compensate for the drift. The resulting point of sail is less efficient and less comfortable. The second inconvenience is a groundswell, which bounces back all the way from Central America when the trade winds slacken at night, causing an uncomfortable rolling motion in the normally sheltered and tranquil west coast anchorages. Deep and narrow bays are best, as the groundswell cannot penetrate the anchorage and breaks up at the entrance. The best way to tell if groundswell is a possibility in a given anchorage is to look at the beach. If the sand on the beach is flat, there will be no groundswell. If the beach sand is steeply sloped towards the water, that slope was caused by wave action.

Seven hours after leaving Antigua, I dropped anchor off the village of Deshaies on the northwestern corner of Guadeloupe and rowed ashore to explore. I found myself in a totally different world from Antigua. The natives spoke French or a type of Creole, but could still understand my more formal French. Cars drove on the right- hand side of the road, and the currency was French francs. Churches were Roman Catholic instead of Baptist or Methodist. The vegetation was far more lush and tropical because the island is much higher than Antigua, so it rains more often. Even though constitutionally Guadeloupe is a department of France, the small villages are very much like those found in any developing country. The infrastructure is excellent with good roads, schools and hospitals. However, the houses are small, and the residents appear to be quite poor, but certainly not as poor as the Antiguans. There are plenty of fresh supplies available and a good variety of French wines, although I find in tropical countries, red wines usually suffer from the heat, while the whites and *rosés* keep their freshness much longer. Ashore, I met a Canadian couple, Stephen and Helen from Toronto, whose boat, *Main Chance*, was also anchored in the harbour. They kindly invited me aboard for an *apéritif* before dinner. They had sailed down from Toronto via Bermuda and were also planning to cruise in the Caribbean for the entire winter. After a pleasant visit, I rowed back to *Muscade* for dinner and a sound sleep.

 The next day, I left Deshaies early in the morning and motored in windless conditions down the scenic west coast of Guadeloupe. At the southern end of the island, the land rises steeply to form a volcano, *La Soufrière*. I was heading towards a small archipelago of islands called Les Saintes, located a few nautical miles south of the main island. As soon as I cleared the landmass of Guadeloupe, the trade winds re-established quickly, so I hoisted sail and stopped the engine. An hour later, I dropped the hook in front of the charming town of Bourg des Saintes.

A short time later Stephen from *Main Chance* pulled up alongside in his dinghy, asked to borrow my portable grill and invited me for dinner. During the evening, he asked me if I would be interested in crewing for him as his tactician and navigator during Antigua Race Week in April. Even though I am no longer much interested in yacht racing, I accepted his invitation. Racing a sailing boat can often be contrary to good seamanship and boat management. Cruising sailors manage their boats with respect for the prevailing conditions, but when racing you are trying to beat nature at her own game by carrying maximum sail and pushing the boat to the limit in order to win the day. This often leads to torn sails, broken gear and stressed crewmembers. I did a lot of racing when learning how to sail. If you are competing in a race with identical boats and someone passes you, the person sailing that boat is obviously a better sailor, and by observation you can learn what you are doing wrong and adjust accordingly.

The following morning, as I was relaxing in the cockpit and feeling pretty good about life, I noticed a French naval patrol boat entering the harbour, towing an inflatable Zodiac dinghy. Just as I was thinking that some incompetent novice had failed to tie up his dinghy properly, causing the navy to go to the rescue, I glanced to the stern of my boat and realized that it was my Zodiac they were saving. I finished my coffee quickly, dove into the harbour and swam ashore to claim it back from the navy. I returned aboard highly embarrassed and extremely grateful that my luck was still holding.

Next on my agenda is a sail from Les Saintes to Pointe-à-Pitre, the capital of Guadeloupe, where I am meeting my next guest in a few days. It will be a tough sail, as the heading is directly into wind and current. Guadeloupe is such a large island that the current is forced to sweep around both ends, which increases the strength of the flow. *Muscade* will not sail any closer than fifty degrees to the wind, so getting to my destination will require a lot of zigzagging or tacking. When sailing close to the wind and into a current, the normal sideways drift or leeway combines with the current to pretty well eliminate any forward progress. To overcome this, I will motor-sail using both sails and engine. The engine increases the boat speed through the water, which cuts down the time that the current affects the tack. It also allows me to steer much closer to the wind.

After a six-hour slog, I arrived at the marina in Pointe-à-Pitre and went alongside my assigned dock. I was in heaven. The marina complex housed many French restaurants as well as a huge supermarket, a well-equipped parts and repair facility, and hot showers. I do have a hot shower on Muscade, but carry a limited quantity of water, so the ablution has to be brief. When at anchor, I usually swim several times a day, then rinse off with a fresh water shower after the last dip. Here at the marina there is a fresh water tap on my dock, so I have the luxury of unlimited showers.

I have been doing half an hour of stretching exercises every morning for years and now do them on Muscade's foredeck, much to the amusement of passers-by. Ironically, the overweight and unfit observers ridicule me the most. I have always been an inveterate walker and consider hiking a great way to stay healthy. When I was working as a pilot, I used to walk for miles on layovers, especially during the nights in European cities when the effects of jet lag made it impossible to sleep. Here in the tropics, I find it more difficult to make time for walking. The air temperature is very uncomfortable during the heat of the day, and the roads are not always conducive to safe hiking. Long beaches are ideal, and very early in the morning is by far the best time. When at anchor, I often swim ashore in the morning, do my stretching exercises on the beach, go for a long walk and then swim back aboard for breakfast.

Today, my friend Terry Jones arrived at the marina for a ten-day visit. Terry was a farm neighbour and is married to an Air Canada flight attendant. During a convivial reunion dinner, we decided that we would sail down to the southeastern tip of this butterfly-shaped island, and explore the towns of Sainte Anne and Saint François along the way. With this in mind, we set sail the following morning into fairly stiff trade winds and a strong counter-current. The current was so strong that we only made it as far as the Club Med near the village of Ste. Anne. Almost as soon as our anchor was set, we were inundated by Canadians staying at the Club, who were very curious about the presence of a Canadian boat so far away from its homeport of Montréal. We soon made the acquaintance of some sailors from Québec City who invited us ashore for a buffet dinner and show at the resort.

The following afternoon, we weighed anchor and proceeded inside the barrier reef which protects the village of Ste. Anne. Here we re-anchored, swam and settled down to some quiet reading with the intention of rowing ashore later for dinner at a beachside restaurant. Terry was in the aft guest cabin, and I was in my cabin in the forward part of the boat. Just as it was starting to get dark, I heard a woman's voice calling, *"Bonjour Muscade,"* from the stern of the boat. Thinking that this might be a beautiful mermaid, and that this might be my lucky day, I grabbed a flashlight and hurried to see who was there. When I peered over the side into the water, I saw my wife Ginette clutching the rudder of the steering vane for dear life. What a shock! Apparently, she had found out from Terry's wife that I was cruising around Guadeloupe and flew down to find me and discuss our future. She had inquired at the Port Captain's office in Pointe-à-Pitre and learned that I was intending to cruise in these waters. Spotting the boat at anchor from her bus just before sunset, she had left her belongings at a beachside restaurant, changed into her swimsuit and swum out to the boat, risking the strong currents and the danger of predatory fish. I completely surprised myself and shocked both Terry and Ginette with my angry reaction to what I considered to be a total violation of my privacy. Furious, I insisted that Ginette leave the boat immediately. However, by the time the three of us had rowed ashore and found a table for dinner, I had calmed down considerably and was ready to have a civil conversation.

As we were sipping our drinks, while we waited for Ginette to retrieve her clothes and dress for dinner, Terry convinced me that this could be a very opportune time to negotiate the terms of our divorce. I had to concede that Ginette, who is not a strong swimmer, had been pretty courageous, if not foolhardy, to swim out to the boat after dusk. The fact that she had come all the way down to Guadeloupe to find me showed a strong commitment and a serious desire to solve our problems. That night, over a delicious dinner, lots of wine, and with Terry's help, we agreed on the terms of our divorce.

During the negotiations, I thought that it might help my cause if I casually reminded Ginette that I had once saved her life. It happened one cold February night, soon after we moved to the farm. Ginette had gone to the opening of an art gallery with Terry's wife, Ann. I was under the weather with a particularly nasty case of flu, so was sound asleep in bed when Ginette got home. Not wanting to disturb me, she had crept upstairs in the dark. On entering the bedroom, she lost consciousness and collapsed. Fortunately, she fell on top of a wicker wastebasket and the ensuing crunching noise woke me up. When I finally fumbled the bedside light on, I saw her lying on the floor unconscious and not breathing. I was still half-asleep, very groggy from medication and had no idea what was happening. My first thought was that she had choked on something, so I performed the Heimlich maneuver to no avail. By then I was in a state of near panic, but remembered the first aid advice from Boy Scout days about making sure the breathing passages were clear. I discovered that a dental plate had indeed jarred loose when she fell and was effectively choking her. As soon as I removed the obstruction, she immediately gasped for air, began breathing again and quickly regained consciousness. I was now as wide awake as anybody can possibly be and soon figured out that Ginette had suffered carbon monoxide poisoning from a malfunction in her car's heating system. I immediately phoned Ann to warn her and make sure that she had not succumbed to the same toxic gas. The next day, we scrapped the car.

Back in the beachfront restaurant, and with a glad heart, I extended an invitation to Ginette to spend the night aboard *Muscade*, the boat on which we had shared so many sailing adventures during our ten years together. I was happy to acknowledge that this woman, whom I married in Bermuda eight years before, had not lost any of her nobility. Our priorities had changed, as had our dreams and aspirations for life. Clearly, it was time to go our separate ways with no regrets or loss of respect. An amicable divorce was in the offing.

The next morning, the three of us had a rollicking sail to St. François where I anchored *Muscade* in the protected inner harbour, and rowed Ginette ashore in the dinghy. We said our goodbyes and agreed to follow through with the divorce proceedings when I get back to Montréal in early summer. I knew that the jealous Tosca would jump to the wrong conclusion and suspect that the meeting with Ginette in Guadeloupe had been pre-arranged, and I dreaded telling her the real story. Sure enough, later that afternoon when I phoned her, she hung up on me, then stubbornly refused to answer subsequent calls. I have always thought jealousy to be such a destructive and useless emotion. If Ginette and I had really wanted to continue our marriage, there was absolutely nothing Tosca could have done about it, except to take solace that her jealousy had been justified. While I still have strong feelings for Tosca, it is becoming sadly evident that our relationship cannot last much longer.

I am reasonably pleased with the way my first winter is unfolding. I am enchanted by everything about the West Indies and am gaining confidence daily as I navigate between the islands, either alone or with friends as crew. I have already had the privilege of meeting people from all walks of life whom I never would have met from the cockpit of my Air Canada jet. I am finding that the balance between having friends on board and being alone is just about right. I tend to meet more people when I am by myself. If *Muscade* is at anchor, and another privately-owned vessel anchors close by, I am sure to have much in common with the owner, as we have travelled similar paths to end up in the same anchorage. In our adopted lifestyle, we are down to one degree of separation. Meeting new people on these chance occasions is always a worthwhile exchange. I still have lingering doubts about having left Air Canada at the high point of my career and sometimes wonder what the future holds for me. I am curious as to what the "moving finger" will write about me, in years to come.

I have not had much luck catching fish this winter, so today I asked some local fishermen from Les Saintes for their advice. I have never been a sport fisherman, but I love to eat fresh fish and know that these waters are teeming with tuna and dorado. The fishermen instructed me that the best technique is to trail a small plastic squid on the end of a long line (at least three hundred feet) behind the boat. Early mornings and evenings just before sunset are the optimum times. The best locations are naturally those close to reefs and known feeding grounds, not in the deep ocean waters between islands. Fish can be caught in the open ocean if one happens to be sailing through a migrating school, which can often be identified by swooping birdlife, or the presence of dolphins.

Armed with this information, I bought myself a sturdy reel, a thousand feet of high-test line and some plastic squid lures. The fishermen told me that the size of the lure determines the size of the catch. The speed of the boat is also important, so *Muscade* will have to be traveling close to her maximum speed for me to snag a tuna or dorado. Slower speeds will attract barracuda, which should not be eaten due to possible toxicity in the fish. In extreme cases, this poison can cause severe illness or death. Because barracuda are territorial, there are some locations in the Caribbean where they can be eaten. Local fishermen say that, south of Martinique, barracuda are edible because the type of coral which causes the toxic build-up (ciguatera) is not present in that area. Barracuda eat small reef fish, which feed on the toxic coral. Because the effect is cumulative, the bigger the barracuda, the more likely it is to be poisonous. I have attached my new reel to a teak handrail just behind the wheel, so I can wind in my catch without leaving the cockpit and I have sworn never to eat barracuda. Tomorrow, I will be single-handing back to Antigua to take part in the annual Race Week celebrations and I am looking forward to trying out my newly acquired fishing gear.

Antigua Race Week was started several years ago by charter boat crews, who congregated in Antigua at the end of their West Indies winter season for a bit of fun and relaxation, before crossing to the Mediterranean for the summer. It has evolved into a major event on the world yacht-racing calendar. I will act as navigator and tactician aboard the yacht, *Main Chance*, owned by Stephen and Helen Cerny whom I met in Guadeloupe last January. We will be competing in one of the cruising classes. Race Week offers a combination of hard racing during the day and non-stop partying in the evenings. Each class of boat has its own start, and each race presents different challenges. One of the highlights of the week is a beach party sponsored by Mount Gay Rum, but there is something special going on every evening. The sweet sounds of reggae or steel band calypso music provide a perfect backdrop for a rum-enhanced post mortem of the day's race.

All things considered, it was an enjoyable week. Tosca, after finally realizing that Ginette's visit to the boat had resulted in a pending divorce agreement, flew down to Antigua to join in the fun. *Main Chance* did fairly well in her class, but we had to withdraw from the last race because of a torn sail. The owner proved to be highly competitive, disregarded my advice most of the time, took the boat too close to shallow water for my liking and carried too much sail in high winds. I later found out that he had some Olympic experience in smaller boats, which explained his competitive spirit. At the end of the week, we parted the best of friends and agreed to meet in Canada during the summer. I am glad I accepted Stephen's offer to participate in Race Week. It definitely honoured my father's advice to "never refuse an invitation."

My first full winter in the Caribbean is drawing to a close. I am reflecting on this while sailing *Muscade* from English Harbour around to Crabb's Marina on the north coast of the island. As I sail inside Cade reef, my fishing reel suddenly releases and rapidly spools out. I slow the boat by turning into the wind, tighten the reel tension and slowly crank in tonight's dinner, a two-pound yellow-tailed snapper. Tomorrow morning, I will make arrangements to leave my trusty boat in dry storage for the summer.

It's been a good winter, but I am still a little unsure of myself. It is obviously going to take more time before I am completely convinced, and totally comfortable with my new life. It is exciting to contemplate what the summer has in store for me. I will initially stay with Tosca at her lakeside house while I negotiate my divorce. Then, if all goes well, I will fly to the U.K. and spend some time with my parents who live on the island of Anglesey in North Wales. I am also considering a tour around Scotland, the land of my birth.

Today, the 26th of June 1985, Ginette and I ended our marriage amicably. We convened at the courthouse in St. Jérôme with a very sympathetic judge and one lawyer, representing both of us. The judge approved the divorce routinely. Then, while I was still in the witness box, he asked if I would mind answering a few questions about sailing in the West Indies. It was all quite amusing and convivial. The judge, who either had a dream of doing the same thing himself one day, or was living my dream vicariously, seemed fascinated and got quite caught up in the exchange. Our lawyer took advantage of this amicability to ask my latest best friend, the judge, if he would approve the final divorce immediately instead of making us wait the usual thirty-day cooling-off period. He heartily agreed to have the papers ready by the following Monday, and we all left the courthouse chatting together, if not exactly arm-in-arm.

The divorce agreement is quite simple. According to Québec law, we are each entitled to half of the farm. I agreed to sell my half to Ginette for considerably less than the market value. I gave her a twenty-five year mortgage with no down payment and a five per cent interest rate. The current mortgage rates are eighteen to twenty-two per cent, so it is a very fair arrangement. Ginette agreed to pay me monthly until the loan is paid off and the farm becomes hers. *Muscade* remains my property because I had owned the boat before our marriage. I gave Ginette all of the furniture in the farmhouse, with the exception of one antique pine refectory table, which I had bought when I first arrived in Montréal. The standing joke among my friends was that I had bought an antique farmhouse table; then felt obliged to buy a farm with a farmhouse to put it in. Ginette agreed to store the table for me at the farm.

The euphoria over my satisfactory divorce settlement is proving short-lived, and I am wondering if all men are as stupid and naïve as I am when it comes to relationships with women. I could add the adjective "cowardly" to my rhetorical question. I am referring to the beautiful and vivacious Tosca, who naturally has her own version of our future. I have been so focused on my new life and so obsessed with my new-found freedom that I have largely ignored the Tosca dilemma and now must face it head-on. When we first met, I didn't have the courage to tell her that our relationship had little chance of long-term success. She was in no position to give up her life to hitch up with a newly-minted vagabond, and

I was not about to abandon my long-nurtured dream. Under different circumstances, Tosca and I could have continued a happy relationship for a long time. We have decided to break things off. I will transfer my few belongings from her house to a friend's basement. I don't have much to store: some clothes, books, personal papers and my winter things including skis. I have no car and all the rest of my "stuff " is on board *Muscade* in Antigua.

I have been asked to deliver a Dutch, Trintella 42 yacht from Montréal to Antigua after the hurricane season next November, and have gladly accepted the challenge. Stephen and Helen Cerny (from Antigua Race Week) want me to help them evaluate a new boat at the Ted Hood yard in Marblehead, Massachusetts, later this summer, and I have agreed to meet them in Boston. Ted Hood is a famous American sailor, sail maker and boat builder. It will be a pleasure to meet him. His company, Little Harbour, has just finished building a boat called *American Promise* for Dodge Morgan, who will attempt to break the single-handed, non-stop, round-the-world record with his new boat. The Cernys and I have been invited to the commissioning ceremony, on the same day that we are going to sail and evaluate a Little Harbour 55 sailing boat with Ted Hood. These are the sorts of opportunities I was hoping might materialize, now that I am free to accept them.

Nonetheless, it is with a heavy heart that I leave Tosca and the beautiful Laurentian hills and lakes to travel to the U.K. for the summer. My ties with Montréal seem precarious. After eighteen exceptional years, during which I fell in love with Québec and embraced the culture and language wholeheartedly, I am moving on. Québec is a principal creative dynamo for all of Canada, and Canadians are fortunate to have such an incubator for artistic talent. Many Canadians from outside Québec fail to recognize this asset and sometimes denigrate their French-speaking countrymen. It is discouraging to hear people say: "If they spoke proper Parisian French, I would consider learning it." The irony is that the language spoken in Québec today is purer than that spoken in France. The pronunciation and usage in "The New World" can be traced back to the first colonists during the reign of King Louis XIV. Isolated in North America for four hundred years, the language has evaded corruption, so has far fewer Anglicisms than the French spoken in France. Non-French speaking Canadians from outside Québec tend to lump all francophones together, not realizing that there is no love lost between Québecers and their French cousins. If anything, there is mutual animosity. The theory that Québecers are conspiring with the French to reconstruct a French nation in Canada could not be farther from the truth. Years ago, when President Charles de Gaulle tried to interfere in Canadian politics, Prime Minister Lester Pearson quickly showed him the door.

Fortunately, my departure this summer is only an *au revoir*. I will be back very soon and will continue to make Québec my home, but it does seem a little strange to be returning to the country of my birth as a free agent for the first time since I came to Canada at the age of eleven, when my father was posted to Ottawa with the British High Commission.

I am sitting in the first-class section of an Air Canada Lockheed Tri-Star bound for London, wondering if I would rather be in the captain's seat, instead of being an unemployed passenger on this flight. My decision to leave Air Canada was not based on any economic rationale. Rather it was a passionate attempt to get the very most out of my life. I also wanted to prove to myself that I really did have the courage of my convictions. Until I left Air Canada, I had never really been tested, and although I did not receive any financial help from my parents after leaving home at age eighteen, the solid base they provided paved the way for a very easy ride. Life's choices can only be evaluated in retrospect, so I must be patient, as it will be many years before I find out if my decision to follow the "old enchanter" was the right one.

I am on my way to visit my parents, who live in the picturesque seaside village of Beaumaris on the Welsh island of Anglesey. They moved to this idyllic location several years ago, after my father retired from his job as a senior executive in London. Their house sits on a hill overlooking the Straits of Menai with a magnificent view of the Snowdon Mountains in the far distance. The local joke is: if you can't see the mountains, it's raining, and if you can see them, it's going to rain. My sister Diana, who was the catalyst for our parents' move to Wales, also lives in this area with her husband and their two sons. It is always a great pleasure to spend some time with my family, and I consider myself very lucky to be in their company several times a year.

A fortunate reality, and one which makes for a harmonious relationship, is that neither I, nor my three siblings, have surpassed our parents' accomplishments, so our status in their home is much as it was when we were growing up. My father, known affectionately by the shopkeepers in the village as "the Admiral," still acts as if he is in charge of the world. He runs his household and takes care of most of the logistics, as my mother is practically blind. He also holds court in the clubhouse of the Royal Anglesey Yacht Club where he plays bridge, sips single malt whiskey, and sometimes gets involved as an official for their sailing races. I joined this club ten years ago to take advantage of reciprocal arrangements with many other yacht clubs around the world. Dad still plays golf at a local goat track, which serves as the golf course. It is on the property of Sir Richard Williams-Bulkley, the fourteenth Baronet of Penrhyn, who sometimes grazes his sheep on the course, adding extra hazards to an already challenging and perverse game. My mother has always been a very keen gardener. She reluctantly left her beautiful acre of English country garden in Surrey when my parents relocated to North Wales. As a consolation, my father agreed to give her *carte blanche* with the garden at their new house, so she has completely redesigned and terraced the property. I have inherited my mother's love of gardening and enjoy helping her with the incredible amount of weeding and pruning needed in this rainforest-like climate.

I have been hiking in the Snowdon Hills and walking around the bucolic country lanes of Anglesey. My sister and her husband, an orthopedic surgeon at the near-by county hospital, have kindly invited me into their social circle. One of their doctor friends enlisted me as crew for an overnight race from Anglesey to Dublin. In the middle of the night, when I was at the helm, one of the gorillas on the crew handed me up a very large, thick bacon sandwich from the galley. As I squished the bread slices together to make it small enough to get into my mouth, copious quantities of bacon grease spilled out and congealed on my foul weather gear. This, and lashings of hot tea, were our sole onboard sustenance. When we arrived at the Royal St. George's Yacht Club in Dublin the next morning, it was all hands ashore to see how much Guinness we could consume before the return race the next day. All of this confirmed my preference for ocean cruising, and I politely declined an offer to crew in next year's Fastnet race. There are sometimes limits to accepting invitations.

Towards the end of my stay in Wales, I borrowed a car from my parents and headed up the east coast of Scotland to check out my birthplace, the fishing port of Arbroath. In January 1941, my father was flying Swordfish torpedo bombers with the Royal Navy out of a naval airfield close to Arbroath. I had the good sense to leave Scotland at the tender age of nine months, when my father was posted to a similar base in the Orkney Islands. During my time with Air Canada, I had enjoyed many layovers in Prestwick, on the west coast of Scotland, but had never visited my birthplace. After looking around this fairly prosperous fishing town, which seemed to have done quite well without me all these years, I continued further north to Inverness, where I spent a couple of days hiking and scrambling in the Scottish highlands before returning to Wales to pack my bags for the trip back to Canada.

The Air Canada flight from London to Montréal was chaotic. The flight attendants had just started strike action against the company, and scab crews were poised to operate the aircraft. At the last minute, Air Canada decided to let the regular crew work their way back to home base, while the scab crew travelled back as first-class passengers on the same flight. It was a recipe for disaster, which the captain should never have permitted. As anyone could have predicted, the service was horrible, and one small act of protest was committed during the flight. I knew all of the Montréal-based flight attendants well and had much sympathy for their plight. There was one bad apple among them who carried out the vandalism and tried to instigate trouble, but the rest of the crewmembers were making the best of a very bad deal. Meanwhile, the captain was oblivious to what was happening to the rest of his aircraft beyond the cockpit door.

I have arrived in Montréal and am sitting on my bed in a hotel room at the Dorval Airport Hilton, feeling very sorry for myself and on the verge of tears. For one thing, I detest hotels, having spent much of the last eighteen years in so-called "five stars." For another, I had not anticipated that all of my friends would be out of town, including the friend in whose house I had stored my belongings. My real home is several thousand miles away in a boat yard in Antigua, so I am really marooned. My feelings are further depressed, knowing that on previous occasions Tosca would have been at the airport to meet me, drive me to her comfortable home and pour me a glass of wine. Instead, here I am in the city which has been my home for over twenty years with nowhere to go except this lousy hotel room.

CHAPTER FIVE

THREE HURRICANES

What a difference a day makes! I am back to my usual self, in good spirits and feeling a little ashamed of all the self-pity of yesterday. I suppose that I was due for a bit of a downer having left my job, divorced my wife, sold my farm, moved to my boat and left my girlfriend all in the same year. I have rented a car and, later today will meet the owner of the boat which I am delivering to Antigua next month. The friends who are storing my belongings are back in town, so I will stay with them until I depart for the West Indies.

Air Canada has fired all of the flight attendants who worked my flight back from London yesterday, which I think is very unfair. I have contacted the flight attendants and their union officials to offer my support and have accepted a request from their lawyer to testify on their behalf as an expert witness at an upcoming labour tribunal.

It is now September, and I am completely back in my element as a delivery skipper aboard the yacht, *La Brunante*. Her name is a French-Canadian word, which dates back to colonial times and is no longer used in France. Roughly translated, it means the period in the evening between sunset and nightfall, or perhaps, late twilight. She was recently built by the Trintella Company in Holland and is beautifully and luxuriously appointed. The boat will be my home until I reach Antigua. I have been commissioned to deliver her to the same boatyard where I left *Muscade* for the summer. This is very convenient, and gives me the opportunity to stock up with spare parts and non-perishable food supplies for my own boat. I am with two good friends, both Air Canada captains. They will crew for me from Montréal to Annapolis. After hurricane season, I have arranged for other friends (there is no shortage of people, who wish to try ocean sailing) to join me for the second part of the trip. We will depart from Norfolk, Virginia, sail to Bermuda, then carry on to Antigua. The owner of the boat, André Lussier, will make up part of my ocean crew, but I will remain the captain and ultimate authority. André is a charming gentleman, who made his money in the early days of cable television by importing and selling hardware to that industry.

Hurricane Gloria is roaring up the East Coast of the United States and is expected to hit New York City in two days. It is a category four storm, and should be taken very seriously. I am presently in Catskill Creek on the Hudson River about a hundred miles north of New York City, where I am re-stepping the mast, which had to be lowered when transiting the Champlain Canal system. My options for weathering the hurricane are: either to stay here at the marina and risk a flood surge in the creek, which could wash away the docks, or anchor out in the Hudson River and - take my chances - once I know the expected wind direction. After consulting with the locals about previous storms, I have decided that it is safer to stay at the marina. This plan has an added advantage because the marina is home to a decent restaurant and a lively bar. Gloria has been named the "storm of the century," and many buildings in New York have been evacuated, including the World Trade Center.

It is now several days later, and although Gloria inflicted huge damage on everything in her path, we came through unscathed. Most of the channel marker buoys in New York Harbour were displaced by the storm, so I had to revert to basic navigation when transiting from the Hudson River to the open Atlantic. The next day, while almost becalmed in light airs at the mouth of the Delaware River, we were treated to a rare spectacle when a huge orange cloud of migrating Monarch butterflies drifted through our sails on their annual journey to Mexico. The rest of the trip up the Delaware River, through the canal, and down Chesapeake Bay was uneventful, and we arrived in the historic town of Annapolis on schedule.

At the beginning of November, my ocean crew arrived, and we sailed down the Bay to Norfolk, getting there just in time to hole up for hurricane Juan. After Juan had safely past, I decided to set sail shortly after a cold front passage to take advantage of the strong northwesterly tailwinds behind the front. This strategy backfired when, shortly after our departure from Chesapeake Bay, the yacht's main steering system broke. We found ourselves hurriedly installing the emergency tiller as the boat floundered in forty-knot winds and high seas. We were forced to beat our way back to Norfolk into a strong headwind, but got some relief when I discovered that the autopilot was connected to the rudderpost below the break. As a result, we didn't have to steer with the manual tiller. Shortly after getting back to the marina in Little Creek, we located the break in the steering pedestal, fixed the problem and set sail immediately, as I did not wish to lose the advantage of the tailwind. We arrived in Bermuda in record time, after four and a half days of boisterous sailing. Just before making landfall, the owner panicked when we lost the Loran C, coastal navigation signal. To reassure him, I took a quick sun sight with my sextant to confirm that we were on track for the island. When we were safely alongside in St. George's harbour, he complained of heart pains, so I rushed him to hospital. He was diagnosed with dangerously high blood pressure and had to return immediately to Montréal. Unfortunately, this means that he will not be able to continue on to Antigua, but will fly down later to join the boat.

The day after our arrival in Bermuda, when I was treating my crew to a celebratory dinner at the Carriage House in St. George's, I was surprised to spot Dodge Morgan dining at an adjacent table. He was supposed to be on a solo voyage around the world. I introduced myself to Dodge, reminded him that I had been at his commissioning ceremony in Marblehead and asked what he was doing in Bermuda. His boat, *American Promise*, had incurred some serious mechanical problems early in the voyage, forcing him to break off the circumnavigation and put into Bermuda for repairs. He was planning to restart his attempt to break the record the next morning. I promised to be there to wish him *bon voyage* and help cast off his lines.

As it is now getting close to the end of hurricane season, it should soon be safe to leave for Antigua, but the latest forecast has hurricane Kate heading directly towards Bermuda, and I am starting to feel a little jinxed. Having to avoid three hurricanes in one delivery trip is probably a record. Ancient mariners used to say about hurricanes, " June too soon, July stand by, August a must, September remember, October it's over." With global climate change, this rhyme no longer holds true, as hurricanes are now becoming quite common in November, and even in December.

The trip from Bermuda to Antigua was very enjoyable, and I am now fully comfortable and relaxed during these ocean passages. *La Brunante* is a pleasure to sail and very easy to handle with all of her modern conveniences. My crew consisted of Peter Waddell, his wife Gisela, and Ernest Mellows, who was hitching a ride back to his own boat. Gisela had crewed for me once before, from Cape May, N.J. to the Bahamas and had been chronically seasick on that trip. She bravely wanted to give ocean sailing one more try. Unfortunately, she was sick again and will have to forgo future ocean trips. Chronic seasickness is actually quite rare. Many people get sick for a day or two and then can be quite productive crewmembers for the rest of the voyage. According to naval history archives, Admiral Horatio Nelson suffered from chronic seasickness. The jury is still out on the causes of this debilitating condition, although there are numerous theories. We had steady favourable winds all the way, avoided the doldrums, and the boat and her crew, apart from poor Gisela, performed admirably.

After anchoring *La Brunante* in front of Crabb's Marina, I went ashore to check on the condition of my own boat. All was well. We sometimes forget that inanimate objects do not share our concept of time. I am often asked who takes care of *Muscade* when I leave her for long periods. My answer is that objects such as boats, cars, cottages, and houses don't require daily care, so it is useless to be concerned about them. I will continue to live aboard *La Brunante* at anchor in the harbour until *Muscade* is ready to be launched. This is a wonderful arrangement, one much envied by the other yachties in the boatyard, when I meet them every evening in the marina bar to compare notes on the day's work and the winter's cruising plans. Living on a boat out of the water is far from ideal, as the toilets and sink drains cannot be used, and access is by ladder.

I have a dream winter planned. After spending the holiday season in Wales, I will cruise gently down the entire West Indies chain to Trinidad to arrive there in time for Mardi Gras. The list of my intended ports of call reads like a romantic pirate story: Guadeloupe, Les Saintes, Dominica, Martinique, St Lucia, St Vincent, The Grenadines including Bequia, Mustique, Canouan, Grenada and finally Trinidad. I can hear echoes of Robert Louis

Stevenson's Long John Silver: "Aharr miss Purity, thar'll be no more rum 'til we reach Portobello." I can palpably and dramatically feel a transition occurring as the type of life, I have dreamed about for so long gradually becomes my reality. Another ambition has been to have my own boat in Trinidad during the carnival celebrations. With any luck, it will come to pass next February.

I became enamoured with Trinidad's carnival many years ago when I was a navy pilot. The Canadian aircraft carrier, *Bonaventure*, was on a courtesy visit to Port of Spain during this amazing event, which is undeniably a celebration for the local people, not an event contrived for tourists. Preparations for the next carnival begin immediately after the hangover from the current one has worn off. Trinidadians spend a huge part of their disposable income, to say nothing of incredible amounts of time and effort, preparing their costumes for the annual Road March, which is always accompanied by steel drum bands pulled on wheels. Not even the most conservative, stiff and proper Anglo-Saxon could resist leaping to his feet and swaying his hips to the rhythm of the music, when a steel band starts to play. Local Calypso singers compose original music for each new carnival season. The lyrics often have political comments or social messages, which add extra dimensions to the already spectacular music. All of this made quite an impression on a twenty-three year-old, single navy pilot with time on his hands in a tropical paradise. When flying for Air Canada, I always made sure to select flights which included layovers in Trinidad during carnival.

Alas, the scuttlebutt among the cruising crowd is that the Trinidadian Government has placed a restraint on foreign yachts during carnival, restricting them to the busy commercial harbour of the capital, Port of Spain. Apparently, yachts wishing to visit other parts of the island during the festivities require a written invitation from a yacht club. This imposition will definitely cramp my style, as I was planning to moor at the Trinidad and

Tobago Yachting Association during carnival. However, I recall that André Lussier, the owner of *La Brunante*, knows someone working for Bell Canada on assignment in Trinidad. This person is supervising the installation of a new telephone system and could possibly be my saviour. I have left a message with André in Montréal, asking if his friend can help me to get an invitation.

I am presently in Martinique, still determined to be in Trinidad for carnival. Today, I phoned Montréal again and got some very good news. André's friend Lise has offered to sponsor my stay in Trinidad. She will obtain the required invitation from the T&T yacht club, where she is a member, and will generally pave the way for my visit. After getting this great news, I invited my sister Diana and her husband to join me for the carnival celebrations. From here in Martinique, I will single-hand to St Lucia, where friends from Wales will join me to crew the rest of the way to Trinidad.

"Jump up" parties are held for several weeks before the actual carnival begins and serve as a warm-up for the main event. When I sailed into the Trinidad Yacht Club, after a fabulous three-week meander from Martinique down the Caribbean chain of islands, the club manager greeted me with a warm welcome and presented complementary tickets to the club's "jump up," to be held that very evening. What fabulous timing!

I am dancing to the music of a twenty-piece steel band on the clubhouse patio of the yacht club. My partner is a beautiful Trinidadian woman, whom Lise brought along as my date. Intoxicated with the music, mellowed by the rum-punch, beguiled with my dance partner, and enchanted by the entirely amazing scene, I glance up to the starlit sky and realize, for the first time and without any equivocation, that choosing this adventurous life was absolutely the right thing to have done. This moment marks an important, pivotal milestone for me because from now on, I shall embrace my decision wholeheartedly and never look back.

Without the initial step of leaving Air Canada, none of the adventures of the last year and a half would have happened. Now, I am beautifully positioned to continue for as long as this life remains compelling, or until another dream takes precedence. The umbilical cord, connecting me to a conventional life has been completely severed. I hope that the "old enchanter" is as pleased as I am.

During a break in the music, as if to bolster my newfound confidence, Lise announced that she has arranged for me to actually take part (*play mas*) in the carnival parade, the Road March. I will join a "band" of her friends, some of whom are B.W.I.A. pilots. We will form a group of about one hundred dancers dressed up as tropical trees. My costume fitting is scheduled for tomorrow afternoon; then there will be "jump ups" every night for the rest of the week, leading up to Mardi Gras itself. My sister and her husband will arrive from Wales two days before carnival, and Lise has arranged for them to view the parade from her apartment balcony, which is opposite the reviewing stand. From there, they can cheer me on and wish me luck on my merry dance, which lasts for twenty-four hours.

The carnival is over. *Muscade* is anchored in Scotland Bay on the north coast of Trinidad. Sister Diana, brother-in-law John and I are swimming, relaxing and catching up on our sleep, after the magnificent carnival experience. Tonight we will make the crossing to St. George's, Grenada, a sixteen-hour passage. I prefer night crossings because there's no sun exposure, and it is much easier to spot shipping traffic and identify the lighthouses, which I use for navigation. As usual, I am using the "dead reckoning" method of navigation, by which I keep track of the boat's position using compass heading, estimated boat speed and estimated effects of current. There is a new system of satellite navigation available now, but it's extremely expensive and beyond my budget. The cruise with my sister will take us back up through the Grenadines to St. Vincent, then on to St Lucia, where they will disembark.

Then I will single-hand up to Martinique to join other friends who will sail with me to Guadeloupe. Finally, I will single-hand from Guadeloupe to Antigua, arriving there in about six weeks from now. I then plan to leave *Muscade* tied safely to the mangrove trees in Nelson's Dockyard, while I spend a month skiing in France.

The French ski resort of Chamonix is reputed to have some of the best off-piste skiing in Europe. My good friend Jean Milette, who was with me on *Muscade's* maiden voyage thirteen years ago, has bought an apartment there. The building, one of the original Alpine hotels built in the early 1900s, has recently been converted into condominium apartments. Jean's apartment on the second floor was originally a solarium-style dining room. It features floor-to-ceiling windows, which afford a spectacular, panoramic view of the entire Chamonix Valley and frame the majestic massif of Mont Blanc in the distance. Jean is an expert skier and qualified mountain guide, as well as being a masterful *raconteur* and *bon vivant*, so I will be in excellent company both on and off the slopes. The famous French yachtsman and solo around-the-world sailor, Eric Tabarly and his delightful *Martiniquaise* wife are the other owner/occupants on Jean's floor. Eric, a French naval officer, has competed in just about every race available for both single-handers and crewed yachts. In 1964, he won the single-handed transatlantic race and was awarded the prestigious, *Chevalier de la Légion d'Honneur*. He was also a French navy pilot, so we have a lot in common.

I have been enjoying some challenging skiing, and in the evenings, have had the chance to meet some of Jean's interesting friends and enjoy their hospitality. To repay their kindness, I donned my chef's *toqué* and have hosted several dinner parties. One of our larger-than-life guests was Jean Fernandez, who was involved as an impresario at the famous Hippopotamus Club in New York City. He goes to Kathmandu every year for high-altitude trekking, and I have become quite intrigued by this idea. I have never been to that part of the world, so have penciled in a trip to Nepal and India later this year. According to Fernandez, November is a great month to be there, as the skies are clear, and mountain vistas superb. He has recommended a guesthouse in Kathmandu, so it is highly possible that we will meet again next autumn. For the present, I will bid *au revoir* to the French Alps, fly over to Wales to see how my parents are doing, then continue on to Antigua to finish the rest of the winter aboard *Muscade*.

Arriving back in Antigua was just like returning home. *Muscade* was patiently waiting for me in the mangroves. I had only been on board for a short time when Bonnie and Michael Briggs from *Artemanti* came by in their dinghy to invite me for dinner. Michael, formerly a London solicitor, had decided to exchange his law practice for the cruising life, as had his lovely wife, who gave up her career as a dancer with the English National Ballet. When they bought their boat, a British-built Nicholson, it was named *Diana*. Michael was in a quandary: he didn't like the boat's name, but was superstitious about arousing the wrath of the sea gods by changing it. As Diana was the Roman goddess of the hunt, and Artemis was her Greek counterpart, he changed the boat's name to *Artemanti*, with no negative consequences to date.

This year's Antigua Race Week is in full swing, but my guests and I are enjoying the event as spectators and partygoers. The Race Week activities are a fitting way to celebrate the end of yet another season, but I have one more trip to make this year. I have decided to single-hand up to Barbuda for their carnival celebration, before hauling *Muscade* for the summer. The island of Barbuda lies about twenty miles north of Antigua and is part of the same country. I recently met a couple from Paris, Michel Cordier, and his friend, Jacqueline, who have taken a year off to cruise their home-built steel boat, *Bel Ami*, from France to the West Indies and back. I have persuaded them to sail up to Barbuda to join me for the carnival. Michel works as an aircraft maintenance technician for Air France in Paris.

The Barbuda carnival (not to be confused with Mardi Gras) was well worth the sail up to that isolated island. It was a festive weekend, celebrated by the locals without a tourist in sight. There were only three visiting boats in the anchorage, including *Muscade* and *Bel Ami*. My fishing techniques have improved considerably. I caught a fish, both on the trip up and on the way home. After the carnival celebrations, Michel and Jacqueline came aboard *Muscade* for a grilled tuna dinner, which I served with homemade breadfruit chips and salad. We then said our goodbyes. I was leaving early the next morning for Antigua, as soon as the light was sufficient to allow me to pick my way through the uncharted coral heads. Michel and Jacqueline were leaving for Bermuda, *en route* back to France. We promised to reunite aboard *Muscade* sometime in the future - in Paris.

I have just learned that Dodge Morgan aboard *American Promise*, has arrived back in Bermuda after completing his solo, non-stop, round-the-world voyage in only 150 days, cutting the previous record in half. The article said that he was a fighter pilot in the U.S.A.F. before retiring to make his fortune manufacturing radar detectors. There seems to be a definite connection between pilots and ocean sailors. I feel privileged to have attended his boat's commissioning ceremony and to have been there as he re-started his record-breaking attempt from Bermuda last November.

At the end of May, I left *Muscade* once again at Crabb's boatyard for the summer and headed back to Montréal. Before leaving I wrote in my ship's logbook: "Thanks Muscade for a most fantastic winter - the best of my life to date - many new friends met and many exciting places discovered. See you next winter."

It's true that boats take on personalities of their own and can become friends and almost members of the family - or have I been alone too long? On that subject, I am now sharing a house in

Montréal. Even though I am rarely in Canada, I do feel detached and sense the need for a land base again. My house-mate who is going through a difficult divorce, can use the extra income. I have also acquired a used car, so it seems that I am reverting to a more balanced life, after two years of trying to find the right equilibrium. My finances are working out very well, mainly because my expenses are much lower than my income. For income, I have my reduced Air Canada pension, some revenue from a life annuity, investment income and monthly payments from Ginette, who continues to buy my half of the farm. To her credit, and not surprisingly, she has not missed a single payment. My expenses are almost all discretionary, with boat maintenance being the largest, but still very modest outlay.

Today, I received a phone call from my friend Jean Milette of Chamonix fame who told me that he has just purchased a seventy-two foot aluminum ketch. He has invited me to join him in Boston when he takes ownership of his boat later in the month, then help him sail the boat down the American east coast to Annapolis, where he hopes to go into the charter business. It sounds like a wonderful project for my summer, an activity which I will pair with a trip to Wales to do some intensive hiking in preparation for the trip to Nepal in November.

Jean's new boat is named *Ayacanora*, after the beautiful heroine in the classic popular novel "*Westward Ho.*" She is a most impressive and luxurious sailing yacht with many innovative features. She was designed and built in the U.K. as a large and comfortable vessel which could be easily handled by two people. Her accommodation consists of a large main salon with fireplace, a full dining room for ten people with a mahogany, self-leveling dining table, a huge owner's aft cabin with bathroom, a large well-equipped galley, three other guest cabins, several other bathrooms, plus crew living and sleeping quarters in a separate section up front. All of the sails are self-furling and can be hoisted and adjusted with electric winches. She is extremely well balanced and very easy to sail and maneuver. Jean bought her fully equipped, and I was fortunate enough to join him in Boston for the maiden voyage.

We spent most of the summer slowly meandering down the east coast of the United States to Annapolis. Sometimes, we had friends and girlfriends as crew: at other times, it was just two of us aboard. Highlights of the trip were an overnight in Plymouth, one of the first settlements in the American colonies; an extended visit to Newport, Rhode Island; sailing down Long Island Sound tracing the same path that we had taken on *Muscade's* maiden voyage, exactly twelve years before; an overnight at the Indian Harbour Yacht Club in Greenwich, as guests of friends I had met in the West Indies; a night sail down the New Jersey coast where we were taken by surprise, and boarded by a United States Coast Guard SWAT team looking for drugs; some great cruising in the northern part of Chesapeake Bay, and finally our night-time arrival in Annapolis, where we brought the boat to anchor in front of the Naval Academy under sail only, as the engine would not start. Even though *Ayacanora* is primarily a sailing boat, if the anchor had failed to hold on the first try, the consequences could have been drastic and very expensive. It was a very enjoyable summer, and one which confirmed the old adage: "Small boats small problems - big boats big problems." Jean certainly will have a full-time job and large expenses to maintain this beautiful boat. After conferring with several brokers, he has given up the idea of chartering and will keep *Ayacanora* as his private yacht.

CHAPTER SIX

INDIA AND NEPAL

It is now time to prepare for my trekking expedition to Nepal. I am in North Wales training for the trip. In this part of the world, climbing, trekking, and hill running are all very popular sports. It is here that Sir Edmund Hillary prepared himself for his conquest of Mount Everest. It is not hard to find trekking companions, and I often hike with my brother-in-law and his friends. They are planning a more serious expedition to northern Pakistan next year and have invited me to join them. Apparently, a young Pakistani medical intern, who is working in the local hospital under the supervision of my brother-in-law, is very keen to help organize the trip. His father, General Sawar Khan, is a former Governor of the Punjab and good friend of the President of Pakistan. This is shaping up to be another "once-in-a-lifetime" opportunity.

During my physical training, I have been staying at my parents' house in Beaumaris. Next week, I will take the train to London and overnight with my brother Angus who is a buyer for Harrods, while I arrange my visas for India and Nepal. I would also like to include Tibet, but it is impossible to get a Chinese visa in England at the moment. I have heard that it is much easier to obtain a visa for Tibet in Kathmandu. When my papers are in order, I shall hitch a ride on the first available Air Canada flight to Bombay and begin a new adventure.

When I was a young man, the prospect of going to India and other parts of Asia was overshadowed by dreams of visiting the European capitals, the Greek islands, the Alps in winter, and the resorts of the West Indies. Today, India is number one on my travel list, and I am looking forward to discovering and learning about the culture of the Sub-continent. Even before the airplane touched down in Bombay, the aromas of wood smoke, incense, and cooking spices infiltrated the cabin through the air conditioning system, stirring my imagination. As usual, the Air Canada flight attendants spoiled me rotten. The word is out that my testimony at the labour trial of the laid-off flight attendants helped them to get their jobs back. Only the ringleader, who committed an act of vandalism by activating a handheld fire extinguisher in-flight, was dismissed.

Soon after disembarking in Bombay, I learned my first lesson: never travel on an airline-employee standby pass in India, especially at the end of a Hindu holiday. I was trying to catch an Indian Airlines flight to New Delhi, but the flights were all oversold, and the standby procedure consisted of rushing towards the ticket counter, waving handfuls of large-denomination rupee notes. I soon realized the futility of my situation and introduced myself to the flight deck crew of the next Delhi-bound flight. Without the slightest fuss, my problem was solved, and soon I was comfortably tucked into a cockpit jump seat, thanks to the generous, warm and friendly hospitality of the Indian captain and his crew. The next day, the flights had lots of open seats, so I had no trouble getting to Kathmandu.

My goal in Nepal is to hike the well-known Annapurna circuit, so after a couple of days exploring the exotic Nepalese capital,

I jumped on a bus for the nine-hour trip to Pokhara, where I will begin the trek. The bus ride, although long and uncomfortable, was interesting. The terrain along the entire route was planted with rice, growing on meticulously tended, symmetrical terraces. The rice harvest is just beginning, so the terraces have a soft golden hue. Pokhara is the principal starting point for many different treks in this region of Nepal. The shops and outfitters are completely equipped to provide anything a trekker could possibly need. The town has numerous guesthouses and restaurants and has a festive atmosphere. It also appears to be one of the marijuana capitals of the world. Unfortunately, I will have to forgo the Annapurna trek, as it takes almost three weeks to complete, not including the time needed to make the arrangements. I have found a comfortable guesthouse on the lake, from where I will hire a guide and organize several two and three-day hikes. There are many tourists here from France, Germany, Australia and the United States. I have already met quite a number of them and am getting the distinct impression that there is nothing unusual about what I am doing. The food in the local restaurants is excellent and extremely varied. One sits around large communal tables, so it is very easy to strike up conversations and meet fellow travellers.

After ten days of trekking and climbing in the hills surrounding Pokhara, I am ready to head back to Kathmandu and then on to Delhi to discover the delights of northern India. I am disappointed with the commercial nature of the trekking scene in Nepal. It is certainly anything but, "far from the madding crowd." I am consoled that, this time next year, I will have a chance to climb and trek in territory virtually unknown to foreigners, in the Karakorum Mountains of northern Pakistan, adjacent to the Chinese border.

During dinner, on my last night in Pokhara, I met some New Zealanders, who were surprised that I had not yet acquired a supply of brownies for the grueling bus trip back to Kathmandu.

After dinner, they escorted me to a local bakery to make sure that I was properly provisioned for my journey. As it turned out, these marijuana-laced chocolate biscuits were delicious. They greatly enhanced the comfort and seemed to considerably shorten the duration of the ride. Back in Kathmandu, I stayed in another guesthouse where I met up with some of my new friends from Pokhara. During the next few days, we thoroughly explored this intriguing city and shared delicious meals in the many Tibetan-style restaurants. I also linked up for dinner with Jean Fernandez from Chamonix, who had inspired me to travel to Nepal in the first place.

When I was in Wales, getting in shape for this trip, one of my brother-in-law's colleagues casually mentioned that, in his experience, New Delhi was the one city where a prior hotel reservation was absolutely essential. I tend to be quite skeptical and too often make the mistake of dismissing such remarks, so when my flight touched down in Delhi at ten o'clock at night, I was not concerned about finding a place to stay, and his advice was far from my thoughts. Eventually, I did find a hotel room, but not before spending four hours in a motorized rickshaw in the company of two other Canadians in the same predicament. I think we tried every hotel in New Delhi before finally finding a dingy room on the outskirts of town at two o'clock in the morning. At that point, we were completely at the mercy of the innkeeper. Note to self: learn to listen to advice.

I spent the next week touring Delhi, Agra (site of the spectacular Taj Mahal), and Jaipur, the city of the Mogul kings. What a country of contrasts! From some of the poorest people in the world living in abject poverty to multi-millionaires living incredibly luxurious lifestyles, it is a country of extremes. Shiny Mercedes cars share pot-holed roads with elephant and camel-drawn carts. At first, I was appalled by the poverty, but later became more reconciled. Because the poor seemed to accept their lot in life and did not appear overtly distressed, I made an effort to be more accepting as well. I suppose the Hindu religion, which promises a better life after reincarnation, helps to keep things reasonably quiescent. Hindus believe they have a *Kharma* or fixed destiny and that it is their religious and moral duty to play their cards in the best possible way in order to free their souls from the bondage of the body. Through cycles of death and reincarnation, they hope to eventually re-unite with God.

Tourists tend to be a magnet for beggars, but it is rare to see anyone begging in the more remote villages where disadvantaged individuals are accepted by the local people and survive on the auspices of their charity. With time, my digestive system gradually adapted to a different bacterial world. I used iodine-laced water for drinking and kept my mouth firmly closed while showering.

My last day in India was spent by the swimming pool of the five-star Oberoi Hotel in Bombay with the Air Canada crew that would be operating my return flight to London. After staying in three-dollar a night guesthouses in Nepal, it was quite a culture shock. I was in fact lucky to get on the flight back to London. Even though there were lots of seats available, extra fuel was needed to counter anticipated headwinds, so non-revenue passengers were not being boarded due to weight limitations. The captain, whom I knew well, decided that my hundred and seventy pounds would not make much difference and arranged for me to ride in the cockpit. I am quite satisfied with my initial foray into India. I definitely plan to return many times to learn more about the intricacies, diversities and resilience of human nature with the hope of becoming a more tolerant and understanding person.

I arrived back in Antigua yesterday to prepare *Muscade* for our third full winter in the West Indies. André Lussier and his friend Jean-Charles met me at the airport. Jean-Charles has asked me to deliver his forty-seven foot yacht from Montréal to Antigua next November, and I have accepted. This commitment pretty well fills up my dance card for 1987, which will start with wintering aboard *Muscade* with a couple of breaks for some skiing at Whistler and Mont Tremblant. In the spring, I am planning a single-handed voyage from Puerto Rico to Montréal and, if I survive, will spend most of the summer living aboard Muscade on Lake Champlain. In October, I have the expedition to northern Pakistan; then will return to Montréal to deliver Jean-Charles's boat to Antigua.

André and Jean-Charles are great company. They have been helping me fix some electrical problems on my boat. They are both extremely well versed in all things mechanical and have been preparing *La Brunante* for the winter season in the same boatyard where *Muscade* has been stored. This work generally referred to as "fitting out," consists of repairing anything that is broken, installing new equipment as well as carrying out preventative maintenance on anything else that could potentially break or cause problems. I have learned two valuable lessons from these talented gentlemen: never be reluctant to dismantle and inspect something which is broken, and always have the right tools for the job before starting a repair. Their motto is: "If man can make it, man can fix it." Adopting this attitude will stand me in good stead next spring, when I attempt my single-handed trip back to Canada and later on, when I eventually attempt an Atlantic crossing.

In Robert Pirsig's book, "*Zen and the Art of Motorcycle Maintenance*," he emphasizes that, when repairing something, one should be patient, take the time needed, and complete the task with the utmost integrity (no duct tape, please). In the evenings, after a hard day's work in the boatyard, I have been exploring the local restaurants and have faithfully attended the Sunday afternoon rum punch and steel band sunset ceremony on Shirley Heights. This weekly event is a must for anybody visiting Antigua.

Muscade is now ready to go cruising, but I will not launch her until I return from Christmas holidays in Wales. Last night, I was rudely awakened by a violent shaking motion. It took me a moment to realize that *Muscade* was still on dry land. The earthquake caused no damage to the yachts in the boatyard, but it was a reminder of how vulnerable we are to the severe forces of nature, and, in my case, to the fact I have no boat insurance. The entire chain of Caribbean islands was originally formed by volcanic eruptions. The islands are all inter-connected in the molten core of the earth and many still have active volcanoes.

The Christmas holiday visit with my family in Wales is now a distant memory. It is the end of March. I am anchored in Falmouth harbour, Antigua, reviewing my logbook entries for the last three months. It has been a fabulous winter of cruising. My Cajun friends, Harold and Mary-Lou Crochet, who were farm neighbours, came aboard for a week. Harold still has his dairy farm in Québec, and Ginette, my former wife, still lives next door. When I first moved to the farm, Harold helped me transition from the theoretical farming I had learned at agricultural college to the hands-on, practical realities of this most challenging occupation. We used to help each other at haymaking time and co-owned a grain harvester. In those days, Harold was on the Board of the dairy conglomerate Agropur, and I would sometimes help his family with the milking chores when he was away at meetings. Now, as we relax in the warm sunshine and dive off the boat into the turquoise waters of the Caribbean, I am reminded of the times when I had to climb up the outside ladder of Harold's silo in minus thirty degree temperatures to unfreeze the silage un-loader so that his dairy cows could be fed.

Muscade, with her Canadian flag, has become part of the Caribbean scene and is now recognized by the locals wherever she sails. I am on a first-name basis with many of the boat boys who provide invaluable services in the various anchorages. They paddle out in leaky rowboats or on old windsurfing boards to offer advice on the best places to anchor. They sell local produce and are always happy to do work on the boat or run errands. For the consideration of a few dollars, they will faithfully guard your dinghy during a visit ashore. They have even been known to put together a small, floating band to serenade the evening *apéritif*. When they show up, you listen politely for a few minutes, then pay them to go away. A very clever marketing strategy.

I am starting to think seriously about my solo trip back to Lake Champlain in May. I am certainly not a lone wolf, but I would like to experience at least one single-handed ocean voyage, just to see what it is like and to challenge myself. Perhaps I'll have some eureka moment during the trip and make some profound discovery.

I am having trouble with the boat's transmission, which sometimes does not engage, a problem I must have fixed before my solo voyage north. I am off to Montréal tomorrow morning, so today, after making sure the boat was securely anchored, I removed the transmission and dropped it off at a local repair shop to be rebuilt while I am away on my ski holiday. As I was finishing the job, Bonnie Briggs from *Artemanti* came by in her dinghy to invite me for dinner. My first instinct was to politely decline, as I have a very early flight tomorrow morning, but she absolutely insisted. Bonnie has a girlfriend from California staying with her and wants me to make up the party. Am I forgetting my father's advice about invitations?

The dinner onboard *Artemanti* was highly amusing, and I was quite taken by Bonnie's friend, Debbie. She is a graphic artist, lives near San Diego, and is presently working as a primary school teacher. We made a tentative date to have dinner together when I get back next week.

Spring skiing at Mont Tremblant is more about enjoying the mild weather and long lunches on sunny terraces than it is about sliding down mountains. The now ubiquitous artificial snow does not transform into the lovely, easily ski-able, corn snow as natural snow does. Instead, it turns into slushy mashed potatoes as the day warms, making it very difficult to ski well. Still, it is very pleasing to be sipping cold white wine in warm sunshine with old friends. Thinking back to what skiing used to be like in Québec, before snowmaking equipment was invented: there were entire winters when we were forced to ski on thin coverings of compacted snow and ice interspersed with grass and rocks. Most of us kept an old, beaten-up pair of skis to use in such conditions, so I should not complain.

I'm back in Antigua for Race Week, but in spite of several requests to crew, I have decided to remain a spectator again this year. Racing is not really my passion. The transmission is fixed, and *Muscade* is ready for the voyage back to Lake Champlain. I saw Debbie again. We had dinner and took in a few of the Race Week social activities before she flew back to California. She is an adventurous woman who has trekked and travelled extensively. We have a lot in common. When I told her about our planned mountaineering expedition to the Karakorums in October, she practically begged me to include her in the party. I am already regretting my promise to her that I will ask my fellow trekkers if she can come along. I recognize this as yet another one of my character flaws: I have a very hard time saying no to people and now run the risk of upsetting my trekking companions. I have a need to be liked, so try hard to please everyone. However, practically speaking, what are the chances of a woman from California showing up in Northern Pakistan to share a mountain adventure with four men she does not know?

My solo trip back to Lake Champlain next month is now at the top of my agenda. I have been studying the U.S. Navy ocean planning charts for the month of May. These charts contain an amazing amount of data, accumulated and averaged over many years. What interests me most is the probability of storms, the winds that I can expect along the route, the prevailing ocean currents, and the shipping lanes where I will have to be extra vigilant. I will take my departure from San Juan, Puerto Rico and sail north, leaving the Bahamas well to the west. When clear of the Bahamas, I will alter heading to make landfall at Beaufort, North Carolina. As I get close to my intended entry point, I will have the option of changing my destination by continuing around Cape Hatteras and sailing on to Norfolk, if weather permits. The planning charts indicate light-to-moderate easterly winds, very little probability of storms, and some periods of calm. Initially, there will be very little current, but I will pick up a good push from the Gulf Stream, once I am north of the Bahamas. I expect to see lots of shipping until I get abeam the Bahamas, and again when I am in the Gulf Stream on my way up the U.S. East Coast.

Some friends I met in Catskill Creek when I was holed up there during hurricane Gloria, have arrived to help me sail *Muscade* from Antigua to Puerto Rico. We are planning a spectacular ten-day jaunt through the northern islands of the Caribbean including the Virgin Islands. It's down wind all the way with a favourable current, so it should be a real sleigh ride. We are intending to explore the anchorages and towns of St. Bart's, St Martin, the British and American Virgin Islands, and finally Culebra before arriving in San Juan. It is all new and exciting territory for *Muscade* and her skipper.

I am presently alongside at the Club Nautico in old San Juan, impatient to set sail back to Canada. The cruise from Antigua certainly met all expectations. The weather was glorious and the winds most favourable. Highlights from the ship's log book include: an evening in Gustavia, the capital of St. Bart's; an overnight sail from St. Martin to Virgin Gorda; some very pleasant but crowded anchorages in the Virgin Islands; a nostalgic visit to the town of Charlotte Amalie, a place I had not visited since navy pilot days, and an equally nostalgic entry into San Juan harbour past the historic San Felipe del Morro Castle, which has guarded the entrance since 1539.

During the last winter that I served as a navy pilot, my squadron was detached to Roosevelt Roads Naval Air Station in Puerto Rico for rocket and bombing practice. At that same time, the new Canadian maple leaf flag was commissioned, and in honour of the occasion, we carried out a multi-plane, low-level fly-past over San Juan, sporting the new flag, freshly painted on the tails of our aircraft. Looking back on my time in San Juan, I am reminded of my encounter with a self-professed witch - albeit a very beautiful one - completely devoid of hairy facial warts.

I met her at a party in the Naval Officer's Club and subsequently invited her out for dinner. The evening was going along swimmingly, until she asked me if she could read my palm. This action precipitated a most unusual and worrying occurrence. After examining my palm for a very short time, she abruptly let my hand drop and turned as white as a sheet. Even though I have absolutely no belief in anything occult and have no faith whatsoever in any religion, I was curious. Ana-Maria refused to divulge anything, so the evening turned into a dismal failure. Several days later, after much cajoling from me, she revealed that I was going to die in a spectacular, catastrophic accident when I was in my mid-thirties. I was twenty-four at the time. Her credibility as a witch was later corroborated in a letter, which I received from her on arrival back in Halifax. She recounted dreaming of events which could only have been known to the aircraft carrier's crew. In spite of this alarming evidence, I totally disregarded the whole prophecy. Nonetheless, I am very happy to be sitting here today in my mid-forties enjoying the view of old San Juan. I have absolutely no intention of renewing my acquaintance with that misinformed witch. This is the first time I have thought about her since that ominous prediction, twenty-two years ago.

CHAPTER SEVEN

SOLO VOYAGE AND SHIPWRECK

Early in the afternoon of May 14, I motored out of San Juan harbour past Fort Morro and set heading for Cape Hatteras. The weather was clear and the northeast trade winds well established, so I hoisted full sail and stopped the engine.

"Heidi" is keeping the boat on course, and my voyage has begun with *Muscade* rushing northwards at maximum hull speed. For planning purposes, I have assumed an average speed of five nautical miles an hour, which should make it about a ten-day trip. I don't have the latest satellite navigation equipment yet, as it is still too expensive, so I will be relying on an accurate compass course for direction and a trailing log line spinner for distance. I will update my estimated position with astronavigation fixes whenever the sky is clear and sea conditions favourable. Since before Christopher Columbus, navigators have been measuring the sun's altitude when it crosses the local meridian to determine latitude. Without getting too technical, this method will be impractical on this trip, as the sun's altitude will be almost ninety degrees at meridian passage, making it hard to measure accurately. I will compensate by measuring accurate sun altitudes in the morning and again in the afternoon, when the sun is between forty-five and sixty degrees above the horizon, and then reconcile the two position lines to get a navigational fix. At night, I can use the star Polaris, to determine latitude and will also be able to fix my position using other stars, the moon, and planets. I did verify the accuracy of the boat's compass during my trip from Antigua to San Juan. "Heidi" can steer a very true course, provided the wind direction is steady. On the negative side, the spinner that measures distance tends to get fouled by Sargasso weed, which will be prevalent all along my route. Over the years, I have lost spinners to large fish, so I carry several spares. Another potential problem could be the lack of wind. "Heidi" needs some detectable wind to steer the boat properly, so I might have to steer manually if forced to motor through periods of calm or fluky winds. This proposition is too tedious to contemplate.

I should emphasize that hundreds of sailors, both men and women, have completed single-handed voyages. I have already mentioned my friend Paul Johnson who crosses oceans on a whim, the famous French sailor Eric Taberly, as well as Dodge Morgan aboard *American Promise*. One of the main differences in my case is that during the first third of the trip and the last third of the trip, I will be transiting very busy shipping lanes and will have to be extremely vigilant, which will preclude me from sleeping for long periods of time. My strategy is to catnap in the cockpit at night and then go below for longer periods in my bunk during the day, trusting "Heidi" to keep the boat on track. This plan assumes that ship's crews will be more alert and less likely to hit me during the day, and if there is a collision, at least I'll be able to see what's happening.

It has now been twenty-four hours since I left San Juan, and all is well. The wind has been holding nicely, and *Muscade* is one hundred and fifty nautical miles closer to her destination. I am feeling exhilarated and find that, in some ways, solo sailing is more enjoyable and less stressful than having to be concerned about the well being of crew members. I can eat when I am hungry and catnap when tired. There is no worry about running out of fresh water, so I can have a shower whenever I feel like it. As anticipated, there was lots of shipping traffic last night, and I expect this will continue for another day or two, until I am east of the Bahamas. I am feeling well rested and in good spirits as I experience the ultimate test of self-sufficiency: alone in my own little world where survival is the main consideration. There is something heady about not having to depend on anyone else and being completely responsible for one's own actions.

Day four: the trade winds are still holding well, and I'm relaxing in the cockpit, sipping coffee and listening to the CBC program, *Sunday Morning*, on shortwave radio. There was no shipping traffic last night, and nobody has intruded into my ten-mile circle so far today. I am up-to-date with my navigation, which shows that *Muscade* has averaged six nautical miles per hour since departure. I do have a mechanical problem with the engine, which overheats whenever I use it to charge the batteries. It's probably a partially- blocked heat exchanger, and should resolve itself once we encounter cooler ocean temperatures. The weather is still tropical, so I am standing my night watches in a short-sleeved shirt and shorts. The daylight hours are long, the sunsets spectacular, and the moon is full.

My logbook entries for days six, seven and eight record an extremely frustrating period. I had to transit through the middle of a high-pressure area, and the winds during that time were either very light or completely calm. I would have been quite happy to lower the sails, wait for wind to re-establish, and catch up on my sleep, but that proved impossible. Even though the sea was oily calm, there was still too much erratic swell motion to sleep.

For three long days, it was non-stop sail changes as I alternated innumerable times between motoring through calms and sailing whenever there was just enough breeze for "Heidi" to steer. Eventually, the high-pressure area moved off to the northeast, and southerly winds piped up enough for *Muscade* to sail properly, and for her skipper to put his head down. By this time, I was north of the Bahamas and into the Gulf Stream. The weather was much cooler with occasional showers, so I had to wear a sweater and jacket at night. On day ten, after copying an excellent weather forecast, I made the decision to go around Cape Hatteras and into Norfolk. On the evening of day eleven, I made landfall by sighting the Cape Hatteras lighthouse. On day twelve, I sailed up the Virginia coastline in a stiff westerly breeze, rounded Cape Henry, entered Chesapeake Bay and docked at the Little Creek Marina just before sunset.

Everyone here at the marina has been most generous. I have been enjoying amazing hospitality from the resident yachtsmen, who have been treating me like a long-lost hero. I have repaired the heat exchanger, re-stocked the boat with food, water and diesel fuel, and am ready to "sail on the morning tide" for New York City, a distance of three hundred nautical miles. This will be a coast crawl in very busy waters, requiring a constant lookout for pleasure boats, fishing vessels, tugboats and naval ships. I will not be able to sleep at all on this leg of the voyage.

For almost two days now, I have been struggling with very light and variable winds and the dreaded calms. I am exhausted and completely exasperated with constant sail changes and the tedium of having to steer under power for long periods of time. Note to self: before your next trip, install an electric autopilot. To make matters worse, I am still more than a hundred miles from New York. I am delusional and incapable of making sound decisions. For some reason, I have a serious case of get-home-itis. I should have put into the protected harbour at Cape May several hours ago and anchored for a good night's sleep. It is now two o'clock in the morning. I am unable to stay awake, and there are no anchorages on this section of the New Jersey coastline. *Muscade* is under full sail in very light winds and making painfully slow progress up the coast. I am completely out of options and ideas, so I have turned on all the boat's deck lights, set the alarm clock for a one-hour sleep and collapsed in the cockpit.

I have just been rudely awakened by the sickening sound of fiberglass pounding against hard sand. I am aground. While I was sleeping, during my fourth hourly stint, *Muscade* altered course ninety degrees towards the coast, sailed through a series of rocky reefs and has just run aground on the beach in downtown Ocean City, N.J. Because of my stupidity, lack of judgment and supreme over-confidence after a successful solo ocean trip, I have lost my beautiful boat. *Muscade* is lying parallel to the beach in the roaring surf and is being flipped violently towards the beach with every incoming roller, then flipped back and pounded in the other direction as each wave recedes. I quickly radioed a distress call to the Coast Guard, and fired off a couple of red flares to indicate my position. I then said good-bye to *Muscade* and offered her my apologies for precipitating such an ignominious end. I was sure that she would soon break up in the pounding surf. Almost at once, I completely internalized and accepted the inevitability of the uninsured loss, even as future options for life were forming in my mind.

With great difficulty, I lowered an anchor and some heavy chain over the bow to try to stabilize my position on the rising tide. I managed somehow to lower the sails and secure the flailing boom. It was broad daylight, and already a crowd had gathered on the beach to watch the show. *Muscade* had hit the beach halfway between two huge stone retaining walls designed to prevent sand erosion, and people were climbing out on the rocks for a better look.

Before long, a Coast Guard cutter showed up, but remained off shore, unable to help me, as it was too dangerous to approach my position. The captain of the cutter politely radioed that they were in the business of saving lives, and I was obviously not in any danger and could easily swim ashore. I was desperate. I asked them to arrange for a salvage company to pull me off the beach, before *Muscade* broke up. By this time, the local police had organized a surfboat with two oarsmen. They were standing by on the beach to come to my rescue if necessary. Luckily, *Muscade* was still in one piece when the salvage boat showed up about an hour later. The surfboat crew was able to row out through the breaking waves to the salvage tug and bring back a long towline, which I secured to cleats on the bow. A few moments later, the tug dragged me off the beach to seaward of the rollers into deep water. Less than two hours after hitting the beach, *Muscade* was afloat again, disaster had been averted, and my beautiful boat, containing all of my worldly possessions had been saved. It was now time to take care of the salvage costs.

The laws pertaining to salvaging a vessel are complicated and claims for fair compensation usually end up in court. Costs vary depending on whether the incident took place in international or sovereign waters. Generally, the law recognizes that compensation paid to a salvage company should be commensurate with the degree of risk involved, the value of the rescued vessel, and the level of difficulty. Another important consideration is whether the owner of the distressed boat remained on board or abandoned ship. According to a friend who works for Lloyds in London, I was very fortunate. Even after considering the good weather, lack of difficulty and practically no risk or danger to the salvagers, he said that a fee of ten thousand dollars would have been deemed reasonable. In extreme cases, involving abandoned vessels in international waters, the fee can equal the total value of the boat.

As soon as the salvage crew had recovered their towline, they pulled up alongside *Muscade* and asked me if I had insurance. When I told them that I did not, they shrugged and then asked me to explain how I had managed to run aground on such a lovely morning. After hearing my sad story about over confidence and fatigue, they agreed to settle for three hundred dollars. I quickly went down below, signed over all of my remaining U.S. dollar traveller's checks totaling five hundred dollars and gratefully handed the money over to my benefactors.

All of this to say that my luck is still holding, and *Muscade* continues to be a charmed vessel. The next order of business was to thoroughly inspect the boat, and clean up the shambles down below where every drawer and cupboard had emptied during the pounding. I donned my wetsuit and inspected the hull and rudder for damage. Miraculously, everything below the waterline looked normal, and on deck, the mast and rigging were intact although the rigging had stretched, so the mast was leaning slightly to port. What an amazing testament to the Hallberg-Rassy company.

Everything below is now back in its place. *Muscade* is sailing beautifully up the Jersey coast towards New York with a good southerly breeze, and I am enjoying a hearty breakfast and a brand-new lease on life. Ironically, I am now well rested, having slept for four one-hour stints before hitting the beach. My adrenaline level is still off the chart, so it would be impossible to sleep anyway. I really do not deserve to have escaped so easily after such stupidity and gross negligence. Now that my brain is functioning again, the reason for *Muscade's* ninety-degree heading change towards the beach is clear. A well-known phenomenon known as a sea breeze must have altered the wind direction from south to east, while I was sleeping. A sea breeze occurs in the morning when the land heats up faster than the water, creating a pressure difference and causing the air over the water to blow towards the lower pressure over the land. "Heidi" maintains a constant angle to the wind, so the boat's heading altered towards the shore when the wind changed. How *Muscade* avoided the reefs and the stone jetties will forever remain a mystery. I first learned about sea breezes twenty-five years ago, while studying meteorology for my naval pilot's wings. This was another classic case of "forgetting by experience." I am suitably humbled.

This afternoon, I tied up to my mooring in the perfectly sheltered Pelots Bay, Vermont, exactly three weeks after leaving San Juan, and almost three years after having left this idyllic spot to begin my grand adventure. The friend with whom I have been sharing an apartment in Montréal has a new lady in his life, who has moved in, so I will give up my room and live permanently aboard my boat. I am looking forward to a relaxing summer of cruising on Lake Champlain and hiking in the Green Mountains of Vermont in preparation for my Pakistan expedition in October. It will be a great chance to catch up with my Montréal friends and to take in the Jazz Festival.

André Lussier has asked me if I would like to skipper *La Brunante* in the Caribbean next winter. His health is failing, so he is no longer able to handle the boat himself. He is offering me unlimited use, so I would be free to invite friends at any time. André will try to get down occasionally during the winter if his health permits. He has also asked me to sail *La Brunante* back from Antigua to Montréal next spring, so he can carry out a full refit before putting her up for sale. I have agreed to all his requests, as the arrangement dovetails very nicely with my plans. After mountaineering in Pakistan I will return to Montréal to skipper Jean-Charles's boat to Antigua. On arrival, I will move aboard *La Brunante* for the winter. This will allow me to leave Muscade in storage near Montréal during the coming winter, so she will be well-positioned next spring for a full refit before possibly sailing her to Europe. It is quite amazing how opportunities come along when one is free to accept them.

It is now September. One of the most enjoyable summers of my life is already fading into memory. *Muscade* is out of the water and fully winterized in a marina south of Montréal. I am in North Wales training intensively in the hills of Snowdonia for the trip to Pakistan, along with my three climbing companions. We realize that, no matter how hard we train our bodies physically, even the fittest athletes cannot prepare for altitude sickness. It remains to be seen how each of us will cope with this condition, which can occur when climbers ascend too quickly and are unable to get enough oxygen from the air they are breathing. Climbers have died from altitude sickness, which is manifested by a severe headache. The rule is: if you get a severe headache, descend immediately to a lower altitude. Debbie from California is still interested in joining us, and my three companions have agreed to include her if she shows up next week on our British Airways flight to Rawalpindi. I am in good company, as my three companions are all doctors. My brother-in-law John is an orthopedic surgeon, Wil is an anesthetist and Chris is a general practitioner.

The day before our flight to Pakistan, we got together at my brother Angus's London house for a celebration. My brother is thirteen years younger than I am. He returned to England as a five-year-old at the end of our father's appointment in Ottawa, when I left home for Naval College. He is married to Maria and has two young daughters.

I have fond memories of Angus during my early days with Air Canada, when I was flying the DC8 to London. He would sometimes accompany me on the crew bus to our departing aircraft, where the flight attendants would always spoil him with goodies from the first-class trolley. Those were the good old days before any form of security screening was considered necessary. Friends and family, who were not travelling, could actually board the aircraft to say good-bye to their loved ones. On arrival in London, flight crews were picked up by a company bus on the tarmac below the aircraft and driven directly to the layover hotel. Very occasionally, there would be a customs spot check, but usually we just signed a standard declaration form.

On one occasion, I was flying to London with a captain who had just shot a moose on a hunting trip. I made the mistake of mentioning to him that I had never savoured this delicacy, so on our next flight he brought along a large chunk of moose meat for my parents' Sunday dinner. He figured that my lucky family would probably be the only ones in Britain dining on delicious roast moose that evening. Of course, the inevitable happened. Once we were sequestered aboard the crew bus, when it was too late to ditch my present, we were informed that we had been randomly chosen for a customs spot-check. The British in those days were paranoid about raw meat and the threat of foot-and-mouth disease, so I figured I was in big trouble and stoically awaited my fate. In the customs hall, I dutifully lined up my baggage for inspection: a flight bag, a suitcase and a huge lump of moose meat wrapped in brown paper and tied with string. The friendly and courteous British customs officer had a cursory look in my suitcase and flight bag, but completely ignored the brown paper package. That evening, my family dined on roast moose, but from their oblique comments after the meal, I surmised that they would have preferred any other four-legged domesticated mammal. I didn't mention it to my captain.

CHAPTER EIGHT

KARAKORAM EXPEDITION

If this were a novel you would predict that, after we were comfortably seated aboard our British Airways flight to Pakistan, but just before the main cabin door was closed, and just as we were breathing a sigh of relief, Debbie from California would show up at the very last minute. That is exactly what happened, so now we are five.

Shortly after our arrival in Rawalpindi, it became obvious just how privileged we were to have as our host and benefactor, General Sawar Khan, former governor of the Punjab, former Vice Chief of Army Staff, and right hand man to President Zia-ul-Haq. As I have already mentioned, General Khan's son, Omar, was completing his training as an intern at a Welsh hospital under the tutelage of my brother-in-law and fellow climber, John Barnes. Our co-host in Pakistan was Brigadier Iftikhar, the father of Omar's wife and good friend of General Sawar Khan. These two gentlemen were determined to make sure that everything about our trip went off without the slightest hitch, and their hospitality, in this part of the world where hospitality had its origins, was without precedent. All to say that on arrival, after the briefest of formalities, we were whisked away in staff cars to Flashman's Hotel, where we were to stay while completing the final planning details of our expedition. All the resources of the Pakistan Tourist Bureau had been placed at our disposal, and General Khan was expecting us at his home that evening for a reception. One of the best mountain guides in the country, Hunar Baig, had been engaged to oversee our entire mountain experience. He had previously led successful expeditions to the top of K2, the second-highest mountain in the world.

Following Hunar's recommendations, we have decided to attempt two separate climbs. For the first one, we will proceed by minivan up the Karakoram Highway to the village of Passu, then climb to the top of the Batura Glacier and back. For the second trip, we will start near the Naltar Lakes then climb up and over the Dintar Pass, reaching an altitude of about 16,000 feet. We are all very excited about these plans and can't wait to get started, but first we are to have dinner with our hosts, General Sawar Khan and Brigadier Iftikhar, and unwittingly cause an embarrassing incident. We had neglected to mention to the General that a woman had joined our group, and he had planned an all-male evening. After greeting us in a most gracious and charming manner, General Khan whispered a few words to an aide, and in no time the wives appeared, and the evening was saved. After the reception, we were invited to a sumptuous feast at a restaurant, located up in the hills overlooking Islamabad. Of course, there was not a drop of anything alcoholic.

The Karakoram Highway was a joint construction project by the governments of Pakistan and China. It took over twenty years to build and was officially opened last year (1986). Following the route of the ancient Silk Road, it begins in Kashgar and winds southwards through some of the most inhospitable territory in the world to Gilgit, then follows the Indus River to Abbottabad and on to Rawalpindi. More than a thousand workers died during construction, mostly due to landslides, which are still very prevalent.

I can say unequivocally that I have never seen such spectacularly beautiful scenery anywhere else in the world. Every bend in the road presented a different and totally unexpected, breathtaking panorama, and glaciers abounded. We spent the first night at a government hotel in Abbottabad then proceeded to Gilgit, where we stocked up with supplies before continuing to the village of Passu. The next day, with Hunar Baig leading the way, and with our contingent of ten porters and two cooks, we started our ascent of the Batura Glacier. Baig had chosen the itinerary well. Unlike the well-worn treks around Annapurna and those leading to the Everest base camps, our trails were practically in virgin territory. There was absolutely nothing touristy about this trip. The paths we were following such as they were, had been broken by nomadic yak herders seeking grazing areas for their stock during the summer months. It was clear that Baig was using this first trek to condition us, teach us some mountaineering techniques, and determine if we were able to tackle the Dintar Pass climb. The weather was spectacular: warm days and cool nights, sunny and crystal clear, affording unrestricted views of "the roof of the world," where mountains under 20,000 feet don't even have names. The days were long, the hiking and climbing strenuous, but we were all invigorated by the mountain air and spectacular scenery. We were fed local dishes prepared by our two cooks and slept like logs tucked into our arctic sleeping bags. Debbie proved to be an able climber and a pleasant, uncomplaining companion, in spite of the extremely primitive conditions.

I had found out before leaving Passu that Debbie would be marking her birthday during the Batura Glacier climb, so I had asked Baig if it was possible, in this strictly Muslim country, to acquire a bottle of something stronger than goat's milk to celebrate the occasion. He was most accommodating and sent a runner across the Chinese border for a couple of bottles of *eau-de-vie*, which he duly stored in his rucksack. On the morning of Debbie's birthday, we noticed that one of our cooks was hiking along with a stray kid goat cradled in his arms, leading us to believe that perhaps these fierce tribesmen might possess a modicum of compassion. Both our illusions and our appetites were slightly diminished that evening when curried baby goat was served for Debbie's birthday dinner. The Chinese *eau-de-vie* went down smoothly, and after several glasses of this potent poison, I summoned up the courage to act out an off-colour joke, which uses hand signals and whistling instead of words to make the point. I was delighted and relieved when, after I mimed the punch line, our Muslim porters rolled on the ground with laughter. As Freud postulated, all humour is either sexist or racist. I would add that sex is the one subject which crosses all ethnic lines and serves as a common denominator for human communication.

After reaching the source of the glacier, we attempted a day climb to the highest peak in the area. None of us had any altitude sickness problems upon reaching the summit of about 16,000 feet, which bodes well for the next part of our adventure. Several days later, after having trekked back down the glacier to Passu, we set up camp for the night in a plantation of mulberry trees. The next day, Debbie, who is a teacher in California, taught an English lesson at the Aga Khan School in Passu. This area, which includes the Hunza Valley and Karimabad, is part of the Aga Khan's domain and is one of the most enlightened parts of Pakistan, where even girls go to school. It is a veritable Shangri-La. Later, we had the incredible privilege of being invited by one of our cooks to his yurt to have tea and sweetmeats with his wife and children, who looked upon us with awe and fascination.

We have decided to treat ourselves to the comforts of a hotel in the town of Gilgit before starting the second half of our expedition. We are all in need of a hot shower and a comfortable bed, after ten days of camping with very little water. This whole area was originally part of Kashmir, and has been a disputed territory between

Pakistan and India since partition in 1947, when the British Raj artificially created Pakistan. Even though the population of Kashmir was over seventy per cent Muslim at the time of partition, politically it was ruled by a small Sikh minority, which lobbied for the territory to be awarded to Hindu India. Pakistan was apportioned about a third of the territory - mostly mountainous and sparsely populated areas - and India got the rest. Over-flying helicopters were a constant reminder of this ongoing border war, but General Sawar Khan had made sure that the numerous military checkpoints posed no problem for us. I don't know what was written in Urdu, on our *passe-partout,* but every time we handed over our papers to the soldiers manning the barriers, they snapped to attention, saluted, and waved us through without further ado.

Our second climb began with a long, treacherous and hair-raising jeep ride from Gilgit to the beautiful Naltar Lake region. Baig had engaged the same two cooks from Passu, but was obliged by custom to hire local porters for this climb. The men he chose look like a gang of ruffians and are obviously very poor. Some are wearing cut-off rubber boots and some only have flip-flops for the climb, which will certainly be above the snow line. We rummaged in our backpacks looking for any spare socks or sweaters to give them. Baig confided in me that the whole gang could mutiny at any moment, especially if the going gets rough. He tagged me with the affectionate nickname, "Jumbo-Wallah," when he found out that I had been an airline pilot.

We soon left the aqua coloured, crystal clear Naltar Lakes behind and started the climb. The turquoise coloured lakes reminded me of the sea colour in the Bahamas, but the water temperature here is only just above freezing, so although the lakes look inviting, bathing is completely out of the question. After a couple of days, the porters seemed to be settling down, but as we were now above the tree line, we had another problem - there was not enough firewood available. Each night, after we were tucked into our sleeping bags inside our alpine tents, everyone else in the party huddled together and dozed around the campfire, so it was essential to find enough wood to keep the fire going all night. Our cooks also needed wood. The night before our final ascent to the Dintar pass, we camped above the snow line, and our porters were definitely not amused.

Shortly after our enthusiastic celebration at the summit, Baig informed us that it was too dangerous to descend the other side of the pass. The snow levels were too deep, the overhanging cornices unsafe, and there was a distinct avalanche risk. At least the porters were now happy as we retraced our steps back down to the valley floor. We managed to convince Baig that there was enough money in our budget for another night in a Gilgit hotel, a farewell dinner, and a flight back to Rawalpindi instead of an uncomfortable, two-day mini-bus ride. We only had to mention General Khan's name, and all doors magically opened. Baig arranged for me to fly back in the cockpit of the Pakistan International Airlines turbo-prop aircraft. These flights operate using visual flight rules, which means that the pilots cannot fly in cloud and must maintain visual reference to the mountains at all times. This type of aircraft does not have the capability to fly higher than the surrounding peaks, so must navigate through the valleys. Flights are often cancelled because of bad weather.

Back in Rawalpindi, General Khan had arranged a farewell celebration at his residence, but insisted on dragging us into the bazaar for some last-minute souvenir shopping before dinner. There, we were given a lesson in the art of bartering, as the tall and imposing General towered over an obsequious and diminutive carpet dealer who ended up writhing on the floor, bravely trying to defend his exorbitant prices against the General's harangues and insinuations about the legitimacy of his birth. Much to the General's chagrin, to say nothing of the carpet dealer's angst, none of us bought anything.

I am planning to travel on an airline employee's standby ticket back to London, so today I went to the British Airways office to see if there was a seat available for me on tomorrow's flight (my four trekking companions have confirmed reservations). I introduced myself to the Pakistani agent, who assured me there were lots of open seats and that he would make sure we were seated together. Early the next morning, when we arrived at the airport, the same British Airways agent was waiting for us at the check-in counter. With a big smile and warm handshake, he handed me five first-class boarding passes with the rejoinder, "Here you are, Captain - there will be no riffraff near these seats." As it turned out, we had the entire upper deck of the 747 to ourselves, and the captain offered an open invitation to visit the cockpit. Probably the best part of the return flight was the champagne, very much appreciated after three weeks in a Muslim country with nothing alcoholic except Chinese *eau-de-vie*. On arrival in London, Debbie flew back to California, I flew back to Montréal and John, Chris and Wil returned to North Wales.

After hardly enough time to catch my breath, I have moved on to the next adventure. I am aboard the forty-seven foot yacht, *Le Pat-Mar*, in Catskill Creek awaiting delivery of some emergency equipment, including a life raft, before setting sail for Bermuda and Antigua. The boat's name is a contraction of the owner's sons' names, Patrick and Martin. Jean-Charles, who has become a good friend, is upset today, as the world's stock markets have just crashed (Oct 1987). I remind him of the advantages of being "independently poor," but he fails to see the humour.

The bar, restaurant and clientele at the Catskill Creek Marina have become very familiar, after my many stays here with *Muscade*, and the extended wait during hurricane Gloria two years ago. Jean-Charles will make up part of my crew, along with his son Patrick and my friend Ernest Mellows, who is once again hitching a ride back to his own boat in Antigua. This will be the first ocean passage for *Le Pat-Mar*, so there are bound to be some surprises. The good news is that the boat is equipped with the latest sat/nav equipment, so I won't have to rely on my sextant for navigation. Sat/nav provides periodic fixes, depending on the availability of polar orbit satellites, but does not give constant position data.

The trip to Bermuda was not without problems. We departed Staten Island in strong westerly winds and a favourable five-day forecast. At first, the seas were quite boisterous, and we began to take water into the boat from the poorly sealed cockpit lockers. Jean-Charles and I worked well together and were soon able to overcome this, as well as several other problems, and pump the boat dry. Two days out of Bermuda, I copied a weather forecast, which predicted that a severe cold front would overtake us before our arrival. We had lots of time to prepare the boat, so when the bad weather hit, the sails had already been reduced to a storm jib and a handkerchief of mainsail. We were about half a day northwest of Bermuda, surfing downwind like a small sailing dinghy, with fifty-knot winds blowing from dead astern. I was concerned that if anything happened to our rig, we could be blown on to the barrier reef which extends a long way north of Bermuda. Consequently, I altered heading towards the east to enable an approach to St. George's harbour from the much safer, northeast quadrant.

After a twelve-hour sleigh ride, during which time none of my crew felt confident enough to take the helm, I made my approach to Bermuda. I kept the reefed mainsail up until we were well inside the shelter of the harbour, so that if the engine faltered while we were motoring directly into a forty-five knot wind in the extremely narrow entrance cut, I would be able to spin the boat around and sail safely back out to sea. Once secured alongside, it was time to share a stiff rum with my crew and with my friend Jean Milette, who met us on the dock. His boat, *Ayacanora*, which I had last seen in Annapolis harbour, was in Bermuda awaiting passage to the Virgin Islands. Rum and coke with lots of lime juice (Cuba Libre or rum and scum as we called it) is the preferred drink of navy pilots. Invariably, the first sip reminds me of that welcome drink in the wardroom of the aircraft carrier, after a difficult landing on a dark and stormy night.

It seems Bermuda was always destined to play a major role in my life. It was my father's favourite place on the planet. As a young man, he was based here aboard *HMS Orion* as part of the Royal Navy's West Indies Squadron. He was flying amphibious aircraft, which were catapulted from the cruiser and then recovered by the ship's crane after a water landing. His memoirs express a true passion for the island. Bermuda was my first real taste of the sub-tropics. In 1963, I came here as a member of the Royal Canadian Navy rugby team. We were competing in a tournament against the American Ivy League colleges during College Week, and I felt that I had discovered a veritable paradise. Subsequently, my naval air squadron was often detached to Bermuda as part of our N.A.T.O. training with the U.S.N. I was there the day President Kennedy was shot and recall a very solemn group that evening in the U.S.N. Officers Club. As you know from this narrative, I based *Muscade* in Bermuda during the winter of 1975-76 and eventually got married there. Since leaving Air Canada, I have visited the island every November on various yacht delivery trips.

After a week's break, during which we made some modifications to *Le Pat-Mar* and fixed all the problems we had encountered coming from New York, the weather was ideal for our departure to Antigua. I had advised Jean-Charles to expect a fast sail for the first part of the trip, then a day or two motoring through the doldrums, followed by a rollicking sail once we encountered the northeast trade winds. As it happened, we transitioned to the trades without the calm break the doldrums usually provide and arrived in Antigua in a record time of seven days.

After a couple of days celebrating in English Harbour, Jean-Charles and I sailed around to Crabb's Marina on Antigua's north shore where I moved aboard my luxurious winter sailing home, *La Brunante*. She has been stored out of the water for the summer, so I will need to spend several weeks preparing her for the coming winter's cruising, before heading back to Wales for the pre-Christmas parties. I plan to launch the boat early in the New Year.

It is now mid-December, and I am on a flight from London to Los Angeles. Debbie and her parents have invited me to spend Christmas with them in Fallbrook, California. I accepted, albeit with a sense of foreboding and inevitability. Debbie was the wild card on our Pakistan trip and came through with flying colours. She endeared herself to the entire group and adapted to the arduous conditions, without the slightest complaint or hint of bad humour. On the other hand, she has a mysterious nature and an unconventional approach to life, which I have observed before in extremely artistic people. She appears to live in a world of her own making and seems perfectly content with that existence. This attitude manifests itself as an indifference to accepted social conventions, giving her an entirely unpretentious manner. As a graphic artist, she worked on the first *Star Wars* film (all the animation was done by hand), and is now a primary school teacher. She divorced after a short marriage and is living with her retired parents. I have never met a woman like Debbie before and admit to being fascinated by her refreshingly honest view of life and her refusal to conform or compromise her ideals. Her thirst for adventures and readiness to embark on them is also appealing. As my British Airways flight approached Los Angeles, I wondered what was in store for me in California. I was excited by the prospects, but apprehensive as well.

Debbie met me at the airport. We had a warm reunion and a chance to catch up on things during the two-hour drive to her parents' house. It had only been two months since the Pakistan adventure, but a lot had happened in the interim. Debbie would be busy for the next couple of days, until her school closed for the holidays. It soon became clear that she and her parents had planned a very full schedule for my visit. They were wonderfully hospitable and did everything possible to make me feel at home. Their attractive ranch style house was perched on a cliff, with a swimming pool overlooking a canyon. It was located in a citrus and avocado grove, which was Debbie's father's retirement project. I had obviously landed among a family of successful achievers.

There was the usual round of pre-Christmas parties, where I was introduced to all of the high-flying family friends. At one party, I met Julia Child who, as a chef and author, introduced French cooking to American housewives. On Christmas Day, the rest of the family showed up for dinner. Debbie's oldest sister Carol works as a scientific computer programmer. Her husband, a vice-president at Ford Aerospace, had been short-listed for Secretary of Defense in the George H.W. Bush Cabinet. Another sister, Lauren, is a film director. Debbie's twin brother, Rob, a marine biologist, is a professor at Stanford and a prominent member of the U.S. Antarctic research team. They all seemed very interested in what I had to say, and could not have been more charming or welcoming. Being a forester, I was keen to help in the grove and learned a good deal about avocado, macadamia nut, and citrus farming.

As a guest at a local Rotary Club meeting, I witnessed the fervour of American patriotism among this staunchly Republican group. Interestingly, these same people are able to turn a blind eye when hiring illegal Mexicans to work in their gardens, houses, and plantations. I learned about the critical water shortage in southern California and witnessed the gridlock on the freeways. There were obviously a few incongruities in this paradise. When too many of her family members were present, I noticed that Debbie retreated to the sidelines and seemed somewhat intimidated, anti-social and disinterested. I flew back to Montréal to celebrate the New Year with friends then hopped a flight down to Antigua to begin my winter aboard *La Brunante*.

La Brunante, at forty-two feet, is much larger than *Muscade* and much more comfortable. Boats are like balloons: it's not just the added length which counts. The extra width and height both make a huge difference to the living space. In addition, she had been equipped by a wealthy individual for luxury cruising whereas *Muscade* was equipped on a tight budget for safe and reliable ocean passages. This means that *La Brunante* has many extra features not found on *Muscade*: self-furling sails, an electric anchor winch, an electric autopilot and an entire console of the latest navigation and radio equipment. I am able to talk to the owner in Montréal on single sideband radio, and never have to take my sextant out of its box. Down below, the spacious galley is fully equipped with fridge and freezer. The boat is also air-conditioned, an unheard-of luxury for vessels of this size. I have organized my winter in the usual way with a balance between solo time and time with guests. Cruising friends, suppliers, and boat boys will have to get used to seeing me on a different vessel this winter.

In late January, one of my best and oldest friends joined me for a few days. Dermot was a senior of mine in Naval College, where we played on the same rugby team. After graduation, we continued our friendship as pilots, based at the Royal Canadian Naval air station in Dartmouth, Nova Scotia. He is now a captain with Canadian Airlines based in Vancouver, where he keeps his own boat, and is a very good sailor. After a brisk sail from Antigua to Guadeloupe, we anchored for the night in the village of Deshaies. Over a couple of rum and cokes, we reminisced about the time thirteen years ago, when he and his girlfriend Katie (now his wife) had spent some time with Ginette and me on board *Muscade* in Bermuda. We talked about the notorious seafaring scoundrel,

Paul Johnson, whom we both had met for the first time during that visit and speculated on his whereabouts.

The next day, we motored down the windless west coast of Guadeloupe and, after clearing the island at Basse Terre, set sail for Les Saintes. On arrival, as I was looking around the harbour for a suitable place to moor, I could hardly believe my eyes when I spotted Paul Johnson's boat, *Venus*, riding at anchor, so I dropped the hook within hailing distance. Just before sunset, Paul appeared on deck and, after quickly scanning the horizon, yelled over to us, "Malcolm, you are on the wrong bloody boat." Paul and his latest girlfriend had arrived that afternoon from the Canary Islands, having crossed the Atlantic, as most people would paddle across a stream.

One of the much-played, popular songs at the moment is by a group called Foreigner, entitled, "I Wanna Know What Love is." My question is: who wouldn't want to know if they are really in love? Most of us learn, when growing up, how to interpret our emotions and are eventually able to recognize what makes us angry, sad, elated, satisfied, or disappointed, but have no idea how to identify, or even define, love. Getting it wrong has caused couples endless problems, triggered huge divorce rates, and led to multitudes of single-parent families and conflicted children.

Several times in my life, I thought that I was in love, but on each occasion, I was wrong. The initial physical attraction is often just a camouflage for lust, fascination, curiosity, alluring expectations, or intellectual attraction, which can all be false positives for love. Are Hollywood movies, glossy fashion magazines, and Madison Avenue advertisements skewing our judgment by whetting our appetites for the unattainable? Ginette was a truly wonderful person, but in retrospect, I was never in love with her. It was more a question of thinking that I had better latch on to this good woman, because I probably would never find a better one. In most western societies the decision to marry, or not, can be more difficult for women than for men, because women have to decide, almost on the spot, if they should accept a marriage proposal or wait for a better offer, which may never come. On the other hand, men have to deal with the whole issue of rejection. I have already mentioned that someone once said: "Marry the girl next door." I suppose that concept aligns the couple from a cultural point of view, probably engenders more realistic expectations of life, and promises better relationships with the extended family, all arguments used to justify arranged marriages.

When I first joined Air Canada, I often flew with a captain who had his own unique ideas on many subjects. He was a delightful character, one of the few Spitfire pilots to survive World War Two. We had many interesting conversations during the long and boring trans-Atlantic flights. On one occasion, when I was ineptly chatting up a particularly attractive flight attendant in the cockpit, he sighed, "Oh Malcolm, if only I had your age and my experience." He was convinced that our system of boy-meets-girl, boy-marries-girl, and boy-stays-with-girl-forever was completely wrong and a recipe for unhappiness. I have forgotten the exact formula he was advocating, but it went something like this: young men from age eighteen should partner with women aged thirty-nine, live together for seven years, then move on. Similarly, young women from age eighteen should live with men aged thirty-nine for seven years. The resulting group of twenty-five year olds, having left their older partners, would then mate, raise children, then dissolve the relationship, when they were thirty-nine and restart the cycle. His thesis proposed that both young men and young women would be properly introduced to sex and life by experienced partners, so that they would be better prepared to raise children and find contentment. That's about as far as he got with his theory before it was time to recheck the weather, and prepare our aircraft for a landing in Paris.

I am back in California for the March school break. I have asked Debbie if she would like to share my adventurous lifestyle by moving aboard *Muscade*, sailing with me to the West Indies next autumn and then crossing to Europe the following spring. It is a huge commitment for both of us, but especially for Debbie, as she will have to leave her job and give up her comfortable life in California. We both decided that to seal our commitment and to give Debbie a modicum of security, we would marry. It just seemed like the right thing to do.

I must admit that, from my point of view, this is more about companionship and sharing experiences than love. Debbie realizes that we will not be able to have children, as I had a vasectomy about ten years ago. I overheard Debbie and her mother discussing whether such operations were reversible, so obviously neither she nor her parents are entirely thrilled about my reproductive potential. I am delighted to welcome into my life such an easy-going free spirit and am looking forward to the opportunities our partnership might create. We will marry in April then deliver *La Brunante* back to Montréal. The voyage will be an extended honeymoon cruise. When I phoned my sister, Diana, in Wales to announce our engagement, she told me that I was mad. Tomorrow, I will return to *La Brunante* in Antigua and live aboard until our wedding day.

CHAPTER NINE

SECOND MARRIAGE

We were married in the garden of Debbie's parents' house by a judge friend of the family. A couple of days later, we headed to Los Angeles to fly to Antigua and join *La Brunante*. At the airport, I had my first indication that a smooth transition to married life was not going to be easy. As a result of some public relations work I had done for Air Canada, the Vice President of Marketing had arranged first class seats for Debbie and me on our flight to Toronto. For reasons known only to her, Debbie could not accept this arrangement. She spent the entire flight gazing out the window and would not even accept a glass of water or a hot towel. The flight attendants, whom I knew, tried in vain to give us newly-weds their very best service and were totally bewildered by Debbie's behaviour. Needless to say, I began to question my recently changed marital status and wondered if my sister's caustic comment had hit the mark.

Once we were comfortably settled aboard *La Brunante* in Antigua, Debbie became her old self again and cheerfully joined in our daily life as we prepared the boat for the trip back to Montréal. When the boat was ready, we cruised up to St. Bart's and then on to St. Thomas in the Virgin Islands, where we met our third crewmember, Jean-Charles, who will help us sail the ocean part of the trip to Morehead City, N.C. Debbie and I will then have a relaxing cruise through Pamlico Sound, the Alligator River, and the Virginia cut to Norfolk, Chesapeake Bay, Delaware Bay, New York and finally up the Hudson River and the canal to Lake Champlain. Once we reach Morehead City, we will follow the magnolia blossoms northward.

On the ocean trip, Debbie showed the same fortitude and resilience as she had in Pakistan, and proved to be a competent sailor and watch keeper. Jean-Charles was his usual charming self and very good company. I kept my crew well fed and managed to augment our diet by catching a sizeable yellow fin tuna. The weather was perfect, the winds favourable, the boat and crew performed flawlessly, and before we knew it, we were having a celebratory dinner in Morehead City where we consumed so much wine with dinner that we all overslept and were rudely awakened the next morning by the chauffeur who had been hired to drive Jean-Charles to the airport. The rest of the trip north was a delightful saunter. Each night, we would anchor in a picturesque bay, or moor alongside in a marina. In Annapolis, Debbie's sister Carol and her family came aboard for lunch. Once we got to the marina on the Richelieu River where *Muscade* had been wintered, we made arrangements with the owner to stay aboard *La Brunante* until *Muscade* was refitted and ready to launch.

Debbie and I have now been together for seven months and are slowly adapting to married life. I am starting to realize what a huge compromise, to say nothing of a giant leap of faith, Debbie had to make when she agreed to join me on this adventure. She quit her teaching job, put her belongings into storage, sold her car and moved out of her parents' comfortable home in California to embark on this alternative lifestyle. She had to do exactly what I did when I left Air Canada, except she aligned the future direction of her life to a pathway which I had blazed. Now that I have a wife, much has changed for me as well. Going forward, I will have to weigh Debbie's best interests in the balance when mapping our future together. I have traded complete freedom of movement for shared adventures, and aloneness for companionship. It must be said that while Debbie can certainly be very unconventional, she is undemanding, to the point of being frugal. She rarely complains and is easy to live with. Naturally, I feel responsible for our combined well-being and wish to deliver the exciting and fulfilling life we are both expecting.

For the first time since leaving Air Canada four years ago, I'm starting to wonder about the future and sometimes ask myself how long we can continue to live this way. Will we ever tire of living on a sailing boat? Will we ever have to transition back to a more conventional way of life? For the moment, Debbie and I are on the same wave length and share many dreams of future adventures, including sailing *Muscade* across to Europe next summer and exploring the Mediterranean. I do suspect that Debbie would eventually like to settle down in California some day, something I would find difficult to do.

A lot has happened since last May when we successfully sailed *La Brunante* from Antigua to Montréal. On arrival, we continued to live aboard at a pretty marina on the Richelieu River, while totally refitting *Muscade* for her future voyages. The refit included removing and rebuilding the engine and transmission, and replacing all of the engine accessories. We also installed a proper refrigerator/freezer unit, which will make us far more self-sufficient, preclude having to buy ice every few days, and ensure a fresh-food supply on long ocean passages. However, the summer was not all work. We often went to Montréal or to the Laurentian hills to see friends, take in the Jazz Festival or try a new restaurant. Debbie is fairly fluent in French, which delights my French-Canadian friends, and makes socializing so much easier.

In mid-October, it was time for *Muscade* to leave Lake Champlain for the last time. I gave my car away to a friend for use as a winter clunker. He drove us to the boat and waved goodbye as we gathered up all the anchor gear and began our long voyage to Antigua. With considerable nostalgia I steered my faithful boat down the Hudson River to New York. It was her sixth round trip in fourteen years - and it would be her last. We had to wait for a week in a Staten Island marina for a satisfactory weather forecast before leaving for Bermuda, but we should have waited even longer.

The trip to Bermuda was extremely rough. We were severely beaten up by a series of cold fronts and had to furl the sails, leaving *Muscade* to the mercy of the gales under bare poles. The wind was so strong that it blew the tops off the waves, which had a flattening effect on the huge seas. We were forced to stay battened down below decks. All we could see outside the cabin windows was horizontally blown spume. Visibility was reduced to a few hundred feet, so we had to hope that no ships were in our vicinity. The boat careened downwind at hull speed with "Heidi" precariously holding course. By the time the wind finally subsided two days later, we had been blown by the gale and pushed by the Gulf Stream miles off track, so we had to approach Bermuda from the northeast. It was the worst weather I had ever encountered at sea, but *Muscade* was undamaged and Debbie took it calmly in stride.

Ocean sailing is a little like taking a wild roller coaster ride: it feels so good when the motion stops. I was never as happy to be anchored in calm, pleasant surroundings as when we finally dropped the hook in St. George's harbour. After a wonderfully relaxing week in Bermuda visiting old friends, and cruising couples who were also heading south, dining out on succulent fresh fish and taking long walks along Bermuda's bucolic, hibiscus-fringed lanes, we set sail for Antigua, arriving a week later.

We had steady easterly winds for the entire trip and no doldrums. I still used my sextant for navigation, but this will probably be the last ocean passage using this antiquated and difficult method. New satellite navigation systems are becoming much more affordable, and it will be a real luxury to know the boat's exact position by simply flipping a switch.

Relying on astro-navigation can be very stressful because, during cloudy conditions or rough weather, several days can elapse without getting a proper fix. During these periods, I have to plot my position using imprecise data. This best guess of the boat's location can easily be many miles in error. On top of that, the mathematical calculations required to reduce star sights to position lines are challenging enough in a naval college classroom, let alone in a sea-tossed boat. It follows that, in an emergency, I would not be able to transmit an accurate position to search-and-rescue authorities. This newly acquired, more responsible attitude is quite a change for me. On the original trip to Bermuda in 1974, I had no radios on board and navigated with a plastic sextant. It appears that I'm becoming more prudent with age and less willing to take chances.

It is now clear that the ideal crew for *Muscade* is two competent sailors and one reliable self-steering device. Logistically, things are far easier with only two people aboard, and as long as both are responsible watch keepers, everything runs smoothly. We have devised a watch system which works well on these ocean trips. During daylight, as long as one of us is on deck and can scan the horizon every fifteen minutes, we do not keep formal watches. As soon as it gets dark, one of us assumes the watch and remains responsible for the lookout until too tired to continue. Fatigue triggers a watch change. Whoever is on duty at night must be harnessed to the boat and must never leave the cockpit without informing the other person. If Debbie sees any lights during her watch, she immediately wakes me, as she is not yet qualified to assess collision dangers by interpreting ship's navigation lights. Unless there is an emergency - like a sudden squall or an unexpected increase in wind speed - we try to do all the sail changes during our watch turnovers, when we are both awake, dressed and on deck. This system allows the watch-keeper freedom to read in the comfort of the cabin, make hot chocolate, or get a bite to eat when on duty. The person off watch sleeps in a snug, cradle-like bunk, equipped with canvas leeboards, which is warm, dry and secure, even in the roughest conditions. It is so important to stay warm, dry, well-fed and well-rested during an ocean passage. As I learned on the beaches of New Jersey, fatigue is the enemy.

Muscade is back at anchor in English Harbour. Debbie and I are relaxing in the cockpit and making travel plans. During the first phase of our recent trip from Lake Champlain to New York, my mother suffered a stroke. Because her condition was stable, my father judged that there was no need to interrupt our trip south, but now that we have completed the voyage, we are going to Wales to offer support. If my mother is still making steady progress, we will continue with our plans to spend Christmas in New Zealand with Debbie's twin brother and his wife, who are on sabbatical in Wellington at the University of Victoria. Debbie's parents will also join us for Christmas in the sunshine. While we are away, we will once again leave *Muscade* here, at anchor in the hurricane hole, with her stern tied into the mangrove bushes as an extra precaution. She remains uninsured.

Our visit to Wales with my parents was very sad. Mother's stroke has left her with impaired speech and movement. She is no longer able to play bridge or complete crossword puzzles and requires a walker to move around the house. Luckily, my father is capable of shopping for groceries and cooking meals. They have a housekeeper who comes in on weekdays, and my sister lives nearby. As everything was more or less under control, we felt comfortable about leaving for Vancouver *en route* to New Zealand.

New Zealand was simply wonderful. The climate is a perfect solution for any northern dweller looking for eternal summers. We rented a camper van for ten days and toured around the South Island, climbing Mount Cook, hiking around Milford Sound and the glaciers, and visiting Queenstown and Christchurch. It was midsummer, and the weather was spectacular, but there were flies in the ointment. The voracious little insects called sand flies made our Canadian black flies seem very tame indeed. Debbie's parents flew in from California for Christmas Day. When the turkey was stuffed and in the oven, we trotted off to the beach for a swim, returning for a festive meal washed down with copious quantities of slightly-chilled, deliciously-fruity Central Otago pinot noir. When it was time for us to leave, Debbie's brother and his wife promised they would visit us onboard *Muscade* in April.

It is worth repeating that inanimate objects such as boats, houses and Egyptian pyramids are oblivious to the passing of time, although humans do tend to anthropomorphize them, needlessly worrying about leaving their possessions unattended. I am never concerned about such things and was not surprised to find Muscade exactly as we had left her a month earlier. Worry is a useless emotion, which alters nothing, but serves only to increase the anxiety and stress level of the worrier. It is a poor substitute for inaction. If nothing more can be done to improve a situation, the only option is to forget it and move forward.

Ever since I bought *Muscade* fifteen years ago, I have conscientiously kept a logbook and have a narrative for every day spent on board. I have just been re-reading the entries for the winter of 1989, from the time we returned from New Zealand until today, when we are setting sail for Portugal via Bermuda and the Azores. The logbook records an action-packed winter, during which I was keen to share the delights of the West Indies with Debbie. We decided to keep the same routine I had followed when single i.e., a good balance between time for just the two of us and time spent with friends and family. After five winters here, I am getting to know the territory and feel entirely comfortable navigating between the islands and into the various anchorages. It was a rare mooring spot where I did not know somebody, and where a spontaneous drinks party or dinner aboard or ashore did not materialize. Debbie was a deft hand in the galley and seemed to enjoy socializing in small groups.

We did have a dramatic incident one morning in Martinique. *Muscade* was anchored under the volcano, Mount Pelée, near the French colonial town of St. Pierre on the northwest coast of the island. We had arrived quite late the night before, after a non-stop sail from Guadeloupe, and were enjoying a lazy morning in the cockpit. The anchorage is notoriously difficult because the bottom slopes away steeply from the shoreline, so if an anchor drags, the boat will quickly be in deep water with the anchor hanging free. By mid-morning, the only other boat left at anchor was one named *Interlude*, from the USA. We waved to the owners as they went ashore in their dinghy for a visit. There was a very strong offshore wind gusting down the sides of the volcano, and we watched in horror as *Interlude* began dragging her anchor, and started drifting out to sea.

We knew immediately that it was up to us to intervene. There were no Coast Guard facilities available, and no other boats to help. By the time we started the engine and weighed anchor, *Interlude* was a blip on the horizon. As we motored at full speed away from the shelter of the island, the winds picked up considerably, and by the time we got close to *Interlude* there was significant wave action. We put out all the fenders, and, after several attempts, I managed to get alongside *Interlude* and lash the two pitching boats together, then jumped aboard the yacht and pulled up the anchor, which was hanging down vertically. Using full power, we managed to slowly coax the two boats back against the wind into St. Pierre, where we re-anchored *Interlude*.

Just as we were finishing this maneuver, the owners pulled up in their dinghy. After convincing them that we were not trying to steal their boat, we told them the real story. If we had not gone to the rescue, *Interlude* would have disappeared without a trace, and they would never have known what had happened to their boat. They might have guessed that she had dragged her anchor, and a subsequent air search (practically impossible) might have located her somewhere between Martinique and Central America. Needless to say, they were extremely grateful and insisted that we stay another day at St. Pierre and join them for a lavish dinner on board *Interlude* that evening.

CHAPTER TEN

NEAR-MISS IN MID-ATLANTIC

Tonight, we leave for Bermuda on the first leg of a transatlantic voyage to Portugal. It is the 24th of May, and I can still hear the echoes of those seasoned Bermudian sailors whose advice I ignored to my peril many years ago, when they suggested I should wait until the end of May before venturing into the North Atlantic. June is absolutely the best month to sail from Bermuda to the Azores, so we should easily slot into their recommended time period. *Muscade* is ready in all respects as is her crew. We have inspected all of the standing and running rigging, had the seams on all sails re-sewn, completed preventive maintenance on the engine, transmission, and hydraulic steering system, filled up with diesel fuel and water and stocked up on fresh food for our seven-day trip to Bermuda. The navigator has a brand-new satellite navigation system, and his sextant is stored safely in its box for emergency use only. We have a new, rigid-bottomed inflatable dinghy, which is lashed down on the foredeck and equipped with emergency survival gear, in case we have to abandon ship. The captain now has fifteen years' experience aboard his boat, his first mate is fully competent and "Heidi" has proven her worth. As we set course for Bermuda, we are relaxed and confident about accomplishing our mission and excited about taking our floating home to the Mediterranean. We have started studying Portuguese and will persevere throughout the trip, so we can communicate with the natives on arrival in the Azores and later in Lisbon.

After clearing Antigua to the north, and aware of the uncharted reefs around Barbuda, we altered heading to sail safely up the western side of that island, which happens to be the only land obstacle on our route to Bermuda. At midnight, we could see the dim lights of the small town of Codrington, where most of the island's two thousand people reside. The rest of the seven-day trip to Bermuda was fairly uneventful. The northeast trade winds stayed with us for four days. We motored through one day of calms, passed through a spectacular cold front with violent thunderstorms and lightning and sailed into Bermuda with gentle easterly winds and spring-like weather. One would think that the metal mast of a sailing boat would make a perfect lightning rod during thunderstorms at sea, but fortunately this is not the case. There are surprisingly few instances of small sailing boats being hit by lightning.

We spent five delightful days in Bermuda, then set sail for Horta, the capital of the island of Faial in the Azores. Horta is the traditional stopping place for the more than one thousand couples who cross the Atlantic each year in their own sailing boats. Because the distance to Horta is about two thousand miles, it could take up to three weeks to get there, so our approach to this voyage had to be significantly different from previous passages.

That is to say, everything becomes more critical, and the ability to be totally self-sufficient takes on new importance. Even with extra diesel fuel in portable containers, *Muscade* has a maximum range of about six hundred miles so motoring during calm periods is out of the question until we get within striking distance of Horta. Thanks to a state-of-the-art battery charging system, which I installed during last summer's refit, I only need to run the engine for one hour a day to keep the batteries fully charged, but even this limited use will account for twenty per cent of the total fuel capacity over a three-week period. Water is the other precious commodity. It will have to be carefully rationed, so there will be no hot showers for a while. We have stocked up on a large quantity of bottled drinking water.

Food is not a problem. Early sailors, who were forced to survive on hardtack biscuits, salted meat, rotten vegetables and tainted water, were given a daily rum ration to help perk up their appetites. Later, after Captain Cook's research, the Royal Navy added limes to this regimen to prevent scurvy. Fortunately, things are much better today. Besides our well-stocked freezer, we have a large supply of canned foods and plenty of fresh fruit and vegetables. Eggs will last up to a year, as long as they have never been refrigerated. We have flour to make fresh bread as well as rice, pasta and noodles. UHT milk, cream and yogurt need no refrigeration and last for months. We are not going to starve.

We had very light westerly winds and calm seas for the first few days, but still made significant progress under full mainsail and spinnaker. By the fourth day, strong southwesterly winds settled in to our area, and *Muscade* gamboled along day and night at her maximum hull speed rushing towards the Azores like a hired horse galloping back to its stable. Nine days after leaving Bermuda, we crossed the halfway point and celebrated with an elaborate dinner of smoked salmon, followed by roast beef, mashed potatoes and zucchini, with frozen yogurt for dessert. No wine of course. That will have to wait until we are safely in port.

For the first time, I am beginning to experience the feelings of euphoria which long-distance sailors talk about. After nine days at sea, with at least another nine to go, I am really comfortable in our own little world and am in no hurry to return to the big one. Our world is a peaceful place where, apart from the weather, we are in charge of our destiny. Our travelling companions are seabirds, different species of whales, dolphins, porpoises, sea turtles and any fish that dares break the surface. Once or twice a day, we are disturbed by a ship, and have to pay attention until it transits safely over the horizon. To date, we have not seen any other yachts, but this is bound to change when we approach the Azores, and all boats will be homing in to the same destination like moths to a candle's flame.

Today's dramatic events will be etched in my memory for as long as I live. The potentially tragic sequence of errors began this afternoon, when we noticed a very large bulk carrier looming on the horizon astern of us. At the time, we were sailing under mainsail only, with a strong westerly breeze dead astern. This meant that the boom was almost perpendicular to the boat's axis and was securely lashed down to the port gunnel with a preventer line. We were on a starboard tack. Anyone who has crewed for me will acknowledge that I am a very prudent sailor and always take every precaution to avoid collisions at sea. Today was no different, and ironically there was no immediate problem. I had at least fifteen minutes before this huge ship would be in our vicinity. It was daylight and the visibility was excellent. I had lots of time to remove the preventer line (holding the boom in place), disconnect the self-steering vane, start the engine and alter heading away from the ship's track. As I was beginning these preparations, something very unexpected happened. For the first time in my sailing experience, the captain of the ship called me up on the radio to have a chat. He confirmed that he had me in sight and was altering his ship's heading to pass down the starboard side of *Muscade* before resuming course. Speaking with a Scottish accent, he told me that his ship was carrying coal from Vancouver to Europe. As the ship approached, we continued our casual conversation, and I suggested to Debbie that she might want to have her camera handy to snap a picture of this mammoth vessel as it passed down our starboard side.

I was completely disarmed and utterly lulled into a sense of false security by my conversation with the captain and trusted him implicitly to avoid *Muscade*. I had not felt it necessary to complete any of the preparations previously mentioned. The preventer was still attached, "Heidi" was still steering the boat, and the engine had not been started. When the ship was a couple of hundred metres astern of *Muscade*, she altered heading directly towards us. I was incredulous. It was as if the captain was deliberately trying to run us down as part of some macabre, mid-Atlantic game. The ship was on a direct collision course, approaching very rapidly, and only seconds away from smashing us to pieces. Horrified, I leaped to the stern, disconnected the self-steering, then jumped back into the cockpit and spun the wheel hard to port. By now the bow of the ship loomed directly above us, and I said to Debbie, "I see no way out of this situation." As *Muscade* started her left turn, circumstances came together to save us. We were now at ninety degrees to the ship's course. The enormous bow wave pushed us off, thus preventing a head-on collision. Because the preventer rope was still attached to the boom, it was holding the mainsail in the optimum position to take full advantage of the strong wind being channeled down the side of the ship. The mainsail caught the wind and *Muscade* shot forward like a scared rabbit and began making just enough headway to avoid both a sideswipe and being scraped down the port side of the ship. Debbie, calm and cool as a cucumber, snapped a photograph. We had somehow escaped a watery grave.

I was in a complete state of shock and very, very angry. As ridiculous as it seems, I was convinced that the captain was trying to run us down on purpose. He probably thought that he had hit us because from the bridge we would have been completely hidden under his bows. When we were well clear of the ship, and my heart rate had assumed a more normal count, I tried to contact the ship by radio. After several tries, it became clear that they were no longer interested in talking to us. Finally, about five minutes later, a crewmember with a different accent answered my call, identified himself as the first officer and said, "Sorry about that. The captain was just trying to get a closer look at your boat." I was not amused. I can only surmise that the captain had diverted his ship from its course as a minor distraction from an otherwise boring voyage and resumed his course prematurely, before his ship had completely overtaken us. The turn would almost certainly have been done on autopilot. I am guessing that he was trying to get quite close to us, but misjudged the turning radius.

There have been several reported incidents of collisions at sea between large ships and small pleasure yachts as well as many cases, where boats have simply disappeared. A few years ago, I saw a photograph of a cargo ship which had recently arrived in Yokohama. It showed the mast, rigging and sails of a yacht jammed into the anchor hawse pipe. Unfortunately, some of these accidents are inevitable. Solo sailors have to sleep and are well aware of the risks involved. Commercial ships have to make a profit for their owners, so are constantly steered by autopilot and carry the absolute minimum crew mandated under international labour conventions. Besides, even the most diligent lookout cannot be expected to be totally vigilant during a four-hour night watch.

Years ago, as a naval cadet on training cruise from Vancouver to Australia and New Zealand, I often stood night watches, as a lookout on the bridge of a frigate. I remember finding it extremely hard to stay awake for an entire four-hour watch and developed an effective technique for dozing while standing. As previously mentioned in this narrative, small boats, even those made of steel, do not show up well on ships' anti-collision radars, and watch-keeping officers do not necessarily monitor their radar in good weather. *Muscade* has a state-of-the-art radar reflector attached high up on the mast, but it is of questionable value.

On the subject of collisions, in one of my parents' albums there is a photograph of my father shaking hands and sharing a joke with H.R.H. Prince Philip. It was taken years ago during a marine trade fair in Japan where my father's company, Decca Navigation, was promoting its latest anti-collision radar. After Prince Philip departed, several Japanese newspaper reporters approached my father to find out what they had been laughing about. Dad had to invent some story for them, as he could not repeat that Prince Philip had actually said: "Come on McCulloch, we all know that most collisions at sea are radar assisted."

After our close call, we quickly got *Muscade* back on course and Debbie whipped up some lamb chops with rice and vegetables to console her badly shaken husband. I really could have used a stiff drink, or a couple of glasses of good red wine with dinner, but managed to keep my resolution not to drink at sea. The strong westerly winds continued to give us a good push, and when I did my noon-to-noon distance calculation the next day, I found that Muscade had defiantly broken her all-time distance record by clocking a hundred and sixty-four nautical miles in one day, in spite of her close call with *World Spear*.

I suppose that one should never expect to cross the North Atlantic without encountering at least one violent storm. A low-pressure area with an associated cold front is apparently on its way towards us with expected winds of forty knots. The storm warning has generated lots of radio chatter among other yachts in our area as we compare notes on the impending gale and falling barometer. One French yacht, *Mercury*, out of St. Bart's and bound for Horta, came into view, and her skipper asked me for an accurate position, as he did not have satellite navigation equipment. Another boat, *Tangara,* from New Zealand was also in the area, and we made a radio date to meet for dinner, after our arrival in the Azores. The storm arrived as promised, but tossing around under bare poles in high winds and rough seas was an anti-climax after our near-death experience several days before. Debbie and I were completely relaxed, knowing that *Muscade* could easily handle the bad weather.

After the storm passed, the skies cleared and favourable southwest winds set in. We were now only a few days' sailing from Horta, and still had lots of fuel and water, so I approved unlimited hot showers and removed all restrictions on engine use during calm periods. Seventeen days after leaving Bermuda, the verdant shrubbery, lavender-coloured hydrangeas, and cascading waterfalls of the island of Faial came into view. All we had to do was cruise down the southern coast of the island, round the eastern end and enter the yacht harbour. Somewhat impatiently, I decided to increase our speed with engine power, but as I shifted into forward gear the propeller shaft sheared, and we became a pure sailing boat. Luckily, the wind held steady, so we were able to sail right into the port and were nudged into our dock space by the friendly and competent marina staff who used their workboat as a pusher tug.

The marina at Horta is a unique and amazing place, as ninety per cent of the boats here are in transit from North America to Europe. For the first time since quitting Air Canada five years ago, I find myself completely surrounded by like-minded individuals. I am comforted and reassured to be among people who share the same philosophy and the same the attitude towards life. No explanations for my chosen path are necessary here. Even though it is still very early in the season, *Muscade* was the five hundred and seventy-ninth boat to clear Portuguese customs in Horta this year, which puts things in perspective and makes our Atlantic crossing seem quite ordinary. Peter's Bar, the traditional watering hole for visiting sailors, also serves as an unofficial *poste restante*.

Before setting sail, we had told our friends and family about this mail service and, sure enough, there were several congratulatory letters awaiting us. The next item of business was to walk around the marina and locate the crews we had met on the radio during the recent storm. While doing this, we also came across several other couples whom we had met in Bermuda or the West Indies. We were one big happy family. After a delightful seafood dinner with our new friends at one of Horta's many good restaurants, we retired to a full night's sleep in a motionless bunk for the first time in two-and-a half-weeks.

I had read in a sailing magazine that the majority of trans-Atlantic sailors do not allow enough time to discover the charms and beauty of the Azores Islands. Most move on towards mainland Europe far too impatiently after arriving and later regret missing this spectacular part of the world. In view of this, we have decided to stay here for at least a couple of weeks.

There is a long-standing tradition in Horta. Transiting boats are encouraged to record their visit by leaving some form of artwork on the walls surrounding the marina. Sailors tend to be superstitious, so would never risk the wrath of Poseidon by ignoring this established custom: to do so could have unpleasant consequences for the onward journey. Debbie has put on her graphic artist's hat and designed an appropriate logo for *Muscade*. We have staked out a vacant space on the wall, acquired the materials necessary for the job, and hope to please the sea god with her artistic talents. There is an amazing amount of very good artwork here, dating back many years. One can spend hours browsing the walls and enjoying the originality of design and witty comments. I am quite surprised by how many yachts' names I recognize from my short time in this fraternity.

A mechanic has inspected our sheered transmission coupling and determined that we must haul the boat so that he can remove the propeller shaft and carry out a proper repair. It is completely my fault that the transmission coupling sheered. When I reinstalled the engine during last summer's refit, I neglected to realign the engine and propeller shaft. I mistakenly assumed that, as the engine mounts had not been moved, there was no need for realignment. Now I am paying for my mistake. Surprisingly, there is no travel lift on the island of Faial, so I have hired a crane and rented some lifting straps to get the job done. *Muscade* will be towed to the main harbour wall, where she will be lifted out of the water, then chocked up on the dock for the time it takes to do the work, a small job for these enterprising Portuguese artisans whose forbears have been repairing boats for centuries.

During an ocean trip, it is very difficult to get enough exercise, so every day since arriving in Horta, we have taken long walks along the picturesque country roads with their blue hydrangea hedgerows. Today, we took a ferry across to the neighbouring island of Pico and hiked up to the top of the volcano. We picnicked at the summit, where hot steam was hissing out of vents in the rocks. It was a long day, and we were physically exhausted when we got back to Horta, but we felt satisfied with our accomplishment.

We have now spent two weeks in this delightful part of the world, and it is time for us to set sail for Lisbon and complete our transatlantic crossing. *Muscade* has a new, properly aligned propeller shaft, and all of the usual preventive maintenance has been completed. It's eleven hundred miles from here to Lisbon, so we are anticipating a nine-day crossing. The winds should be mostly westerly, and there will be a weak current setting us from north to south. We expect to encounter lots of shipping traffic, especially near the Portuguese coast, where we will have to cross one of the world's busiest shipping lanes. *Muscade*, courtesy of Debbie's artwork, has left her mark on the walls of Horta, so we are hoping for an uneventful and safe trip.

After saying goodbye to our many new friends and promising that we will meet them again in some exotic Mediterranean anchorage, we left the harbour shortly before sunset and headed east to pass between the islands of Pico and San Jorge. Since it was the Fourth of July, I went down to the galley and rustled up an appropriate dinner of hamburgers and fries, followed by ice cream, while Debbie stood the first watch.

We took eight days to reach Lisbon. For the first half of the trip, we had southwesterly winds and smooth sailing. We were then hit with a northeaster, had very rough sailing under reefed sails for three days and finished the trip under engine power in calm and foggy conditions. We crossed the main European shipping lanes in reduced visibility and did not actually see the coast of Portugal until we were only two miles away. Of course, with our satellite navigation system, we knew exactly where we were at all times. I can only imagine how tense it would have been if I had still been relying on my sextant for navigation. While recording our landfall in the ship's logbook, I wrote, "Europe has just been rediscovered," because that's how it felt to me. I had crossed the Atlantic hundreds of times in my Air Canada jet, but this was very different. Arriving in one's own boat, having taken more than one month at an average speed of five miles an hour, puts things in an entirely different perspective. We motored up the mighty Tagus River in the hallowed wake of Vasco da Gama and managed to squeeze *Muscade* into the last available slip at a marina in Belem, a suburb of Lisbon. The marina was appropriately named *Bom Successo.*

Mostly due to our limited Portuguese language skills, which abetted a bureaucratic run-around, it took us hours to find the proper customs office in the city. When we finally did, the officials didn't really know what to do with us, and I began to think that we needn't have bothered. We were politely dismissed without being given any documentary evidence of our arrival. I am quite happy with this type of bureaucratic nonchalance, because it bodes well for the rest of our stay in Portugal.

The whole exercise reminded me of an occasion years ago

when I sailed into New York, having just arrived from Bermuda. When I phoned the United States Customs authorities from a local marina to report my arrival, the officer on duty asked me where I was heading. When I said that I was on my way to Lake Champlain, he told me to keep on going, as it was in Canada. It's true that the northern part of the lake is in Canada, but ninety per cent of the lake is in the U.S.A. This nostalgic flashback reminded me of how trusting border arrangements used to be between the U.S.A. and Canada. The important point is that we are finally here in Portugal, our first European destination, where we will base *Muscade* until next spring. We are delighted to be in this beautiful country, and look forward to exploring every part of it.

I find it amazing that most marinas and yacht clubs in the world are invariably full to overflowing and often have long waiting lists. Very little space is allotted to visiting yachts. Even on weekends, national holidays or peak vacation periods, most local boats remain marina-bound, and it is difficult for visitors to find space even for a few days. This is because many men buy boats to satisfy a yearning for freedom. For these individuals, their boats represent a psychological means of escape from the stresses of modern-day life. Their reason to have a boat is not necessarily to cast off in search of adventure. Rather, their pleasure comes from owning a boat, which is always ready to set sail and offers the potential for a getaway. These individuals spend hours working on their vessels, ensuring that they are immaculately maintained and equipped with all the latest gear, but rarely take them out for more than a short jaunt. Some of these boat owners don't even like sailing. Others plan to get going when they retire in their mid-to-late-sixties, but rarely do. A few years ago, the English magazine *"Yachting Monthly,"* conducted a survey to determine the average use of cruising boats in the U.K. The report concluded that owners used their boats an average of only eighty hours a year. Alas, Lisbon is no exception. The *Bom Successo* marina management has told us that we have to move out. This is unfortunate, because I had promised Debbie a trip back to see her parents in California.

I need not have worried about finding a dock space, as a saviour soon appeared in the guise of retired Portuguese Admiral Ramos, the owner of the local marine chandlery. After one telephone call, he used his influence to secure a mooring for *Muscade* at a marina further upstream in the centre of Lisbon. Even though I had only served a seven-year commission in the Royal Canadian Navy, retiring as a lowly Lieutenant, the camaraderie existing among all former naval officers saved the day.

Shortly after we had moved *Muscade* to the new marina, I invited Admiral Ramos aboard for a drink. With his help and local knowledge, we conjured up a plan for the rest of our stay in Portugal. He suggested that after our trip to California, we use this marina as a base to explore the Lisbon area. Apart from the river Tagus and the river Douro, which are both navigable for a considerable distance upstream, there is not much cruising to be done on the Atlantic coast of Portugal. The Algarve coast is supposedly a much better sailing area, and there is a newly opened, well-equipped marina at Vilamoura where we could berth *Muscade* for the winter. He further recommended that it would be a good plan to tour Portugal by car in the late autumn, after most of the tourists have left - all very good and most welcome advice.

It is now mid-August, and we have just arrived back from a three- week trip to California. We found *Muscade* in good condition, although the deck and topsides were covered with a layer of fine sand, which blows off the Sahara desert whenever there is a strong Sirocco wind. We were delighted to reunite with other boat owners last seen in the Azores. It really is a "movable feast" of yachts and friends.

I seem to be attracted to creative women, given that both Ginette and Debbie are artists. They both, in their turn, have taught me to appreciate works of art by helping me view them through their connoisseur's prism. These thoughts are in my mind as we tour Lisbon's famous Gulbenkian Museum with its wonderful antiquities, chinoiseries and Lalique glass collection. We are coming to the end of our stay in Lisbon, a city built on the pillaging of a vast Portuguese empire, riches which have long since been fully exploited. Like much of Portugal, the capital is in decline because the wealth generated by the former colonies no longer exists to support the motherland, so the country has become one of Europe's poor cousins. This decline, accelerated by a forty-year long, corrupt fascist dictatorship, was finally halted by a military coup in 1975, which paved the way for the present-day democracy. However, it is easy to imagine how magnificent Lisbon must have been at the zenith of Portugal's colonial greatness. The Portuguese have suffered terribly over the years, and this unhappiness seems to be reflected in the mournful genre of their folk music known as Fado (destiny or fate), which is said to have had its origins among melancholy fishermen's wives lamenting the loss of their husbands at sea. Fado singing, still very popular today, is taken very seriously by the Portuguese. We have attended several concerts and folklore festivals featuring this mournful music.

    I have some unfinished business to take care of before leaving the Tagus estuary and pointing *Muscade* south towards the Algarve. It concerns my friend Jean Milette. Back in the Seventies, when we were both airline pilots, we spent many a cold winter's night in Montréal sipping scotch in front of a roaring fire while discussing what our lives would be like after we had left our airline jobs. At the time, Jean was a captain with Canadian Pacific Airlines, and I was quite envious of his long layovers in Lisbon. He told me one of his favourite haunts was a bar in the Albatroz Hotel, which overlooked the yacht harbour in the quaint fishing village of Cascais. His dream was to be in that same bar looking down on his own boat safely anchored in the harbour, having just crossed the Atlantic. It all sounded pretty romantic at the time. Now I was in a position to live his dream.

Admiral Ramos was right: there is not much of interest for a cruising sailor on the Atlantic coast of Portugal between Lisbon and the Algarve, apart from a handful of fairly exposed fishing villages. We did overnight in Cascais, had a delightful dinner at the Albatroz hotel and sent Jean a postcard to let him know that we had realized his dream. During dinner, we did indeed look out on our lovely *Muscade* riding at anchor, although the weather was misty and the anchorage quite agitated, so we knew we were in for an uncomfortable night. The harbour is unprotected from the east, a detail easy to overlook on an airline layover, when having a drink and dreaming about future adventures.

It is becoming clear that, after sixteen years of cruising in the Bahamas, West Indies, and the East Coast of North America, where beautifully-sheltered, picturesque, and un-crowded anchorages abound, I cannot expect to find the same conditions in the Mediterranean. After all, it is the cradle of civilization whose shores have been heavily populated for thousands of years, so I must adjust my expectations. According to sailors who have cruised the Mediterranean extensively, the best cruising grounds where one can still find relatively unspoiled and un-crowded anchorages, are in Yugoslavia, Corsica, Sardinia, and in some areas of Greece and Turkey. We are not as yet in the Mediterranean, but we have been disappointed with the crowded anchorages in the Algarve. On the other hand, there are some interesting fishing towns, the best being Portimao, which is reputed for its *sardinhas grelhadas* or grilled sardines. Open-air restaurants on the dock haul up fresh sardines directly from fishing boats lying alongside and grill them on barbecues next to their customers' tables. This delicious meal is traditionally washed down with *vinho verde tinto,* a young wine which had its origin in the far north of Portugal in the early 1900s. It can be red, white, or *rosé*. I had been under the false impression that *vinho verdi* was always white, and remember drinking lots of it during my misspent youth in Canada along with that other reasonably-priced Portuguese beginners' wine, *Matéus rosé*.

The good news is that the Vilamoura Marina, where we plan to leave *Muscade* for the winter, is a first-class facility. It is part of a huge new resort complex made up of condominiums, golf courses, many excellent outdoor restaurants, and shops of all kinds. The marina itself has excellent amenities and a full-service boatyard. The town of Quateira is only a short walk away, and the entire coastline is one long sandy beach, so walking has once again become a daily routine. We are delighted to be here in the excellent company of a whole community of cruising couples who will be living aboard their boats during the coming winter. Debbie and I have different plans. We certainly have no intention of becoming hostages to the cool, damp and windy months of the Portuguese winter.

It's only September, winter is a long way off, and we are excited about taking Admiral Ramos' advice to tour Portugal by car and stay in *pousadas*, which are luxury hotels run by the government. Most of them are converted palaces, monasteries, castles, or historic homes and boast good restaurants featuring local cuisine and wines. We will try to cover the entire country, including the mountain area in the north, the Douro River Valley, the Templar's castle at Tomar, and the city of Porto. When we get to Porto, I have a mission to find a bottle of 1939 vintage port to serve at my parents' fiftieth wedding anniversary celebration at the end of December. After our tour of Portugal, we will say goodbye to *Muscade*, fly to Nice, and then drive to Tuscany to meet some friends from Montréal for a two-week Italian holiday.

As for next winter, Jean-Charles has kindly offered us the use of *Le Pat-Mar*, which is presently out of the water in Antigua. I have agreed to skipper the boat for the winter. Debbie and I will meet him at various locations in the Caribbean whenever he has holidays.

Today in Italy, I learned that we might have to make alternate plans for the coming winter. Hurricane Hugo, a category five hurricane and the worst one to hit the West Indies in thirty-five years, scored a direct hit on Guadeloupe, then continued north to Antigua, causing considerable damage in the boatyard where *Le Pat-Mar* is being stored. The boat was blown off its storage cradle, and the hull is damaged. The mast stayed in place, but the rigging was stretched, and the entire mast assembly has to be replaced. I am feeling very fortunate because, had we not crossed over to Europe, *Muscade* would have been stored in that same boatyard.

CHAPTER ELEVEN:

A MISTRAL AND THE FRENCH CANALS

It is now the end of December. We are in Wales celebrating the festive season with my family. Last night, we took over a local restaurant for my parents' fiftieth anniversary dinner party. After the meal, I opened the 1939 vintage port. It was a cloudy red brown color, which did not look promising, but it turned out to be the smoothest and most delicious port any of us had ever tasted. Not wanting to take any chances with a fifty-year-old wine getting any older, we polished off the entire bottle. The chef made the mistake of asking my father what he thought of the meal, to which Dad replied, in his own inimitable way, that although he had quite enjoyed the evening, "the Baked Alaska was a bloody disaster." We later found out that the chef had dropped his first attempt at that dessert on the kitchen floor and had to hurriedly whip up another one. My father's diplomatic skills were not improving with age.

We have good news about *Le Pat-Mar*. The hull has been repaired and the insurance company has approved a delivery trip with reduced canvas to Guadeloupe, where an accredited yard will replace the mast. Jean-Charles has asked me to sail the boat to Guadeloupe, supervise the mast replacement, and continue down island to meet him in the Grenadines. Tomorrow we leave for Antigua.

The trip aboard *Le Pat-Mar* from Antigua to Pointe-à-Pitre in Guadeloupe was routine, until we got close to the marina itself and witnessed the appalling destruction of last September's hurricane Hugo. In the anchorage adjacent to the marina, we could see the mast tops of several sunken yachts sticking up above the water. All vegetation as far as the eye could see had been defoliated. Palm trees were topless. The marina itself was in partial operation, so I was able to pick my way between the sunken boats and find a decent dock space adjacent to the dealer who would be replacing the mast. In view of the situation, it was easy to predict that it was going to be a long process, as we were very low on the priority list for urgent repairs. In spite of everything, it was extremely pleasant to be back in the West Indies, and especially to be in this little corner of France, with its well-stocked supermarkets, huge selection of wines, and abundance of good French restaurants. Not a bad place to spend a couple of weeks. After the mast and rigging had been installed and adjusted to my satisfaction, we cruised to the now-familiar islands of Martinique, St. Lucia, St. Vincent, and the Grenadines for a month before meeting Jean-Charles and his family in Grenada. We handed over the boat to him there and flew back to Portugal via Trinidad and Montréal. So ended my sixth consecutive winter in this superb cruising paradise.

It's springtime in the Algarve. All of the yachties have emerged from winter hibernation and are busily preparing their boats for the coming season. We are also eager to get going. We have already taken *Muscade* out of the water for her annual maintenance and spent our second wedding anniversary applying anti-fouling paint to the hull before going out for a sumptuous dinner to celebrate the occasion.

Muscade is now in the water, and we are awaiting an ideal weather window to sail non-stop to Gibraltar. At the moment, there is a strong easterly wind, or Levanter, blowing. One has to wonder, with some apprehension, about an area that gives names to all its various winds, as is the case in most Mediterranean countries. Apart from the Levanter, we will have to watch out for gales caused by the Sirocco, the southerly wind that blows off the Sahara desert, and most importantly the Mistral, an extremely dangerous north wind caused by a venturi effect in the Rhône Valley. The most prevalent area for the Mistral is between Corsica and the Balearic Islands, which is precisely on our planned route. We are impatient for the Levanter wind to abate, because we have made arrangements to meet Jean Milette in Chamonix for some spring skiing. Our intention is to sail from Portugal directly to Gibraltar, then non-stop to Barcelona and finally onwards to Port Carmargue at the mouth of the Rhône River. Jean will meet us there and drive us to his place in Chamonix. After the ski trip, we will convert *Muscade* into a canal barge and proceed up the Rhône River to explore some of the eight thousand kilometres of navigable waterways of France.

Today, the wind finally turned southwesterly, and we bid *adeus* to Portugal. Almost exactly two days later, after a rollicking sail and only two hours of motoring, we passed through the Straits of Gibraltar and pulled into the famous Sheppard's Marina. We were helped into our dock space by a charming Frenchman who complimented us on *Muscade's* name and later invited us for a drink aboard his bright yellow catamaran named *Banana Split*. His name was Pierre Antoine Muraccioli, better known as the French rock star Antoine, who was also notorious for his musical sparring matches with Johnny Hallyday in the Sixties. In 1974, he embarked on the life of a sailor, writer and movie producer. He is preparing to leave on a single-handed voyage to French Polynesia, where his wife is expecting a baby. During our time together, he gave me a comprehensive briefing on sailing in the Mediterranean, including some valuable information about how best to handle the dreaded Mistral. He politely suggested that, on our way to Port Carmargue, we might consider hugging the Spanish and French coastlines instead of going on the direct track I had planned. That way, if we do encounter a Mistral, we will already be under the sheltered lee of the shoreline and better protected from wave build-up. I will certainly heed his advice: I am finally learning to listen to other people's suggestions.

The solid stone mass of the Rock of Gibraltar towers fourteen hundred feet above the sea. It's a most impressive and unmistakable landmark. For my family, it represents a place where both my father and I, at different times in our respective lives, were almost killed.

In my father's case, it was during World War Two in 1941, when the aircraft carrier, *HMS Ark Royal*, was alongside in Gibraltar. A German U-boat captain, seeing the outline of the carrier with his periscope, fired off a series of torpedoes, not realizing that the ship was moored on the inside of a solid stone jetty. When the torpedoes hit the stone wall, *HMS Ark Royal* was severely battered but did not sink, and my father, considerably shaken, lived to tell the tale. It was a short-lived reprieve however, as the ship was sunk soon afterwards by another German submarine off the coast of Spain, in November 1941. Luckily, my father was airborne at the time.

My near miss was in 1964 when the Canadian aircraft carrier *HMCS Bonaventure* was alongside in Gibraltar at the same jetty. Before the ship entered port, I flew off an aircraft which needed a test flight, and landed at a small R.A.F. airfield located on the narrow causeway between Gibraltar and Spain. The next day, when I showed up with my crew to do the test flight, the R.A.F. weather-briefing officer warned us that when the wind was in a certain direction in relation to the rock mass of Gibraltar, extreme downdrafts could develop over the runway. He told us that when these conditions were evident, the airfield was closed without exception, as it was too dangerous to attempt a landing. When we returned to Gibraltar after a routine test flight, the control tower informed us that although the wind conditions were approaching the limits for closing the field, we could still attempt a landing at our discretion. On approach, at about three hundred feet above ground, I lost control of the aircraft in a huge downdraft. Full opposite aileron had no effect on the direction. Pulling back on the stick had no effect on the steep descent. We seemed doomed to crash off to the right-hand side of the runway. Miraculously, just before impact, the aircraft flew out of the downdraft, the flight controls began to respond, and I was able to carry out a missed approach. The tower controller, who thought that we were dead ducks, promptly closed the field.

Now I had another problem. We were very low on fuel, and due to fog and inclement weather there were no alternate airports available on the European side of the Mediterranean. We were given a vector to Oran in Algeria, and I calculated that we had just enough fuel to get there. Algeria had won its independence from France in 1962, but luckily for us the airfield in Oran was still under French Air Force control. When I found the airport, we were almost out of fuel and had no way of contacting the control tower. After observing the wind direction, I landed unannounced on the appropriate end of the runway. We were immediately surrounded by armored vehicles, but soon managed to convince the French that we were N.A.T.O. allies, not Algerian insurgents masquerading as Canadians. After two days of incredible hospitality courtesy of the French Air Force, and a most welcome introduction to Algerian *vin du sable,* we received a message ordering us to rejoin *Bonaventure* at sea. The ship had been diverted back to Canada to pick up a contingent of Canadian soldiers for a peacekeeping mission in Cyprus. I would be part of that operation.

Back aboard *Muscade*, after only one day in Gibraltar, we were compelled to get going again so that we could make our skiing rendezvous with Jean in France. I had certainly planned badly. In retrospect, I should have cancelled the ski trip and spent a leisurely month cruising the south coast of Spain before going up the Rhône for the summer. It would have been wonderful to spend at least a week in Gibraltar, but it was not to be.

The five frustrating days that we took to reach Barcelona gave us our first taste of Mediterranean sailing. The winds were constantly changing, both in speed and direction, with many periods of flat calm. I have never before done so many sail changes in such a short period of time, and we did a lot of motoring. The Mediterranean is reputed to have no happy medium when it comes to winds: they are either light and fluky, or gale force. I guess we'd better get used to it.

We did have one unforgettable experience halfway through the trip. We were becalmed one Sunday morning off the Spanish city of Valencia and were brunching in the cockpit when we were visited by a large pod of pilot whales, about twenty in all. They surrounded the boat and poked their heads above the water, squeaking as if trying to communicate with us. The bulls, cows and calves treated us to an amazing aquatic show and seemed just as fascinated with us as we were with them. I experimented with our stereo system to find out what kind of music they preferred. It definitely was not opera. Country and western seemed to be the genre of choice. I was tempted to join them in the water, but did not have the courage to jump in. After about two hours, they got bored with our music and swam away, leaving us in awe.

By the time we arrived at the *Real Club Náutico de Barcelona*, I was almost ready to trade *Muscade* in for a motorboat, which seemed a far more appropriate vessel for the Mediterranean wind and weather conditions. It was ridiculous that we were only going to spend one night in this beautiful city. After a stroll down Las

Ramblas, an obligatory *Paella* and a quick night's sleep in a calm bunk, we were underway again. I was very much aware, especially after my conversation with Antoine in Gibraltar, that we were now in Mistral territory.

I could not get a proper weather forecast before leaving Barcelona, as it was too early in the Club's season, but clear sunny skies, light southerly winds and a high barometer reading all inspired confidence. We had to motor for most of the day, but after nightfall a southerly wind picked up enough to start sailing. I was on watch, and Debbie was sleeping below, when the wind veered abruptly to the west and increased in speed. I woke Debbie, asking her to dress quickly and come up on deck, so I could start reefing the sails. In the short time that it took her to join me, the wind had veered further to the northwest and increased to gale force. This was undoubtedly a Mistral. Thanks to Antoine's advice, we were only a few miles offshore, abeam Cabo Creus, known ominously as the Cape Horn of the Mediterranean. However, we were not yet out of danger. The waves were enormous and most of them were breaking over the stern of the boat. We were running downwind with a tiny triangle of mainsail and no jib. After about three hours, we managed to coax *Muscade* under the lee of Cabo Creus where the waves were much smaller, although the wind was still blowing a gale. I was surprised to see that we were not alone: there were several large ships sheltering in the same area, waiting for the Mistral to abate. Unlike us, they had access to good weather reports and had been forewarned. By nine o'clock in the morning, the wind began to subside, and we were able to anchor off the town of Roses for a much-needed rest after a sleepless night. We had survived our first Mistral and the roughest, most dangerous conditions I had ever seen at sea.

We slept peacefully in the sheltered anchorage for most of the day, rustled up a delicious dinner, then weighed anchor to begin the final segment of our trip to the Rhône River entrance.

We motored around the headland of Cabo Creus, ironically in mirror-calm conditions, and spent the rest of the trip changing sails, alternating between sailing, motoring and motor sailing according to the wind's annoying inconsistencies. We arrived at the marina in Port Carmargue the next afternoon. The first thing I did was to phone Jean in Chamonix. He and his neighbor, Eric Taberly, had been aware of the storm, knew we were in that area and were not surprised by our harrowing tale. Many years before, Taberly had lost a boat during a Mistral in the same place.

I am upset with myself for not trying harder to get a proper weather forecast before leaving Barcelona, instead of relying on my own knowledge, which obviously has absolutely no application in the Med. There is no excuse for this negligence. Mistrals are always accurately forecast. Looking back on the trip, I remember seeing Spanish fishing boats, which normally work all night, heading back to port a few hours before the Mistral hit. That was an obvious sign of bad weather, which was entirely lost on me at the time.

Spring skiing in Chamonix with Jean as our mountain guide and host was a treat. It proved a welcome change from *Muscade* to be comfortably ensconced in Jean's luxurious condo. We did have an exciting adventure one afternoon while watching para-glider enthusiasts launch into flight at the top of Le Brevent Mountain, on the opposite side of the valley from the main ski area. We were horrified to see one man's parachute contact a cable car suspension wire as he was circling to gain altitude. Fortunately his chute snagged, then wrapped around the wire, leaving him hanging by his harness with a thousand-foot drop to a sure death below him. We took off at top speed down the ski trail to intercept and warn the cable car driver before he began his next ascent. Meanwhile, the man in distress climbed up his parachute harness to the cable, fashioned a sling and proceeded to slide his way down the wire to the cable car station. Later, over a glass of red wine beside the fire, we speculated as to whether the man in question would continue with his sport, or take the hint and quit while he was still alive.

I had skied before with Debbie in California, and she proved to be very competent, easily keeping up with Jean and me. After ten glorious days, Jean drove us back to our boat. He will stay with us on board for a cruise up the Rhône as far as Avignon.

Muscade has transitioned very well to a canal barge or *péniche*. We stored the mast, boom, and standing rigging at a Port Carmargue boatyard, folded away all the sails, and rigged up a permanent cover over the cockpit to keep us snug and dry when motoring. *Muscade* has a full keel, but only draws four-and-a-half feet, so we should have plenty of bottom clearance in most canals. Our seventy-five horsepower diesel engine will be ideal for powering off the mud if we do get stuck and will easily push us against the strong Rhône River currents, presently in spring flood. I am very much aware that if we have any problems with the engine, we will be completely at the mercy of the current. I have prepared two anchors on the foredeck ready to be deployed at a moment's notice. My one concern is that *Muscade*, being a pristine fiberglass sailing boat, is not suited to rubbing shoulders with the uneven stone and cement lock walls. To protect the hull, we have installed a canvas skirt down to the water line, and have tied rubber fenders from bow to stern on both sides. We have acquired a couple of folding bicycles, which will greatly increase our radius of action. It is both exciting and very relaxing to be cruising in the waterways of France.

Barging is the antithesis of ocean sailing. Weather is rarely a concern, and we will be safely alongside in a charming village, on a grassy canal bank, or at a marina every night. The main preoccupations will be choosing a bakery for our fresh croissants every morning and deciding which local wine to order in the bistro each evening. I have decided to do some serious research while we are in the canals. I'm looking for the bakery which makes the best croissants in France, as well as the one making the best bread.

Later in the summer, when we get into the Marne River between Paris and Épernay, I shall try to track down the best champagne producer.

Our first port of call, just a few miles north of the Mediterranean, was the historic, medieval (1240), walled town of Aigues Mortes, the port of departure for the crusade sponsored by King Louis IX. The next day, we locked through into the Rhône River, and went alongside in the city of Arles, the once-famous hangout for the impressionist painters, including Van Gogh. The Rhône is the longest river in France and before it was canalized, used to be wild and un-navigable. It is a very steep river, rising in the Alps and descending all the way to the Mediterranean, which accounts for the strong currents after the spring thaw in the mountains. Before the river was eventually tamed, navigation was only possible going downstream. Goods, including wine, were floated down the river on rafts, which were then abandoned. Thanks to modern engineering, the river is now fully navigable and very user-friendly for small boats like *Muscade*. Even though the locks are enormous, (each lock has a water level change of sixty to seventy feet), floating bollards recessed into the walls make locking easy. Commercial traffic has priority over pleasure craft, but often the lock keepers, with whom I am in contact by radio, allow me to tuck in behind the larger working barges and ships. Mooring alongside, or anchoring in the canalized sections of the river, is not permitted, but all the towns and cities along the way have either marinas or designated dock spaces on the riverbank. We took eight days to get to Lyon, stopping every night in a different town. In Avignon, we bade farewell to Jean who went back to finish the ski season in Chamonix. On the way up river to Lyon, we traced two thousand years of wine-making history, beginning in Provence then cruising through Château Neuf de Pape, Rhône Villages, Cornas, Hermitage, St. Joseph, Condrieu and finally Côte Rotie.

Debbie's parents were joining us in Lyon for a cruise up the Saône River to Dijon so on the evening of our arrival in that gastronomic city, we went ashore to confirm our rendezvous with my in-laws. On the way back to the boat, I was surprised to see, strewn on the embankment, various items which looked very much like my collection of spare parts for *Muscade*. Sure enough, we had been burgled. The robbers had smashed their way into the main cabin entrance and had stolen a small amount of cash and some credit cards. I always turn off the master electrical switch whenever I leave the boat, so there were no lights available down below, and the thieves had to use matches to search the cabin. My assortment of spare parts had been stored in what looked like a large jewelry box, so I guess the thieves were disappointed when they discovered the contents and subsequently dumped them on the riverbank. Ironically, the spare parts were far more valuable to me and much harder to replace than the cash and credit cards. The following day, we managed to retrieve the full inventory of parts, including the box they were stored in. The police were entirely unhelpful and intimated that we should have expected to be robbed in that location. They were right. I later read in the cruising guide that leaving a pleasure boat unattended anywhere in Lyon was not recommended. The robbers had obviously been watching the boat and pounced as soon as we went ashore. The next day, I found a carpenter to fix the cabin doors. *Muscade* was as good as new, and I was again humbled. It makes me question my confidence in human nature and wonder if it's possible to be too trusting. Of course, had I read and believed the cruising guide, the entire incident could have been avoided.

I am not one to dwell on unpleasant events and manage to get over my mistakes quite quickly and move forward, without remorse. More importantly, Debbie seems completely unaffected by the incident and acts as if the robbery was all part of life's journey, which I suppose is correct. She is the most un-material person I have ever met, and no matter how much I discourage her, she insists on repairing her deck shoes and clothes herself, rather than buying new ones.

I think Friedrich Nietzsche would have approved of the way we are striving for a balanced existence between the actual physical world (cosmos) and the world which we perceive. We are trying to grasp that there is more to life than we were led to believe during our upbringing and schooling. We have gone on to idealize what our lives could be like and are trying to make that ideal a reality, which is what the philosopher was advocating when he elaborated on Plato's "doctrine of two worlds." I contemplate this credo as we cruise gently north up the Saône River on a warm sunny day in the agreeable company of Debbie's parents, passing first the vineyards of Beaujolais and then those of southern Burgundy.

Unlike the Rhône, the Saône River is flat, wide and gentle with almost no current at this time of the year, making it ideal for cruising. At the barge terminus town of St Jean-de-Losne, we entered the Burgundy canal system. As the terrain is steep, the locks are close together, and we had to negotiate twenty-five locks in one day, before arriving in Dijon, where we plan to stay for two weeks. Our bicycles are proving invaluable for sightseeing and for running errands. Dijon, apart from being the mustard capital of the world, was home to the rich and powerful Dukes of Burgundy. The city is steeped in history and makes a wonderful base from which to explore the surrounding areas. The marina here is excellent, and the live-aboard sailors have been most welcoming.

It is now June, and I'm happy to report that my search for the best croissant in France is proceeding well, with new data being accumulated most mornings. It is very settling to be in one place for more than a day or two, a habit we shall weave into our lifestyle as we continue the journey through this beautiful and diverse country.

Today, we cycled from Dijon to the famous Burgundian wine village of Gevrey-Chambertin, where we visited the château and picked up a couple of bottles of the exceptional 1985 vintage. I have always been skeptical of the French hierarchal system for designating different classifications of wine coming from the same vineyard and remain less convinced after today's visit. In this vineyard, the vines which yield the grapes used to produce *Grand- Cru* designated wines are immediately adjacent to the *Premier-Cru* vines. The grapes have the same sun exposure, same soil (*terroir*), same climate, same rainfall, same pruning and care, and the same winemaker makes the wine. The only apparent difference is a small stone hedgerow separating the rows of vines - so why should the wine be different? To go one step further, the wine classed as *Château* is produced from grapes grown just a few metres away from the higher-rated vines, so why should it be considered a lower quality wine? You might say that sixty million Frenchmen can't be wrong, but I see it rather as a brilliant marketing strategy.

In the 1860s, there was a terrible blight, which infected and destroyed over forty per cent of the grape vines in France. The only permanent solution to this problem was to replant the vines by grafting them to imported American rootstock, which was immune to the aphid causing the disease. In Burgundy, there are only two grape varieties. All the red wine is made from the Pinot Noir grape and all the white is Chardonnay. There is a growing discussion among wine connoisseurs as to how the new world Burgundies, both red and white, compare to those from France. I certainly prefer the pinot noir wines from Oregon, which are winning blind-tasting competitions in France, as are the chardonnays from California. Interestingly, several prominent French winemakers, looking to the future, have bought land and established vineyards in Oregon and California.

On the way back to Dijon, we cycled through the village of

Fixin, which has the same *terroir* as Chambertin, and yet the wine sells for a fraction of the price. At Marsannay, we stopped at a winery to buy a case of *rosé*, which the owners offered to deliver. They have a boat in the Mediterranean and were very interested to see *Muscade*, so we invited them to stay for drinks and some of my delicious hors d'oeuvres.

The Burgundy canal, with all of its associated culinary delights close at hand, connects to the Yonne River, which in turn leads to the Seine and eventually to Paris. The locks on the Yonne canal system presented a particular challenge. Some brilliant engineer back in the seventeenth century decided that he could economize on the amount of water required for each lock cycle by making the locks V-shaped. This works well for flat-bottomed barges, but it is a very difficult proposition for keelboats like *Muscade*. We solved this dilemma by befriending Guy, the captain of the commercial barge *Balzac*, who allowed us to tie up to the outboard side of his vessel, once he was alongside the lock wall. After the water level was lowered and the downstream gates opened, we would scoot out quickly into the river; then let him overtake us, so he could enter the next lock first, allowing us to repeat the procedure.

After spending most of the day together, we became well acquainted. In the last lock before entering the river Seine, as I was presenting him with a good bottle of wine for his kindness, Guy suggested that we leave *Muscade* tied up alongside his barge and cruise down the Seine with him and his wife in the wheelhouse. He told us that there was a huge community of barging families, transporting goods all over Europe. Their barge was their home for life, and very often, children of barging couples continue in their parents' wake by acquiring vessels of their own. As we approached the Loing river, a tributary of the Scine, Guy slowed *Balzac* just enough to let us cast off and proceed to the town of Moret-sur-Loing for the evening, while he and his wife continued on to Paris. I was in no doubt that the Canadian flag flying from

Muscade's stern, plus the fact that we had crossed the Atlantic to get to France, were door-openers for these personal encounters.

It's Sunday morning in the royal palace town of Fontainebleau, and I have discovered a croissant which will be very hard to beat. The give-away as I was cycling around looking for breakfast treats, was a long line of customers outside a particular bakery. Unlike the English, the French do not like to queue up for anything, so I knew this shop had to be offering something special. My wait in line was well rewarded when we later enjoyed brunch aboard *Muscade*, featuring these really exceptional croissants. For my money, a great croissant has to be crisp and slightly flaky on the outside and soft and tender inside without being doughy. It has to have just the right amount of butter, be neither too dry nor too greasy and must taste divine.

We are now only two days' motoring away from Paris, and I have reserved a space at *Le Port d'Arsenal* in the heart of the city, close to the Bastille and the old Opera House. Some friends from Montréal, Jean-Pierre and Diane, will be joining us there for a cruise along the Marne River through champagne country to Épernay. They are no strangers to *Muscade*, having cruised with me many times on Lake Champlain and in the Caribbean.

On our second evening in Paris, we had twelve people in the cockpit for drinks and hors d'oeuvres. Among our guests were Michel and Jaqueline Cordier, whom I had last seen four years before aboard their boat, *Bel Ami*, in Barbuda, just as they were departing to sail back to France. I had promised them that we would meet again someday aboard *Muscade* in Paris. Another guest was an old friend, Clint Ward, who had captained the Air Canada 747 which brought our friends here from Montréal. Our guests had mentioned to the flight attendants that I was hiding out in Paris, and the girls passed on the news to Clint, prompting him to seek me out. Later the same evening, we all went out for an excellent dinner at Bofinger, the oldest brasserie in Paris. I found the whole experience almost surreal. To be on board *Muscade* in this magical city was yet another dream realized, and to be reunited with friends, all of whom I had known at different times during my life was extremely gratifying. I had been in Paris many times before on layovers with Air Canada and knew the city well, but this was an entirely different experience.

It reminded me of the first time I saw Paris as a young man. I was holidaying in England on Christmas leave from Naval College and was considering a few days' skiing in Austria before returning to enjoy the festivities with my family. My father strongly suggested that it was about time I saw Paris. He recommended taking the boat train and spending a few days there on my way to Austria so, ski boots in hand, I boarded the train, not entirely convinced that this was a great idea. On the Calais-to-Paris train my spirits rose when an attractive girl asked to join me in my no-smoking compartment, as she was cloistered with a group of chain-smokers. By the time we had reached La Gare du Nord, my French had become more fluent, as had Marie's English. I invited her for dinner, and we agreed to share a taxi to her aunt's house, where she was staying for a few days. Her aunt was a charming and elegant widow, and her residence was more like a small *château*. She made a quick phone call to reserve a room for me in a nearby hotel, and my visit to Paris was off to a promising beginning. Needless to say, my ski trip never materialized. I spent ten days discovering Paris with Marie and her college friends as my guides. I have wonderful memories of meals enjoyed in student hangouts, evenings spent in the Latin Quarter jazz caves of la rue Huchette, and finally a dinner party given in my honour by Marie's aunt. I flew back to London on Christmas Eve, ski boots and all.

When the time came for *Muscade* to leave Paris, we dropped down the single lock from the marina into the Seine and put her into service as a *bateau mouche,* completing a river tour of Paris down to the Eiffel Tower and back, then continuing eastward to the locks leading into the Marne River canal system. This canal starts in the Paris suburbs and proceeds through Champagne country, passing very close to Vimy Ridge, then through Épernay on its way to Lorraine.

As we enter the Marne River, the weather is unpleasantly hot and humid. We are enduring a serious heat wave, or as the French call it, *une canicule*. Ancient astronomers noticed that, between July 23rd and August 23rd, Sirius, the brightest star in the constellation Canis Major (large dog), rose and set at the same time as the sun (today is August 3rd). They believed this coincidence to be the cause of the hot weather, which is typical during the same time period. Thus originated the terms *canicule* in French and "dog days of summer" in English. I am fascinated with etymology, and particularly with how that study explains the shared evolution of the French and English languages after the Norman conquests, when English evolved from a Germanic language into a semi-Latin one. Any English speaker trying to learn French should be consoled that the two languages share thousands of words, which are either identical or very similar. The difficulty lies in learning how words with the same spelling are pronounced in each language and recognizing them when heard.

As we lock our way eastward past the town of Meaux, famous for its Brie cheeses, it is tempting to contemplate seeking relief from the heat wave by taking a refreshing dip in the river. We all swore that, because of the pollution, we would never consider such an option, but after three days of suffocating heat, I found a secluded anchorage among some islands off the main channel where the water appeared clearer, if not less polluted. We stopped for the night, took our chances, and jumped into the cool water.

The next day, we arrived in Nanteuil, our first Champagne village, where the hunt for the best producer began. No sooner were our mooring lines secured to the canal bank, than Jean-Pierre and Diane took off on the bicycles to begin the quest. I was skeptical about their chances for success, as it was late on Friday afternoon and the village looked deserted. I shouldn't have worried. Half an hour later, they appeared with a wine cooler filled with ice and a very good bottle of champagne cooled to drinking temperature. They had met a restaurant owner, made a reservation for dinner, borrowed a bucket of ice from him, then found a vigneron who sold them the wine. We were soon toasting our arrival in Champagne country before going ashore for a delicious dinner at *L'Auberge du Lion d'Or*.

The next morning, the air was deliciously cooler, and our guests took off early in search of croissants. As I was mopping up the morning dew from the decks, an elegant lady came walking down the canal towpath with her dog. When she saw the Canadian flag, she stopped to introduce herself, told me how much she loved visiting Québec and asked me if I knew her old friend, Paul Desmarais. Of course, I had heard of this millionaire-owner of Power Corporation in Montréal, but we didn't exactly revolve in the same social circles. The lady's name was Catherine Tolstoy, a writer and member of the *Academie Française*. After a short chat she trotted off, and I immediately regretted not having invited her aboard for coffee. It was early in the morning, we had rather overdone the wine consumption the night before, and I had forgotten my manners. Soon our guests arrived with a bag of farinaceous goodies to "break the fast," and we settled down around the cockpit table with our *cafés au lait*.

I was to be vindicated when Madame Tolstoy reappeared (*sans chien*), toting a bottle of vintage champagne for her new Canadian friends. She accepted my invitation for breakfast, and a most delightful and interesting conversation ensued. When it came time to cast off and get underway, I invited her to stay on board for a cruise up the river. Unable to accept, she proffered an open invitation to stay at her *château*, asked us to give her regards to Paul Desmarais and shed a tear from the canal bank as she waved *au revoir.* Meetings like this are reason and reward enough for having changed my life's direction. Those who do not have the good fortune to realize their dreams are often content to live them vicariously by associating with the lucky ones like me. I am extremely grateful to all of the many individuals who have assisted me so generously along my way.

It was becoming obvious that we were not going to get much help from the locals in tracking down the perfect bottle of champagne although we soon realized that none of the large commercial labels would be in the running, as those companies are just too big to produce a unique wine. The French are very protective of their favourite boutique wineries and often spend their vacation time helping with the grape harvest in order to get first dibs on the latest vintage. As a result, many small vineyards sell their entire production privately to these same people, at the farm gate.

Now that we are getting close to Vimy Ridge, our Canadian flag is getting even more attention than usual. Residents have definitely not forgotten their Canadian war heroes. People often wave and cheer from the bank as *Muscade* glides past, and when we moored in the village of Jaulgonne one evening, we really hit the jackpot. Many villages offer free dockage, water and electricity to encourage boaters to stay for the night, but in Jaulgonne a reception committee showed up with bottles of champagne in hand to invite us, as their guests that evening, to their annual *Michoui* or lamb roast. We were delighted to accept and had a wonderful evening of feasting, dancing and fraternizing with the locals. Naturally, the only alcoholic drink available was champagne. It was as ubiquitous as lemonade would be at a Canadian county fair, proving the adage that one man's luxury is another man's daily fare. I dug out some Québec square dancing music on cassette, which proved very popular. We danced with the villagers as Diane called the steps. After the party broke up, we were whisked off to a neighbouring village for more fun and more champagne. The next morning several people showed up on our dock quite early. Apparently, I had invited the whole village for a pancake breakfast with real Canadian maple syrup.

Sadly, my quest for the perfect champagne was not advanced at last evening's events but at lunchtime, Monsieur Moleur arrived to take us on a vineyard tour of his home village, Marcilly. Originally from Brittany, he was very proud to have served with a Canadian regiment during World War Two. We had a pleasant stroll around the grapevines, then were invited to his house where his wife served up *crèpes* washed down with - what else? After much prying, I managed to glean from our hosts' remarks that a probable place to look for our ideal champagne might be the village of Tréloux.

I had always thought that covering the neck of a champagne bottle with a white napkin when removing the cork was contrived by some pretentious sommelier at Maxim's, but it's actually a practical safety precaution, as bottle necks have been known to explode when the cork is released. This happened more frequently in the early days of champagne production when glass was more fragile and the gasifying process less precise. When the Benedictine monk Dom Pérignon was perfecting his production method, half of his bottles used to explode in the cellar.

We now have a destination village for our search, so today I motored *Muscade* upstream to Tréloux, arriving late in the afternoon. As all the dock spaces in the village were already occupied and the riverbank was inhospitable, I tied up to a private dock in front of a magnificent small *château*, then walked up to the residence to ask if we could stay for the night. The owner of the property was most gracious. He said we could stay at his dock for as long as we liked, adding that I was the first person who had ever bothered to ask permission. I invited him and his wife for an *apéritif* aboard *Muscade*. The evening air was warm and the cockpit seats comfortable as we sipped our drinks and feasted on one of my specialties, fried Camembert, with a crusty breadcrumb exterior yielding to the warm runny cheese inside. We talked about Canada, French politics, and the general state of the universe, but our guests refused to divulge the name of the best champagne producer in the village. I was discouraged. During our third drink, when I complimented our guests on their beautiful property, they reminisced that their daughter had been married in the garden the previous summer. "So who supplied the champagne?" I asked. "Veuve Olivier," they replied, "it's superb."

The next morning we trekked into town and met the widow's son, Monsieur Olivier, at his vineyard. He was a little unfriendly at first, and clearly wasn't interested in selling anything, but soon warmed to us when we related our saga. He gave us a tour of his winery and agreed to part with two cases of his renowned *champagne rosé*. As I had suspected, he sells most of his wines at the vineyard gate to private collectors who come each year to help with the harvest.

Mission accomplished, we continued up to Épernay, one of the two major champagne production towns, the other being Reims (pronounced rance), which is not on the canal system. I maneuvered *Muscade* alongside the town marina, which was just in front of the Castellane and Mercier Champagne Houses. Already docked at the same facility were two other Canadian-flagged vessels. This was most unusual, as these were the only Canadian boats we have encountered since leaving Portugal last spring. One boat a vintage Dutch barge named *Lionel*, was owned by Hart and Melody Massey. Hart was a retired architect and the son of former Canadian Governor-General, Vincent Massey. He has just published a book called, "*Travels with Lionel: a Small Boat in France.*" The barge was named after his brother. Hart and Melody were coming to the end of their barging adventures and were gathering the courage to sell their beloved *Lionel*. Three Canadian boats in one French marina was reason enough to celebrate, so we organized an all-Canadian barbecue and invited the other boat owners in the marina to join us.

The remainder of the summer of 1990 in France unfolded beautifully. After leaving Épernay, we continued eastwards towards the Rhine River, and enjoyed extended stays at Nancy, the capital of Lorraine, and Strasbourg, in Alsace. *Muscade* then climbed the Vosges Mountains, averaging forty locks a day, accompanied by two assigned lockkeepers who leap-frogged each other on motorcycles to ensure that the locks were prepared for us. Having finally reached the summit after several days of non-stop locking, we had to descend an equal number of locks to get back down to the Saône River and complete the circuit we started last May at St Jean-de-Losne.

Going down in a lock takes considerably less effort than going up because the boat enters level with the top of the lock. Then it is simply a question of looping both bow and stern lines around bollards and keeping the bitter end of the rope taut as the boat descends the lock wall. When the water level is all the way down, and the downstream gates have opened, the lines can be pulled back onboard prior to motoring out of the lock. There is no turbulence in a down lock, as the water is simply being emptied out, like pulling the plug in a bathtub. The most important rule is to never tie a line in a down lock because, as the water level goes down, the boat could end up being suspended by the tied line. The rope will eventually snap under the weight of the boat, and could cause considerable damage or injury. I always keep a sharp knife in the cockpit so I can quickly cut the line if necessary.

We have arrived back in Burgundy just in time for *la vendange*, the grape harvest, and the smell of partially fermented grape juice permeates the air. September weather is ideal for cycling, so we are making lots of stops along our route to visit the towns and villages of Burgundy, previously known to us only as names on wine labels: Beaune, Nuits St George, Macon, Chalon *et al.* Further south, we toured the Beaujolais region before passing through Lyon and re-entering the Rhône River. On Debbie's birthday, we were in the wine town of Condrieu, and celebrated with dinner at a Michelin Guide restaurant in the Bellevue Hotel. We reminisced that on her birthday three years before, we had dined on curried goat washed down with Chinese *eau-de-vie* in the Karakorum Mountains of northern Pakistan. Tonight promised to be a better culinary experience.

The meal was delicious, but the wine experience was a total disaster, which caused us considerable embarrassment and put a damper on the evening. The St. Joseph wine which I ordered, while not corked, was sour, musty and undrinkable. The sommelier agreed with me, but was less pleased when I rejected a second bottle of the same wine in the same condition. It seemed to me that the whole batch was probably spoiled, so for the third bottle I switched to a Côte Rôtie, which was drinkable but not great. By now, most of the other customers in the restaurant were aware of our dispute, and the waiter was surly. I should add in my own defense that I am not a wine snob and have been known to accept marginal wines to avoid the unpleasant consequences of rejecting a bottle. Refusing a bottle of wine in a restaurant can harm the conviviality and ambience of the occasion, create tension with the staff, and appear pretentious. However, if the wine is undrinkable, the only recourse is to send it back. I have confirmed with many sommeliers that on average, ten per cent of wines are "corked." This loss is unacceptable in any business model, and has led to the use of synthetic corks and screw tops in an effort to reduce the odds of spoilage.

We have decided to leave *Muscade* in Avignon for the winter, then continue our adventures next spring in le Canal du Midi, the waterway which connects the Mediterranean to Bordeaux on the Atlantic coast of France. On the last day of our trip down the Rhône, just north of Avignon, we had another dangerous encounter with our nemesis, the Mistral. The wind blew up suddenly to gale force as we were motoring down a canalized section of the river, about two miles north of the next lock. The strong wind was directly astern of us, pushing us down river. We could not turn around and head back upstream, as the wind was too strong for our engine. There was no choice but to continue into the lock. When I contacted the lock keeper by radio, he said that the water was already up at our level, and that there was no conflicting commercial traffic. He promised to have the lock ready with the gates wide open when we got there. Unbelievably, there were three-to-four foot waves breaking at the entrance of the lock. With difficulty, I maneuvered *Muscade* alongside the lock wall, using full reverse power to slow the boat down enough so that I could jump ashore with the stern line and attach it quickly to stop the boat's momentum. As soon as the lock gates were closed, the waves subsided and down we went. On exiting, I decided not to press our luck. I found a sheltered backwater, anchored for the night and opened our best bottle of wine.

We spent a week in Avignon preparing *Muscade* for the winter, while socializing with other couples who are living aboard their boats in this former papal city. The ship's logbook records that we negotiated a total of 736 locks during our summer's tour of France. Although Debbie is not complaining, I sense that it is time to move ashore for a while, and I will certainly welcome a change of venue after six years aboard my boat. Furthermore, there is nowhere in Europe that has a climate suitable for living comfortably aboard a small boat during the months of December through March. We have rented a house in the Laurentian ski village of Morin Heights, north of Montréal, and will move in at the beginning of January, after spending Christmas in Wales. But first we are off to sail in the Pacific.

CHAPTER TWELVE

TONGA KILAMANJARO AND OBERGURGL

The Pacific is a vast ocean to cross in a small sailing boat which can only average six miles an hour. I have never had any desire to attempt such a crossing with *Muscade*, as the distances are just too great. The usual route to the Pacific cruising areas from Europe, or from the east coast of North America, is through the Panama Canal, followed by a 4200-mile slog to the first landfall, the Marquesas Islands. The route straddles the equator, so winds are often light and unpredictable. A boat like *Muscade* could easily take two months to complete such a voyage. On the other hand, there are several lifetimes worth of spectacular cruising to be had among the thousands of islands and atolls scattered across this vast ocean.

One solution is to fly to a particularly desirable cruising ground, charter a boat, and enjoy everything that area has to offer without the hassle of getting there with your own boat. After considerable research, I have pin-pointed the Kingdom of Tonga and, more specifically, the northern Vava'u islands. From all reports, it is considered to be one of the most exotic cruising areas in the world. I have rented a boat from the Moorings Charter Company, and Debbie's parents will join us for a two-week cruise.

The Kingdom of Tonga is situated halfway between Fiji and French Polynesia. When British Captain James Cook discovered this paradise in 1773, he affectionately named the archipelago "The Friendly Islands." We flew on Hawaiian Airlines from Los Angeles to Tongatapu, the main island in the Tonga chain, then chartered a small aircraft to take us up to the northern islands of the Vava'u group. Our boat was a brand-new, forty-foot, French-built sloop, which the charter company had just acquired. We rented the boat without crew and fully-provisioned, so no time was lost getting underway. I had provided a *resumé* of my sailing experience, which proved more than adequate to meet the Moorings requirements for a "bare boat" charter (no professional crew required). Debbie's seventy-year-old parents had been with us aboard *Muscade* in the Caribbean and French canals, knew the drill and had no trouble settling into our spacious rental boat.

There are over forty spectacular anchorages in this archipelago. My challenge was to choose the ten best. The area is somewhat reminiscent of the Virgin Islands, with two major differences: the incredible water transparency and the secluded nature of the place. One can clearly detect objects on the sea floor in more than a hundred feet of water, and at night we were usually the only boat in the anchorage. The few boats that we did see during our cruise were owned by cruising couples from Australia or New Zealand. Our most spectacular anchorage, which would arguably make the top ten list in the world, was Hunga Lagoon. Access to this land-locked, tropical saltwater lake is through an extremely narrow passage only a couple of boat's widths across. Once inside, one can anchor in perfect safety anywhere in the lagoon. Sandy beaches make up the shoreline, the water is crystal clear, and the surrounding hilly terrain is lush with tropical vegetation.

I can spot a tourist trap from a distance of two pistol shots and have always given them a wide berth, so was skeptical when my guests suggested that we should anchor off Hinakauea Beach one evening and go ashore for a traditional Tongan feast. The majority ruled, but I need not have been concerned. We were treated to the delightful experience of a sumptuous feast followed by traditional singing and dancing under the light of blazing torches. Crab, lobster and octopus were cooked in a pit filled with hot embers, reminiscent of a Hawaiian *luau*. These delicacies were complemented with tropical fruits and delicious salads, all served on long polished wooden trays. The magic of the evening was further enhanced by the complete absence of tourists. It was like a private tropical dinner party. It seems that tourism has not yet arrived in this part of the kingdom.

It reminded me of a similar experience, shortly after I joined Air Canada in the mid-Sixties. I had been flying all month on the Montréal to London route with the same captain. He was a most amiable and interesting character, a World War Two bomber pilot with an adventurous spirit and a real zest for life. An interested listener can learn a great deal in the time it takes to complete five return transatlantic flights, and by the end of the month, I had become intrigued by his current project. He was planning to take his family to the Seychelles Islands in the Indian Ocean before the airport had been completed. They were going to fly to Mombasa and catch the tramp steamer which supplied the islands, thus beating Mr. Boeing to the punch. A few months later, I accomplished the next best thing by flying to the Seychelles on the inaugural flight. I discovered a completely unspoiled paradise, much like Tonga is today. There was absolutely no tourism. The only souvenirs available were postage stamps, and the taxi drivers would not accept tips, as the concept of "something for nothing" was completely alien to their culture.

I had heard that the waters around Tonga were a breeding ground for humpback whales, so we were constantly on the lookout for these majestic mammals whenever we were sailing in the deep water between islands. I always mention to my crew that spotting the marvels of nature requires concentrated and dedicated surveillance. If you are not constantly observing carefully, you won't see anything. By the time someone says: "Look at that," the subject has invariably vanished. Sailing vessels have an advantage over powerboats, as they are relatively noiseless, although whales can certainly detect their presence. We were fortunate enough to have two humpback sightings. I never cease to be awed by these amazing creatures, which in spite of their huge bulk and lengths of up to fifty feet, are extremely graceful. They always give me the impression that they are far nobler and more intelligent than *homo sapiens*.

Zen masters maintain that the passing of time is only an illusion, which explains why our charter in Tonga seemed to be over before it had started, and why my next hour in a dentist's chair will probably seem like an eternity. Reluctantly, we returned our boat to the Moorings base at Neiafu. During our holiday, I had noticed a few things on the boat that needed some attention. These modifications were absolutely to be expected, as we were the first sailors to charter this vessel. I made a small list of the items which I had not been able to fix and presented it to the manager when we disembarked. He was most appreciative and asked me to walk him through the boat and point out my suggestions. He mentioned that the Moorings' Tonga base is not yet fully established, then asked me if I would consider staying on for a while as his assistant during the initial set-up phase, and double as a charter captain for customers who did not have enough experience to bareboat. Although his offer was tempting, I was in no position to consider it, even if I had been looking for a job. However, it did confirm the value of being in the right place at the right time, and showed how that concept can impact one's life.

I had forgotten just how bitterly cold January could be in Montréal. Having spent so many winters in the tropics, my body has diminished tolerance for such inhumane temperatures. Debbie and I are cocooned in our ski chalet in the Laurentian hills, where sitting in a comfortable fireside chair with a good book has replaced Caribbean sailing for this winter. We are surrounded by ski hills, but there are very few days in January which meet my minimum criteria for skiing: sunny with good light and no colder than minus ten degrees centigrade. We have rented this house from friends who are now working in Paris. Their car was included as part of the deal, and this fully-furnished house is available until the first of May when we will head back to *Muscade* in France. We are using the residence as a base of operations for our winter's travels and will not be spending long periods of time in this frozen wasteland.

I had misjudged Debbie's need for a change of scenery. She does not seem much happier to be living a more conventional life and sometimes lapses into moody periods and irrational behaviour. One afternoon, when we were stuck in heavy traffic in downtown Montréal, she unexpectedly got out of the car without saying a word and disappeared into a crowd of pedestrians on the sidewalk. We had not been arguing, so I was bewildered. Not having a clue what to do, or how to find her, I drove to the airport as a first resort. It was a good hunch. I found her at the American Airlines counter, where she had already bought a ticket to Austin, Texas. She had attended college there and wanted to catch up with her friends. To her credit, she readily accepted my suggestion to postpone her planned visit, and we drove back to our home in the Lauretian hills together.

A lot of people are fascinated by numbers and numerology.

Much to the dismay of some Vancouverites trying to resell their houses for hugely-inflated prices, any address with the number four is taboo to Chinese buyers, who will avoid it at any cost because the number four in Mandarin is a homonym of the word for death. High-rise elevators and airline seating plans often skip the number thirteen, as if nobody can figure out what comes after twelve. Friday the thirteenth is considered unlucky in Christian cultures, as Friday was the day that Christ was crucified, and there were thirteen attendees at the last supper, the thirteenth being a traitor. Similarly, we tend to celebrate "big" birthdays or anniversaries, ones with "round" numbers. We also love statistics and percentages even though they can be misleading - or just plain wrong.

I am no different. Later this month, I am turning fifty and plan to celebrate the occasion by watching the sunrise over East Africa from the top of Mount Kilimanjaro. Debbie has become re-invigorated by the Kilimanjaro project, and we have increased the frequency and distance of our hikes in preparation for the climb. We have invited Wil Roberts from our Pakistan adventure to join us, and he is bringing two friends, making five in all. We will meet in Nairobi on January 18th, proceed to Arusha in Tanzania, and arrange the climb from there.

Today, January 17th, 1991 is the first day of the Iraq Gulf War, code named "Desert Storm." We over-flew the conflict zone onboard a British Airways night flight to Nairobi. The captain cheerfully announced that he could see Iraqi Scud missiles far below our cruising altitude and reassured us that we were in no danger. In spite of his nonchalance, Debbie and I were relieved to arrive at our hotel in Nairobi and meet up with our fellow climbers. Wil Roberts immediately tagged me as Simba, the old lion, in view of my fiftieth birthday. Wil's friend, David, who works with him in the hospital operating room, and a dentist called James, both from North Wales, make up our team. After the obligatory afternoon tea at the famous Norfolk Hotel, we went out for a high protein dinner at the equally well-known Carnivore restaurant. This open-air terraced restaurant serves up roasted giraffe, wildebeest, ostrich and crocodile, all raised on a near-by ranch. Waiters circulate with trolleys and carve the meat to order at the table. Not a great place for vegetarians, but still one of the top fifty best-known restaurants in the world and a fabulous place to begin our African adventure. The next day, we took a minibus south to the Tanzanian border where we were obliged to transfer to another taxi, as our Kenyan cabbie was not permitted to cross. The next stop was Arusha for lunch. There we learned that the tourist business has come to a standstill as a result of the war, so we will have the whole mountain to ourselves. I phoned the Hibiscus Hotel in Moshi at the base of the mountain, to reserve some rooms and to give them notice that we would be hiring guides for the climb. During our drive to Moshi I couldn't help noticing that Tanzania was one of the poorest countries I had ever visited.

Mount Kilimanjaro is in a National Park, and government rules dictate that visitors must always be accompanied by a certified guide. This means that if one of us suffers from altitude sickness during the climb, everyone must abort the mission. After our experience in Pakistan, we presume that Wil, Debbie and I will be able to tolerate the altitude, which is almost twenty thousand feet, but I was concerned about David, who seemed somewhat out of shape. We decided to hire two guides to increase our chances of success. George, our chief guide, suggested that we take six days to complete the round trip, which allowed an extra day to acclimatize to the altitude. There are seven possible routes to the top. We have chosen the original Marangu trail, which is the most convenient and most popular.

The extreme variations of climate and terrain make this climb unique. The trail starts in a lush tropical jungle and finishes in below-zero temperatures on a glacier. Most people in reasonable health would be able to complete this strenuous hike if not for the high altitude. Every year, more than a thousand climbers have to be assisted off the mountain, and ten people die from altitude sickness, so the threat must be taken seriously. Air density decreases with altitude, as do the number of oxygen molecules available in each breath, making it very difficult to breathe normally. Dehydration caused by inhaling dry mountain air adds to the risk. The most obvious symptom of altitude sickness is a headache. If it is severe, the climber must descend immediately, or risk death.

On the first day of our ascent, we took a jeep to the park gate, at 6000 ft. elevation, then hiked up the five miles from there to the Mandara Camp at 8800 ft. We had dinner in a communal dining hut, then slept in a dormitory, using our own sleeping bags. The next day we hiked up seven miles to the Horombo Camp at 12000 ft. and overnighted there. The third day was dedicated to altitude acclimatization. This meant a six-mile hike up to an elevation of 15000 ft. and then back down to Horombo to sleep. On day four, we hiked back up to the 15000 ft. level, rested in the Kibo Hut until midnight, then started the final ascent. The midnight start allows successful climbers to reach the summit in time to watch the sun rise over East Africa and still leaves the rest of the day to get back down to the Horombo camp before dark. Due to the altitude, it was impossible to sleep during our wait in the Kibo Hut. My resting pulse rate, which is sixty at sea level, was racing at ninety-five.

At midnight, George signaled that it was time to get going. We left our gear in the hut, as it would have been impossible to complete the ascent carrying the extra weight. We had six hours before sunrise to climb the 5000 ft. to the summit. George led the way setting the slow pace essential for success. He kept repeating the Swahili word for slowly, *"polé, polé."* Every step was an extreme effort, as we were constantly gasping for breath. No matter how deeply we tried to breathe, there was never enough oxygen to satisfy the involuntary respiratory system. After about an hour, David succumbed to the altitude and had to be helped down the mountain by our spare guide. We all became very aware that the next person to falter would take down the whole team.

We started the climb in pitch darkness using flashlights, but as we neared the summit, the morning twilight helped show the way. After the most strenuous physical effort my body had ever experienced, I managed the final step and found myself on the rim of a vast volcano in the middle of Africa. With success buoying our spirits, we hiked around the rim on a snow-packed trail to the highest point of the mountain, Uhuru Peak, altitude 19341ft. We all had mild headaches, which are to be expected at this altitude. George explained that it was dangerous to stay on the summit for more than half-an-hour, so we were soon on our way down to the 12000 ft. level. After a celebratory dinner, we had a contented night's sleep and hiked off the mountain the next day. My fiftieth birthday wish had been granted: Simba was a happy, old lion.

We were beginning to realize that the Gulf War, presently wreaking havoc in the Middle East, was really working to our advantage in Tanzania. We had the summit of Kilimanjaro to ourselves, and back in Arusha, the safari companies were falling over themselves for our business. After some research and a couple of phone calls to various safari lodges, we decided that we didn't need to use the services of a travel agency. We hired a driver, who was also a certified guide, checked out his virtually new Land Rover and negotiated a deal based on a favourable black market exchange rate for our much-sought-after American dollars. We then reserved accommodation at the same safari lodges used by the luxury tour companies. They were all vacant and eager for our custom.

The next morning, we were on our way to the Serena Lodge, perched on the rim of the Ngorongoro Crater. Our guide proved to be extremely competent and knew exactly where to find all the animals on any big game (photo) hunter's list. We spent two days in the Crater, one day in the Serengeti, and one day at Lake Manyara, before heading back to Nairobi for a wind-up celebration.

Being an amateur forester, I was fascinated by the majestic Baobab trees, which grow around Lake Manyara. I had thought them to be a fictitious species, invented by Antoine de Saint-Exupéry in his book "*Le Petit Prince*," so I was surprised to find out that they actually existed. These trees can live for one thousand years, grow to eighty feet tall and have a diameter of forty feet. This is another example of how beautifully some species have evolved, while man, the rogue animal, is doing his best to destroy himself, the planet and everything on it, including the elephants and rhinos in this part of the world. *Homo sapiens* is the only species of animal that has no predator. Instead, we hunt each other, baiting our traps with political power, social status, and material possessions, knowing that they will be sprung with pride, greed, xenophobia, and arrogance, eventually leading to war, as an inevitable outcome.

I have never had much interest in photography, except for one brief period of time just before I left Air Canada to start this adventure. During my last month as an airline captain, I was paired up with a first officer who was a camera expert. He agreed to give me a comprehensive briefing on the art of photography during our time together. By the end of the month, having absorbed a lot of knowledge about f-stops, shutter times, and lens types, I was ready to purchase my first camera. While waiting in New York to sail to Bermuda, I bought a state-of-the-art Nikon and several lenses (my first officer had in fact recommended a Leica). I'm embarrassed to admit that I never managed to take a decent shot with that camera, eventually chucked it overboard, and haven't owned a camera since. However, due to the generosity of friends who have shared some of my adventures, I have an amazing photo collection, which will enable me to recapture the pleasure of the original experience long after my memory has faded.

Four years ago, when I opened my backpack, shortly after arriving in Rawalpindi for our Pakistan expedition, I discovered that my dear father had stashed his camera and several rolls of film in my luggage. He couldn't believe that I had no intention of taking pictures of that spectacular part of the world. I dutifully loaded up the device with film shamed by my father's thoughtfulness into taking many pictures (always using the automatic feature) with little expectation of positive results. Surprisingly, the photos turned out quite well. The camera in question, a Canon, had been given to my father by his Japanese agent as a sixtieth birthday present and apparently had an exceptional lens. However, this success did not alter my attitude to photography. I still try to capture as much as possible with my brain's camera and rely on friends to supply me with their creations for future appreciation when my brain has addled.

Debbie and I are back in our Laurentian chalet planning the next adventure. Twenty years ago, I invited nine of my best (bachelor) friends from across Canada to join me in the Austrian village of Obergurgl for a two-week ski holiday. I had chosen this village because, at 6300 ft. elevation, it is one of the highest ski resorts in Austria, so I figured we would have the best chance of good snow conditions. The idea really caught on. All nine of my friends accepted the invitation. I rented a farmhouse right in the middle of this tiny village, which gave us a convenient vantage point. As word of our upcoming ski trip spread, other friends and camp followers, including some married couples, singles, and a bevy of flight attendants, decided to reserve adjacent hotel rooms and join in the fun. The holiday was a great success. It was a two-week non-stop party, and the buzz in the village and on the slopes was all about those "crazy Canucks." The ten of us in the farmhouse took great pity on the unfortunate farmer's daughter, who was obliged to interrupt our post mortems of the night before and brave our motley, unshaven company when she brought in the coffee and rolls each morning.

This winter marks the twentieth anniversary of that holiday, and in view of the "round number," I decided last autumn to send out invitations for a reunion. Hoping to enlarge the attendance, I tagged the event "Obergurglers and Friends." While the idea was initially received with great enthusiasm, the final numbers were disappointing. I had obviously misjudged the altered personal circumstances of my friends. Of the original farmhouse ten, one had died of a heart attack on a ski hill in Alberta, only one is still single, one did not respond, and the rest are married with young children in school and have work-related time constraints. Of the original camp followers, only two couples will be attending. Three of the original ten bachelors have confirmed their attendance, and three new candidates will be joining the party, for a grand total of twelve. I have booked the entire group into a *gasthaus*, located very close to the original farmhouse.

At the end of February, Debbie and I flew to Frankfurt, rented a car and drove to Obergurgl for the reunion. From the opening cocktail party in our *gasthaus* to the closing dinner party at the Edelweiss Hotel, the ski week was great fun, but it did not come close to recapturing the spirit of twenty years ago. My attempt to recreate such a memorable occasion was obviously a mistake. The original players had changed, and my expectations, based on the earlier event were overly ambitious. After a wonderful holiday shared with loyal friends, Debbie and I drove back to Frankfurt via the Black Forest and returned to Canada just in time for the maple syrup season.

One of the things I have really missed by not being in Canada during the last six winters is the maple syrup season, which during my farming years, had become a rite of spring. Even though I was managing a thirty-five acre woodlot on my own farm, my friend Peter Waddell had a much more mature maple forest and a full-scale evaporator for making syrup. Each spring, I used to help him in the very labour intensive, but extremely satisfying process of maple syrup production. Maple syrup is the ultimate example of how a particular *"terroir"* is absolutely essential to the quality of an agricultural product. It can only be made from specific types of maple trees, growing in an extremely limited geographic area, where there are very precise climactic conditions. That area is called southern Québec. About eighty per cent of all the maple syrup in the world is made in *La Belle Province,* with the other twenty per cent coming from adjoining provinces and states having similar *"terroir."* Of all the many maple varieties, only the sap from sugar maple or black maple trees is high enough in sugar content to produce good syrup. The trees must grow in the above-mentioned areas, where temperatures remain well below freezing all winter. When the spring thaw arrives, the sap begins to rise from the roots up into the body of the tree. Cold nights below freezing and warm days above freezing are essential for an abundant flow of sap.

Well before the spring thaw, the maples are tapped by drilling a hole a couple of inches deep into the tree and inserting a spigot. There is a hook incorporated below the spigot on which to hang a bucket, after the sap starts to flow. Peter and I originally used the bucket method for collecting sap, then graduated to a pipeline, which is more sanitary and precludes having to slog through waist deep snow to empty the buckets every day. When using a pipeline, the sap is sucked out of the tree with a vacuum pump and delivered into a holding tank beside the evaporator. The sap then has to be reduced until it becomes syrup. It takes forty gallons of sap to make one gallon of maple syrup, which means a lot of boiling and an enormous quantity of firewood. Sap is actually more fragile than milk and must be boiled down quickly, as soon as it is collected, otherwise it will sour. The faster the sap is reduced to syrup in the evaporator, the higher the quality of the finished product.

Whenever the sap was flowing abundantly, Peter and I would be forced to boil all night long to keep the syrup production ahead of the sap supply. We stood watches, taking turns to sleep, just as we had done on board *Muscade* at sea. The length of the production season varies considerably from year to year. Some years it only lasts a few days with very little syrup being made while in a good year, it can last for weeks, and we would make hundreds of gallons. The previous owners of Peter's farm, the Dixon family, had earned a reputation for making prize-winning syrup, so we strove hard to maintain that standard. Often during the boiling process, neighbours and other residents from the local town of Lachute, attracted by the clouds of steam coming off the evaporator, would drop in to keep us company and buy freshly made syrup. This winter I am delighted to be back helping Peter.

It is now April, and soon we will be heading back to *Muscade* in Avignon. Having a land-based residence this winter has convinced me that it would be a good idea to have a permanent home of our own. I feel that we need a solid base from which to leave on our forays out into the world, and to which we could return to recharge our spirits and enjoy a change of scenery. After six years on the go, I am feeling completely rootless and have a strong physical desire, as well as an equally strong emotional need, to be somewhere pleasant when not on the boat. We have many more years of cruising ahead of us in the Mediterranean, but I am starting to realize that we may not be able to live aboard *Muscade* forever. As for Debbie, I still suspect that she would like to return to California eventually, but she has not yet broached that subject. Our ability to discuss issues like this one has deteriorated, and I am concerned about the future of our marriage. I seem to be making all the decisions affecting our lives and desperately long for some input from my wife. In such difficult circumstances, I have a tendency to blame myself and wonder if the cause of her unhappiness is not entirely my fault. I have come to realize that Debbie is extremely attached to her family, and for that reason, during our short marriage, I have made every effort to include her parents whenever possible: twice aboard *Muscade*; a sailing holiday in Tonga; Christmas in New Zealand; and numerous visits to their home in California, but it does not seem to be enough for her. She is moody and uncommunicative.

I have found a delightful house, which suits my needs admirably, and Debbie has somewhat reluctantly agreed to go along with the purchase. It sits on the shore of Brome Lake in the Eastern Townships of Québec, nestled in the northern reaches of the Appalachian Mountains, about one hour's drive east of Montréal. The closest village is Knowlton, one of the most picturesque spots in the province. There is a vast choice of ski hills nearby, including Stowe, Vermont, which makes it an ideal area for year-round living. The house is part of a development designed as a country retreat for busy Montréalers, so there are tennis courts, a large swimming pool as well as shared lake frontage and a beach. When we were closing the deal in the notary's office, the seller's wife was in tears because she didn't want her husband to sell the property. As we were not planning to move into the house until the following autumn, I rented it back to her for the summer, making everyone happy. We bought the house furnished, a common custom in Québec with holiday houses.

We are now back on board *Muscade*, reassured that we have a home in Canada, and looking forward to establishing a base in Knowlton at the end of our summer's cruising. I am pleased that we now have a comfortable house to which we can invite friends and reciprocate some of the many invitations we receive. Debbie, happy to be back aboard, seems much more content with the whole arrangement. We plan to spend all summer in France, first exploring the rivers and canals between Avignon and Sète and then continuing in the Canal du Midi as far west as Toulouse.

The delightfully unspoiled and bucolic area of France known as the Midi is a well-kept secret. Located west of the Rhône River in Languedoc-Roussillon, and stretching out towards the Spanish border, it was exploited in ancient times by both the Greeks and

Romans, who obviously saw the potential for agriculture and wine production. It is the sunniest part of France, Narbonne being the sunniest city. It lacks the pretentiousness of the Côte d'Azur and is far less developed. One drawback is the Mistral, which brings cold north winds in the winter months and can be tiringly relentless. As we cruised past Port Carmargue, where we originally entered the canal system last spring, we retrieved our mast from the boatyard and secured it on deck. Having the mast on board is cumbersome, and will make it more difficult to maneuver in the locks, but will give us more flexibility when the time comes to re-enter the Med and convert *Muscade* back into a sailing boat.

We are now in Cathar country. The Cathars were members of a Christian sect whose philosophy, roughly based on the New Testament and very tolerant of equal rights for women, was completely at odds with the sexist theology of the popes in Rome. Cathars refused to suspend their disbelief in the Eucharist, arguing that wafers and red wine could not possibly represent the flesh and blood of Christ. Their territory stretched from Beziers to Carcassonne to Toulouse to the hill fortresses north of Perpignan, and up as far as Albi. In 1208, Pope Innocent III decided to organize the Albigensian Crusade to eliminate the perceived Cathar threat to his church. The French king declined to lead the crusade, giving the responsibility to Simon de Montfort, who committed untold atrocities in the name of the Roman Church. Twenty years later, the Cathars in the south of France had been virtually annihilated. When the pope was asked how the French soldiers could identify a Cathar, he said, "kill them all, and God will decide."

This genocide is just another example, as if one were needed, of how the lust for power and wealth, disguised as religion, has caused conflict, suffering and death ever since man crawled out of his cave and leveraged superstition and fear into religion, which he then used as a crowd control mechanism. I fully understand that some people need to have absolute faith in a superior being.

For these individuals, faith trumps intellect while assuaging guilt and providing comfort and peace of mind. I have no problem with that harmless concept as long as the religion in question doesn't proselytize and teaches compassion, non-violence and charity. On the positive side, different religions have given us, albeit by default, many magnificent works of art, superb music, sculptures and architectural wonders. The problem occurs when opposing religions, or even different sects of the same religion, come to blows. Blatant examples are the Catholic/Protestant conflict in Medieval Europe (more recently in Northern Ireland), the Shia/Sunni mutual hatred in Islamic countries, the Crusades, the Inquisition, the Holocaust, the massacre of Hindus and Muslims after Indian partition, and in this area of France, the genocide of the Cathars.

A completely unbiased person would distinguish little difference between today's Muslims and the Christians living a century ago. Christianity happens to be about a hundred years further ahead in its modernization than Islam, but not in all respects. A hundred years ago, Christian women had no rights or status, most orders of nuns wore what amounted to burquas, women had to have their heads covered, especially in church, and brides-to-be entered the church fully veiled, with no part of the body showing. Today Christian women still have little status in the Roman Catholic church and cannot be priests. Our unbiased observer would scratch her head in dismay when observing any of the mainstream religions and wonder how they could possibly still exist and be reconciled with our modern, scientific world. The beast has not changed, and religious wars still rage unabated.

When I was growing up, my parents tried to be reasonably objective about religion and left my siblings and me to draw our own conclusions. My mother enjoyed the serene ambiance of church, loved the hymns, and helped arrange the flowers, but refused to take communion. I now realize that my father was a non-believer, but he was expected, as a naval officer, to attend church whenever his ship was back in Portsmouth. It was always exciting to visit a warship, but the best part of these outings for me was the reception in the officer's wardroom after church, a social occasion with coffee, cakes and sherry. When I was a six year old, my father's Captain was amused when he overheard me reciting, "Forgive us our Christmases" during the Lord's Prayer. When I was twelve, my parents sent me off to confirmation classes. I was bewildered by the doctrine and failed to see what memorizing a list of Catechism questions had to do with God. After the second class, I discussed this confusion with my parents, and they wisely agreed to let me discontinue what I considered to be a hypocritical exercise.

Many years later at Naval College, church was compulsory for all cadets. The best part was still the reception afterwards, where we were expected to chat up the College officers' wives, and be evaluated for our "officer-like-qualities." The College's particularly zealous Anglican minister decided arbitrarily that only officers who had been confirmed could be "leaders of men," so he insisted that the six unconfirmed cadets in my year, myself included, had to be confirmed. When I offered as much resistance as a junior cadet at a Naval College is allowed to get away with, he agreed to forget the Catechism study and to compromise by holding a few religious discussion meetings before calling in the bishop to do the deed. On the fateful day when the six of us were on our knees in front of the altar, and the bishop had started his archaic ritual, only the threat of immediate expulsion from the college stopped me from standing up and marching out of the chapel. I had never felt so hypocritical in my life, but managed to keep the wafer and wine in my mouth until I could deliver them into my handkerchief after the service. When I was eventually commissioned as a naval officer, I did not sense that my leadership qualities were compromised by anybody's God, although I do admit that convincing your troops that God is on their side is a powerful motivator, provided you don't tell them that the opposing side is using the same incentive.

I am reading my notes, and reflecting on the summer of 1991 in France. The Canal du Midi, with both banks lined and shaded by magnificent plane trees, is considered to be France's most beautiful waterway. It is hugely popular with the rental barge crowd, many of whom we met during our summer's cruising. Tourists are permitted to rent barges up to forty-five feet long with no license or previous boating experience. These boats are completely protected with rubber fenders and are affectionately known as "bumper boats." The renters are given a quick checkout before being released to the whims of nature and rarely have serious problems. It was pleasing to watch these groups having so much fun in this idyllic setting. The bankside restaurants and other facilities, which have sprung up to service these boaters, also made our lives much easier and more enjoyable.

We spent Bastille Day, the fourteenth of July, in the medieval walled city of Carcassonne. For the occasion and in accordance with naval tradition, I decided to dress *Muscade* with all the courtesy flags I had accumulated since buying the boat (naval ships use their international code signal flags to dress ship). A courtesy flag, as the name implies, is the national flag of the country you are visiting, flown from the starboard yardarm. So far, *Muscade* has accumulated fourteen of these flags and, hopefully, will require many more before our sailing days together are over.

During the summer, I awarded the prize for the best bread in France, as well as the second-best croissants, to La Mie'nervoise bakery in the canal-side village of La Redorte. The best croissant award still goes to the Dardonville bakery in Fontainebleau, which I stumbled upon last summer. We docked *Muscade* in the tiny harbour of La Robine, while we were away in California attending Debbie's sister's wedding. The port is managed by a delightful English couple who live aboard their converted Dutch sailing barge all year round. We have decided that when our summer's cruising is over at the end of September, this will be an ideal place to leave our boat for the winter, so have made that arrangement.

Because sugar maples are the predominant species, the autumn colours in the Eastern Townships of Québec are, quite simply, spectacular. When artists try to capture this colour bomb on canvas, the resulting landscapes often appear to be impossibly vivid, but are in fact understated, when compared to nature's live show. Debbie and I, with our house on the lake in Knowlton, are now part of this scene, and I am feeling incredibly settled and content to have such an idyllic base of operations. I was overdue to become part of a land-based community again, after seven years of vagabondage. Debbie, less so.

There are two types of friends: passive ones who wait to be called, and active friends who make an effort to stay in contact. I am definitely of the latter persuasion and put a lot of effort into "staying in touch." Debbie does not have many friends and does not make friends easily, but does not view this as a disadvantage and has difficulty understanding my need to bring other people into our world. I respect her deep inner strength, but find it increasingly difficult to reconcile her reclusive nature with my gregarious one. It makes me wonder if people are generally attracted by similar personality traits in their friends and lovers. Ginette was also socially reserved, not understanding the concept of having close friends outside the family circle. Social behaviour is related to culture and is often influenced by parental role models, peer influence, and childhood experiences. My parents entertained often, had many friends and considered them to be as important as family members. On the other hand, Ginette's parents had few friends outside the family circle. Baptisms, weddings, funerals and other celebrations were always family or extended family affairs. Debbie's case is perplexing. Her parents are American versions of mine, but she obviously did not inherit the sociability gene. All this to say, it will be more challenging for us to become part of our new community than it would have been had Debbie been more affable. Fortunately, I already know a handful of people living in Knowlton, and we have joined the volunteer staff of the local newspaper to contribute to village life, and speed up our assimilation. I will write articles and editorials, while Debbie will contribute her talents as a graphic artist. Meanwhile, *Muscade* is safely tucked into her berth on the Canal du Midi awaiting her renaissance as a sailing vessel next spring.

CHAPTER THIRTEEN

PANAMA CANAL AND ECUADOR

Just as we were getting settled into our new digs, the "old enchanter" made an appearance and offered yet another exciting opportunity. *La Brunante* has been sold to an Ecuadorian businessman, who has asked me to deliver his newly-acquired yacht from Newport, Rhode Island, back to Salinas in his home country. The buyer, a Dutchman called Jan de Bruin, has asked to be part of my crew, so that I can give him a complete checkout on his boat during the voyage to South America. As usual on these deliveries, I will be the captain. Ironically, during the last six years I have sailed *La Brunante*, or as she is now renamed, *Mi Dushi* (Ecuadorian Indian for "my darling") much more than the owner ever did. Debbie and I will sail the boat from Newport to Fort Pierce, Florida before Christmas and will complete the journey from there to Ecuador with Jan de Bruin early next year.

I have already purchased the nautical charts necessary for the trip and completed the preliminary planning. From Florida, our route will take us south through the Bahamas, then transit the Windward Passage between Cuba and Haiti. After that, it's a straight run to Colon in Panama, skirting to the east of Jamaica. After exiting the Panama Canal, we will follow the Columbian coast down to Salinas in Ecuador, the new homeport for *Mi Dushi*. After two years of motoring in the French canals I am looking forward to some serious offshore sailing. Navigating a boat through the Panama Canal will fulfill yet another ambition.

The prospect of adventure has once more re-invigorated Debbie, and given a boost to our flagging marriage. Debbie is obviously not happy, but unfortunately cannot articulate her desires, leaving me to guess the reasons for her unhappiness and invent remedies, while simultaneously feeling guilty for having invited her into my life in the first place.

During the delivery trip from Newport to Florida, Debbie was her happy, carefree self again. The voyage was almost the reverse of the one we completed during our honeymoon, three-and-a-half years before. After leaving Newport, we sailed outside Long Island, down the Jersey coast to Cape May, then up the Delaware River to the Chesapeake Canal and down Chesapeake Bay to Norfolk. From there, we took the historic Dismal Swamp Canal (built in the late seventeen hundreds) to Albemarle Sound, then the Alligator River and Pamlico Sound to Beaufort, North Carolina. That part of the trip took us ten days, and *Mi Dushi*, having been completely refurbished prior to her sale, performed flawlessly. From Beaufort, we put to sea, sailed around Cape Fear and hugged the coast to avoid the adverse current from the Gulf Stream. Four days later, we arrived off Fort Pierce inlet, but had to wait all night outside the entrance for daylight, as I didn't want to risk a night entry into an unlit channel with strong tidal currents.

It is now late January. Debbie and I are back aboard *Mi Dushi* in Fort Pierce in the agreeable company of her new owner, Jan de Bruin, and his father, Hank, who flew over from Holland to make up our crew. I am anticipating a ten-day cruise to Colon on the

Atlantic side of the Panama Canal. We will then have to hire a canal pilot and negotiate our passage through the canal. It could take some time, as small boat transits are limited to two days a week. Once we are into the Pacific, it will take us about a week to reach Salinas. We should have very good sailing on the way down to Panama, helped by the strong northeasterly trade winds. On the Pacific side, we will be sailing in the equatorial zone, so we can expect fairly light winds and a lot of motoring. The equator itself is only about one hundred and fifty miles north of Salinas, so we will "cross the line" the day before arriving at our destination. We have stocked the boat with non-perishable food for the entire trip, and enough fresh food to get us to Panama.

On our first night at sea, when we were halfway across the Gulf Stream *en route* to the Bahamas, a loud bang like a cannon shot careened through the boat. At the time, we were beating into a strong easterly wind in moderately rough seas. I was on watch, but the loud noise brought the entire crew on deck to find out what was happening. I quickly ascertained that the forestay had snapped at the point where it attaches to the top of the mast. The mast did not fall because the halyard holding the self-furling foresail held fast, helped by a spinnaker halyard, which I had rigged as a back-up forestay. We had no choice but to abandon our voyage, bear off downwind, and limp into Fort Lauderdale for repairs.

After three days in Fort Lauderdale, *Mi Dushi* is as good as new, and we are underway again towards the Bahamas. I am on watch, reflecting on how lucky we were that the masthead fitting gave way when we were so close to one of the best places in North America to have it fixed. Anecdotally at least, it seems that some people have more than their fair share of luck, even to the extent that their misfortunes happen at opportune times. When I look back over my life-to-date, I can conclude that I am definitely one of the lucky ones.

Crossing the Gulf Stream between Florida and the Bahamas has always been a challenge and can be quite dangerous for small boats because of the very strong and unpredictable currents. The incessant northeast trade winds force the water of the Southern Atlantic Ocean into the Gulf of Mexico, where its only escape is through the narrow passage between Florida and the Bahamian banks. In that narrow passage, currents can easily run at more than five miles an hour, presenting a real challenge for small sailing boats like *Mi Dushi*, which average about six miles an hour. It doesn't take a skilled navigator to figure out that in one hour you have gone six miles forward and five miles sideways. In the days before satellite navigation, I would always make this crossing at night, so I could take back bearings on the lights of Fort Lauderdale and adjust my heading accordingly for the effect of the Gulf Stream, until I was able to see the loom of the iconic Great Isaac lighthouse on the Bahamian side of the straits. Tonight, the Great Isaac light is out of service for routine maintenance, so I am very grateful to have satellite navigation. There is now a new and more accurate system available, called GPS (Global Positioning System), but it is still too expensive for the pleasure boat market. GPS gives constant position data, but the United States government, which owns the satellites, has degraded the accuracy of the system for commercial users to prevent nefarious use by hostile forces.

We entered the Windward Passage between Cuba and Haiti at midnight on our third night at sea, as I was taking over the helm from Debbie. Jan and Hank are now qualified to stand night watches with the proviso that they must inform me immediately if they see any shipping traffic, or if they notice a significant deterioration in the weather. Shortly after taking over the watch, I noticed that we were being followed. The shadowing vessel did not have its navigation lights on, but I could see dim lights coming from the wheelhouse. It was keeping station on us a couple of miles astern. I alerted my crew, then tried calling the ship on the radio emergency channel sixteen, which all ships monitor. After several calls, a sheepish voice answered from the bridge of a U.S. Coast Guard cutter. They were indeed tailing our boat with the intention of boarding us at first light for a routine check. They asked that we have all our passports and ship's papers ready. I told the Coast Guard that *Mi Dushi* was an Ecuadorian registered vessel and gave them some details about our crew and itinerary. Several hours later, they informed me that they did not have the authority to board our vessel, so they wished us a pleasant and safe onward voyage to Ecuador. I suspect that the Ecuadorian Embassy in Washington had denied their request to board. Many people are unaware of the role that the U.S. military plays in international waters: protecting shipping, watching for illegal immigrants, and disrupting the drug trade. Private yachtsmen gratefully appreciate their presence.

The closer we got to the Panama Canal, the more the shipping traffic increased. I decided to sleep in the cockpit for the last two nights at sea, so I would always be ready to dodge the steady stream of ships coming from and going to Panama. The traffic density was not surprising, as about fourteen thousand ships per year use the canal. Ten days after leaving Florida, we docked at the Panama Canal Yacht Club in Colon.

There are certain dead-end marinas in the world, where one can see the remnants of shattered dreams and abandoned lifestyles. The obvious clues are the number of boats, mostly in various states of disrepair, with weathered "For Sale" signs dangling from the rigging. Colon is one of those places. The town itself is considered dangerous. We were advised not to leave the yacht club premises, which have armed guards on duty at all times but, as we had to stock up for the trip to Salinas, risked taking a taxi to the *Super Mercado* in town. Armed guards escorted us out of the taxi, and a soldier with a sub-machine gun was posted at the end of each grocery aisle. Needless to say, we were relieved to get back aboard *Mi Dushi* with our provisions. The Club itself was pleasant, and the staff very accommodating.

On the third evening, we met our canal pilot, A.J., who will be responsible for taking us through the locks to the Pacific side. I invited him to join us for dinner in the yacht club restaurant, and we hit it off right away. He was a graduate of King's Point, the U.S. Merchant Marine Academy in New York. There his sailing master, Joe Prosser, was the same man who had taught me to sail at the Naval College in Canada. Joe, a Newfoundlander, had been skipper of our magnificent eighty-five foot training yacht, *HMCS Oriole*. Rain, snow, gale or calm, Joe would always show up on deck in his bare feet. Whenever we arrived at our destination port, his Mercedes 500SL Gullwing would be waiting for him on the dock. He was independently rich, and his naval career served as a pleasant diversion. During dinner, I asked A.J. if he would authorize me to anchor overnight in the jungle at Gamboa in Gatun Lake. My request meant taking an extra day to transit the forty-eight mile canal, and double-duty for the pilot. After taking a long sip of his wine and with a twinkle in his eye, he granted my request and promised to be on board early the next day.

It would be dangerous for small yachts to lock through the Panama Canal in the traditional way they do in most other locks in the world, including the canals of Europe and North America. The locks are too large (110ft wide and 1000ft long), the walls too rough, and the water flow, when the huge locks are being filled, too turbulent. To ensure a safe operation, small boats are tied together in rafts of four, and positioned in the centre of the lock with long lines leading from each corner of the raft to the lock walls to keep the boats in position. Transiting boats are responsible for providing their own lines, but canal employees are on hand to help secure the ropes and adjust them as the water level changes.

According to the regulations, which were agreed upon when the canal first opened in 1914, every transiting vessel must have a pilot on board. I suppose the regulators were not anticipating small pleasure yachts, and the rules have not been updated to meet present-day requirements. Nevertheless, we were pleased with the arrangement and felt very secure having A.J. on board (as well as a pilot in training, called Campos) to show us the ropes. We entered the first of three chambers comprising the Gatun lock, formed our raft, secured our lines, and were lifted eighty-five feet into Gatun Lake. A brisk four-hour sail under spinnaker put us into the Gamboa Reach, where we anchored in the Panamanian jungle for the night. A.J. was clearly delighted to be under sail in a small boat again. He was more accustomed to being on the bridge of huge container ships. During the short passage, Debbie whipped up a delicious lunch for the entire crew, and when we were safely anchored at Gamboa, A.J. and Campos departed. We were left to enjoy a swim, the tranquil solitude of the jungle, and another once- in-a-lifetime experience.

Early next morning, Campos arrived at our anchorage by pilot cutter. He came aboard to guide us through the five chambers of the Pedro Miguel and Miraflores locks and to oversee our eighty-five-foot drop into the Pacific Ocean at Panama City. We were his first customers as a new, fully-trained pilot. To mark the occasion, we presented him with a bottle of single malt whiskey for a later celebration.

A tricky *Trivial Pursuit* question would be: When transiting the Panama Canal from the Atlantic to the Pacific, in what direction would you be heading? The long answer is: Due to the peculiar orientation of the Isthmus of Panama, you would be heading southeast (not west).

During our three-day wait in Colon, the buzz among transiting yachties was all about the danger of encountering drug runners while sailing down the Columbian coast. It was reassuring to learn that the U.S. Navy is patrolling this coastline using ships, maritime aircraft and ship-borne helicopters. I am taking no chances and will stay well out to sea until we cross the extended border between Columbia and Ecuador. With this in mind, after clearing the coastal islands of Panama, we headed out into the Pacific away from the coastline. The next morning, as daylight was breaking, I was consoled to see a U.S. Navy guided-missile destroyer keeping station on us about half a mile away. We were asked to report our crew passport details as well as our intended destination. I got the distinct impression that they were going to track us all the way to Salinas, and that was just fine with me. Being a former naval pilot, I was able to communicate with the ship using the same jargon and naval radio lexicon they were using, which may have added some credibility to our story. In any case, their job was to make sure that we were not involved in the drug trade.

It took us six days of sailing and motor sailing in variable winds to reach Salinas. I encouraged Jan to take charge of making the many sail change decisions, as he is now fully checked-out on his new boat and will soon be the skipper. We had contact with the U.S. Navy every day, usually with an accompanying fly-past, either by helicopter or P3A maritime patrol aircraft.

On the day before our arrival in Ecuador, we were shocked to witness dolphins on a killing frenzy, when a large school of tuna zoomed past the boat, chased by an equally large school of dolphins. The dolphins were randomly killing the tuna, and the sea was red with a long trail of fish parts and blood as far as the eye could see. I had always considered the dolphin to be a noble and reasonable mammal and had no idea that they killed gratuitously. One more illusion shattered, and my unequivocal belief in the orderliness of nature put into reasonable doubt.

A hero's welcome awaited our arrival at the Yacht Club in Salinas. Jan's wife and children were on hand to greet us and to inspect every detail of their new yacht. Debbie and I gratefully accepted a generous invitation to spend a few days at their home in Guayaquil. After a fabulous lunch of the best tuna ceviche I had ever tasted, we packed our bags and said *adios* to *Mi Dushi*, the boat that had played such a large part in our marriage. Jan and his father Hank, who had both been competent and willing crew members, were delighted with their delivery voyage experience. Jan kindly offered to lend us *Mi Dushi* in the future if we ever felt like returning to Ecuador for a cruise to the Galapagos Islands, which he knew was on my wish list. After a couple of days in Guayaquil, Debbie and I bade farewell to Jan and his family and flew north to Quito.

When we first agreed to deliver *Mi Dushi* to Ecuador, we had thought of combining the trip with a climb of the 19350 ft. volcano, Cotopaxi, which is located about thirty miles south of Quito in the Andean Valley of the Volcanoes. However, after further investigation, we realized that we didn't have the right equipment to climb the icecap at the top of the volcano, so we settled for a climb up as far as the glacial ice.

The next day, we decided to hike up El Panecillo, a hill overlooking the old town of Quito, which affords a splendid, panoramic view of the entire city. A series of paths and stone steps lead up through a slum housing community to an observation deck on top of the hill. Our guidebook clearly stated: "Visitors are strongly advised to take a taxi to the lookout, rather than risking the climb up the path." I thought I knew better, so we naïvely disregarded this warning and hiked up the hill, albeit at a very fast pace. During the climb, we were heckled several times, and had a couple of water balloons thrown our way, but we made it safely to the top. On the way back down, we were not so lucky. Two young men armed with knives jumped us from behind, and one of them snatched my camera bag.

I had mentally rehearsed my reaction to a mugging many times: I would give the robbers exactly what they wanted and be thankful to get away with my life. Unfortunately, I did not react as planned because instinct overcame logic. Obeying my gut reaction, I started to chase the thief to get my camera back. A few seconds later, I saw that Debbie had been pinned on her back, and was kicking bravely at the second mugger who was trying to cut the belt on her fanny pack. I snapped to my senses, went to her rescue, threw off her attacker, pulled her to her feet, and started to run hand-in-hand with her at top speed down the hill. Luckily, the robbers did not take chase, apparently content to have stolen the camera, so we escaped further injury. I sustained a superficial knife wound on my arm, but thankfully Debbie was unhurt. I had read somewhere that shouting "Police" during a mugging can be effective, so I tried that tactic throughout the incident.

When we reported the attack, the authorities had no sympathy for our case, and rightly so. We should not have been anywhere near that area, where even the police fear to tread. Once again my stupidity, arrogance, skepticism and "know-it-all" attitude almost got us into deep trouble as I took advantage of Debbie's trust in my judgment and put her life in danger. Sadly, all of the undeveloped films taken during the trip from Florida to Salinas were in the camera bag, but we considered that a very cheap price to pay for our misadventure.

Charles Darwin theorized that we are programmed to have one of three reactions to danger: Fight, flight or faint. I was programmed to fight, in spite of my intellectual pre-calculations, but made a swift correction to the flight mode, after assessing the danger. Over dinner that night in the comfortable Colon Hotel where we were staying, we decided that it was time to head back to our refuge in Knowlton, recharge our batteries, and enjoy some spring skiing in nearby Vermont.

I don't think that either Debbie or I can specifically identify the reasons that our marriage is failing. When we first met, our incompatibilities were camouflaged by a common thirst for adventure. We were thrilled that our paths had crossed. I truly believed that I had found the ideal woman, who was not only willing, but also very able to be an equal partner in confronting life's exciting challenges. I had been extremely impressed with her gracious and able manner during the Pakistan expedition and continued to marvel at her fearlessness during the Atlantic crossing. However, I had seen, but chose to ignore, the warning signs during my visits to California before our marriage. At that time, as I stated earlier, she appeared to be living in a world of her own creation, was often very distant and sometimes exhibited bizarre behavior. On those occasions, her parents had always managed to get her back on track, something I now have great difficulty accomplishing. They obviously liked me and wanted to promote my future with their daughter. I blame myself and willingly accept most of the responsibility for our marriage failure. If anything, I rushed Debbie from friendship and shared interest into marriage much too quickly, thinking it was the honourable thing to do and keen to begin the adventure with her. I was excited and ready, after five years alone, to invite Debbie into my world and was anxious to solidify the partnership. I disregarded love, the many inconsistencies in our social attitudes, and the premise that she might also want to have a say about our future. Whatever happens, I will always be grateful for the time that Debbie shared with me and will fondly remember her refreshing attitude and unpretentious, almost childlike, manner. I am sure that she doesn't have an enemy in the world because she embraces everyone she meets cheerfully and with equanimity. I sincerely hope that I did not harm Debbie in any way, and that she will take away something positive from the time we spent together.

Québec's divorce laws have been considerably modernized since Ginette and I split seven years ago. Back then, divorces were only granted for adultery, physical cruelty or mental cruelty, and one had to prove adultery. This morning Debbie and I consulted a lawyer in the village about divorce proceedings. He advised that childless couples, with an uncontested agreement, are now granted an automatic divorce after one year's trial separation. We are not even required to appear in court when our case comes up before a judge. When asked about fairness, he suggested that I should pay monthly support payments to Debbie for three years after the divorce, so she could re-establish her life. I am happy to do this and will give her half the equity in our Knowlton house. She had brought a considerable investment portfolio to our marriage, which fortunately we haven't touched, so that will remain hers. Our separation will start in May, when I head back to *Muscade* for the summer. Debbie will alternate between Knowlton and California until she decides what to do with her life. She has been considering the possibility of staying in Canada. In the meantime, she will continue to have the use of our house, car and shared bank account. If the above narrative gives the impression that our divorce proceedings were without anguish, considerable emotion, and many tearful moments, that is not correct. We agonized over every step.

CHAPTER FOURTEEN

CORSICA

I am reunited with *Muscade* in the Canal du Midi. I am fifty-one years old, eight years into my adventure and back to my status as a solo sailor. The big difference is that now, thanks to Debbie's help, *Muscade* is in Europe, and a lifetime's worth of cruising and exploring awaits me. My first priority is to transform the boat from a canal barge back into an ocean sailing yacht. To this end, I asked some old friends from my navy days to help me cruise down to Agde, the nearest access point to the Mediterranean.

My friend Colin has just retired from the Canadian Forces as a General and is living with his wife, Nancy, in Provence. They joined me in Narbonne for a week's cruise down the canal to Agde. Colin's last appointment was as the Canadian Military Attaché in London where Nancy had occasion to give H.M. Queen Elizabeth a few pointers on bringing up children, when attending various royal receptions. Nancy has forgiven me for Colin's appearance in their wedding photos. When I was opening a bottle of champagne in his dressing room before the wedding, I lost control of the cork, and it flew off, cutting him above the right eye. This did not constitute an emergency for naval pilots, and we have been close friends ever since.

It was a delight having them aboard. Colin is extremely well read and recommended enough non-fiction books to keep me going for years. He has written an interesting study paper, making the case that if there is a God, he must certainly be an atheist. He lists six good arguments for this thesis, the first of which is that theists believe in a higher power, and God does not, so he must be an atheist. Nancy, at the other end of the religious spectrum, never missed a chance to pop into the nearest church to light a candle for her two irreverent shipmates. On reaching Agde, we locked down into the Hérault River. *Muscade* was once again in salt water with unobstructed access to the Med. It took only a few days in Allemand's shipyard to apply the anti-fouling bottom paint, re-step the mast, and inspect the sails and rigging.

Last year, on Bastille Day in Carcassonne, I met a professor from the University of Montréal when he motored into the canal port aboard his Canadian-registered sailing boat. Over drinks, he told me that, after five summer's cruising in the Med, his favourite place was the island of Corsica, which was not even on my list. With his enthusiastic recommendations in mind, I plan to sail there from Agde and spend the rest of the summer exploring that exotic island. I know that I will not be able to single-hand any trips longer than twenty-four hours, because sleeping is out of the question in the Mediterranean, just as it was when I almost lost *Muscade* on the beaches of New Jersey, five years ago. To get from here to Corsica, I have to cross the shipping lanes leading into Marseilles, and avoid the busy naval traffic around Toulon. Add to that numerous ferries, pleasure craft, and fishing boats, and one can appreciate the need for a constant lookout.

A retired Air Canada captain, who now lives near Hyères, joined *Muscade* for the trip to Calvi, a town on the northwest coast of Corsica. His wife was a little apprehensive, as she had never been aboard a small boat at sea. She need not have worried. Even though we had to cross one of the most dangerous areas for the Mistral, there was not a breath of wind, and we motored all the way to Corsica on a mirror-calm sea with the sails furled.

The good burghers of Calvi will tell you that Christopher Columbus was born there around 1440. This is much disputed by the citizens of Genoa who also claim him as their native son. At the time of Columbus's birth, Corsica was ruled by the Genoese, and since Corsicans had a bad reputation, Columbus may well have been reluctant to own up to his real birthplace. He always referred to himself as a Genoan, but it's entirely possible he was born in Corsica when his father was posted there. In any event, one can visit the house where he was supposedly born in Calvi.

Contrary to popular belief, Corsicans (not to be confused with Corsairs) are not sailors. Centuries of being raided and pillaged by every marauding pirate group and invading tribe, going back to before the ancient Greeks, forced the islanders from the sea into the mountains where they became hill farmers and herdsmen. Corsican villages are hilltop fortresses, located as far from the sea as possible. Flour was obtained by grinding chestnuts, which proliferate in the mountains, and ancient Corsicans made a living by raising sheep and goats.

Caporal (headman) Napoleon Bonaparte was a Corsican and achieved a most outstanding career path by making it all the way up the chain of command from army officer cadet to Emperor of France. Two other corporals have had a profound effect on my life: One was Corporal Hitler, who tried his best to wipe out the allied forces, including many members of my family, during World War Two; the other was Corporal Hellyer, Canada's Minister of Defense in 1968, who did succeed in wiping out the spirit of the Canadian Forces. Hellyer obviously did not understand the principles of leadership and knew nothing of *esprit de corps* when he merged the three Canadian forces and put them in drab green uniforms.

It is now the middle of October, and I am preparing to leave *Muscade* for the winter in Campoloro Marina on the east coast of Corsica, just south of the ancient capital of Bastia. By reading the ship's logbook, I am re-living and savouring one of the most enjoyable summers of my life. I began my Corsican adventure last June by sailing down the scenic west coast, stopping at Ajaccio to pick up friends, then crossed over to the islands of northern Sardinia. From there, I continued up the east coast of Corsica to Bastia. The west coast is rocky and indented with plenty of sheltered bays and fiords, while the east coast is one long sandy beach.

After exploring Bastia, I stopped into the marina at Campoloro to reserve a dock space for the winter and to visit some French friends who used to live in Montréal. They are now retired on their family farm, a fifteen-minute drive from the marina. Gérard and Marie-France now share the family property with Marie's brother. They grow cash crops of kiwis, plums and almonds. Marie's father, the French Prefect in Algeria at the time of the uprising against the colonial power was assassinated there during the hostilities. Marie's mother and her children were evacuated and resettled by the French government in Corsica. They were given tracts of land, as were many other French families who were forced to leave Algeria at the same time. This group is known collectively as *pieds noir*. These French Algerians were given impenetrable brush areas (*Maquis*) to homestead and worked hard to clear the dense bush before painstakingly converting the land into the fertile and highly productive farms of today. In France during World War Two, members of *la résistance,* who carried out sabotage attacks against their Nazi occupiers, were called the *Maquis*. This was a allusion to the practice of hiding out in the wild, almost impenetrable shrubbery of Corsica, which is still the preferred method of criminals trying to escape capture from Corsican authorities, today.

During a dinner party at my friends' charming colonial farmhouse, I had my first encounter with Alzheimer's disease. I was seated to the right of Marie's mother, who was very much the lady of *le manoir* with exquisite manners, impeccable taste and a regal air. She chatted amicably with me about my life and was curious to know what I was doing in Corsica. After our lengthy conversation, she turned to talk to the person on her left, returning to me a few moments later with, "Good evening young man and what are you doing here in Corsica?" I was disconcerted, but kept chatting with her as if nothing was unusual.

Finding Corsica very much to my liking, I am seriously considering spending another summer here. The cuisine, which incorporates many seafood delicacies, is superb, and the local wines are excellent. One day when I was anchored in the Lavezzi Islands off the south coast, the locals taught me how to harvest sea urchins, then eat them by dipping crusty pieces of baguette into the egg yolk-like centre of this utterly delicious echinoderm. *Soupe de poisson* is a specialty all over the island, and the preferred *apéritif* is *pastis* served with lots of ice and a splash of water. For meat lovers, genuine wild boar is a good choice on menus during the autumn hunting season. French is the principal language, but long-established Corsican families speak a dialect of Italian amongst themselves. I learned my French in Québec, and Corsicans can tell from my accent and usage that I am Canadian, which usually works in my favour, especially among the separatists, who consider me a brother-in-arms.

One night, when anchored in the inner harbor of Ajaccio, I was rudely awakened by a huge explosion in the port. Corsican separatists had blown up a French pilot cutter as a protest against alleged discriminatory hiring practices by the French-owned ferry companies. The separatists seem content to concentrate their disruptive tactics on destroying French property, rarely targeting or harming people. A recent poll concluded that over eighty per cent of Corsicans want their island to remain part of France. A similar survey in France indicated that roughly the same percentage of Frenchmen wouldn't mind if Corsica became an independent country. In any case, Corsica is a very popular island destination. It is completely inundated with French and Italian tourists during July and August. Ferries disgorge thousands of camper cars, motorcycles and other vehicles filled with holidaying families, intent on enjoying the huge variety of campsites, beaches, mountain resorts, hiking trails (some of the best in France), and the many charming towns and villages.

Debbie spent the summer in California with her parents, and I phoned her often to see how she was coping. I still suspect that she will choose to resettle there after our divorce. Today I had the sad task of packing her belongings, which I will take back with me to Canada. I am amazed at how few possessions she needed, and how little she had accumulated during her four years as *Muscade's* first mate. It was not without feelings of remorse, guilt and nostalgia that I collected her things and put them into a duffle bag. While putting *Muscade* to bed for the winter, I met most of the other cruising couples, wintering their boats in this marina, but the local Corsicans, who dock their boats here, are less friendly. History has taught them not to trust strangers, even if they are relatively benign Canadians.

Back in Knowlton, I am continuing my work as a writer for the local newspaper and expanding my network of friends. I am surprised at how cooperative most people (especially politicians) can be when being interviewed for a news story or an editorial. I suppose the same ego and need to be recognized also fuelled their drive to run for office in the first place. I have been attending the town council meetings and writing up the details for the paper, which is proving to be a fast-track introduction to the community. Remembering the complications between Ginette and Tosca and being aware of small village gossip and the machinations of the rumour mill - but mainly out of respect for Debbie - I am determined not to get involved in any new relationship until after our divorce is approved next spring. Jean-Charles has asked me to skipper *Le Pat-Mar* in the Caribbean again next winter, as his job leaves him little time to use the boat. I am pleased to accept this offer and will commission the yacht in early January, after spending Christmas in Wales. He has offered me the same arrangement that I had on *La Brunante*. I will be able to invite friends at any time throughout the winter. My only commitment will be to pick up Jean-Charles and his family in the Grenadines in March, and deliver them up to St Lucia, where he intends to leave the boat for the summer.

However, I am considering taking a pause to consolidate my life. I am really enjoying the house in Knowlton, as well as the stability that village life provides. I am reconnecting with friends in Montréal after my second failed marriage. I have rejoined *Le Club de Jeudi Soir,* a group of single friends who get together for dinner at a different Montréal restaurant every Thursday evening. It's a mixed group with an unwritten rule that members should stay friends, enjoy one another's company, but not get romantically involved. I am privileged to be the only Anglophone member.

Another compelling reason to consolidate my affairs is my growing attachment to Corsica. I now have an ideal base for *Muscade* and have a strong desire to get to know the island more intimately. It is an easy commute from Montréal via Paris to Bastia, so I can come and go as I please between April and November, then spend my winters in the Caribbean as skipper of *Le Pat-Mar*. Now that I have a secure place to leave *Muscade*, I will avoid Corsica in July and August, when it can be too hot and crowded with tourists. Fortunately, those two months are ideal in Québec and in Wales, where my ageing parents appreciate my support. It always takes time to weave oneself into the fabric of a new place, befriend its people and grasp its culture. I have no wish to move on too quickly and miss those experiences.

It is also a good time to remind myself that, had I not followed the advice of the "old enchanter," none of the events described in this book would have happened. It is true that completely different events would have filled that same timespan of my life, but everything has worked out far better than I could have imagined. Even the unfortunate happenings, the brushes with disaster, and my divorce from Debbie are pieces of the same time-management puzzle, which will eventually make up my entire life story. The circle analogy is appropriate. We talk of having a "circle of friends" or about "moving in the same circles." As we progress, our circle moves with us, overlaps with other people's networks and greatly enhances our social opportunities. When I worked as an airline pilot, I would board my aircraft, make a sharp left turn into the cockpit and close the door, precluding (with apologies to my first officers) most chances for social interactions. This book is a testament to how all that changed after I liberated myself and allowed myself the freedom to interact randomly and spontaneously. On the day before I die, the way I have spent my allotted time will be extremely important to me, but will mean absolutely nothing to anyone the next day.

Looking back on the day I submitted my resignation letter to Air Canada, I now realize that some subconscious spirit was challenging me to make the most of my life. It was certainly not my pragmatic self that made the philosophical decision to quit and try something completely different. My inner voice kept repeating: "Take this seemingly irrational leap of faith, or you will always regret missing the opportunity." Coming to terms with one's mortality is another very important piece of life's time riddle. Accepting death as inevitable, and realizing that life is finite, sharpens the desire to squeeze the most out of every day and underlines the fragile nature of human existence. It dictates an urgency to live for the moment, which can lead to genuine peace of mind. Day-to-day problems and frustrations fade away, becoming trivial when they are viewed in the perspective of a finite lifetime. Making mistakes is absolutely the best way to learn, but it is equally important to move on quickly from those mistakes and not dwell on how they could have been avoided. Looking backwards with remorse can spoil the enjoyment of the moment, as can over- anticipating future events. Unreasonable longing for something in the future makes the present seem like a valueless period, or a time which must be endured until something more exciting comes along. I have never understood the strange concept of "killing time."

Acquisitiveness and its enabling henchmen - greed, envy, and lust for power - can easily get in the way of a meaningful life. Acquisitiveness has no limits: it becomes a thief who steals precious time which could be spent to better advantage. You can do two things with money: "Buy stuff or do stuff." Certainly money has no intrinsic value. Some *homo sapiens* are still hunters, some still gatherers, but some have managed to evolve into more noble creatures. Could it be that collecting unnecessary items, accumulating much more than is reasonable, hoarding loot, and not being able to share or throw anything away are all inherited traits from our cavemen-gatherer ancestors?

The unvarnished reality is that most people are forced to work and earn money in order to survive. We sell our time for money. Our worth is measured according to the talent or experience we bring to the workplace. Expectations and ambitions dictate the amount of money we think we need. To live as an average person in a typical "third world" country requires an annual income of less than one thousand dollars. That is the basic survival end of the scale. The upper end amount is determined by each individual and is predicated on various combinations of the following: societal norms, personal expectations, feelings of entitlement, delusions of grandeur, levels of competitiveness, peer and family pressures, insecurities, moral responsibilities and identity issues. In a free enterprise society, there is no upper limit to wealth accumulation. Individuals can try to use their skills, talents or nefarious activities to amass whatever amount of wealth satisfies their personal aspirations. Most people come to the realization during the process of acquiring wealth that being materially rich does not guarantee self-esteem, fulfillment or happiness. The fear of eventually becoming old, sick, and poor can be incentive enough for some individuals to keep hoarding riches, even though the pains of sickness, old age and terminal illnesses cannot be assuaged with money.

By contrast, most West Indians are happy people. I have seen the boat boys who paddle out to service boats at anchor, workers that pick up odd jobs cleaning and polishing mega yachts, and dockside laundry ladies make fun of the millionaire boat owners when they appear disgruntled and out-of-sorts with their lives. Their typical reaction is: "Take it easy man," delivered with a big smile. Why are they so content with their lives? Perhaps it's the year-round equitable climate, and the fact that there is always something available to eat: bananas, sugar cane, mangoes, fish etc. I have become very attached to these people and greatly admire their attitude to life.

My winter aboard *Le Pat-Mar* in the Caribbean was amazing. Once again, all of the other players had to get used to seeing me on a different boat. I spent most of the time sailing in the Grenadines, which have become my favourite islands. The island of Bequia, with its steel-band dances every Thursday at the Frangipani Hotel, conch fritters at Mac's Pizza, sunset walks for a rum punch at Spring Hotel, pristine beaches with clear turquoise waters, and evenings at the Harpoon Saloon, is a treat. The boat is extremely well-appointed with three double cabins offering all the comforts of home. Many friends and family members accepted my invitation to share part of my winter aboard. Towards the end of the season, I picked up Jean-Charles and his family at Union Island in the Grenadines, and sailed with them down to Grenada, then back up to St Lucia.

It's springtime in Knowlton, Québec. Today, our lawyer phoned to say that the Provincial Court has approved the divorce. Debbie has decided to resettle in California, and I have been packing up her belongings, which I will send by courier to her parents' address. The nearest U.P.S. office is in nearby Richford, Vermont, but when I tried to cross the U.S. border with a carload of boxes, the female customs officer was not helpful and demanded a full written inventory for the contents of each box. When I explained that most of the goods had been acquired in the U.S.A. and were being returned to my American former wife, she took pity on me and let me pass. She then gave me her work schedule, which will enable me to bring down a second load tomorrow when she is on duty again. I could have hugged her, but settled for giving her a box of chocolates on my last trip. I will support Debbie for three years and have given her half the equity in our house. Shortly after the divorce, Debbie's mother wrote me a letter, saying that I would always be considered part of their family and was welcome at any time in their Californian home. Needless to say, I was relieved to receive that gracious note, which caused me to shed a tear for our failed marriage.

Back in Corsica, I am gradually being accepted by the locals who keep their boats all year in the marina at Campoloro. They call me *"le Canadien."* I'm on friendly terms with the usually taciturn Port Captain and am beginning to feel welcome. I have befriended Rocchi, the owner of the excellent restaurant, *A Casarella*, in the old citadel of Bastia. During a dinner there with visiting friends, he honoured me with a certificate, naming me one of his restaurant's *bon vivants*.

On one of my commutes back to Knowlton, the Air Inter passenger agent at the check-in desk told me that the flight I was attempting to take to Paris was oversold. The rule when travelling on a stand-by ticket is never leave the airport until you see the aircraft take off, as there can always be a last-minute chance for a seat. With this in mind, I strolled down to the restaurant for some breakfast. There, I spotted the flight crew and introduced myself. The captain, a former French navy pilot, was upset because his cockpit jump seat was already occupied, so there was no space for me on his aircraft. When it came time for him to board, he escorted me across the tarmac, saying, "There's no way I'm going to leave a fellow navy pilot stranded." I crouched in the cockpit during takeoff and landing and sat in the flight attendant's seat for the rest of the short flight to Paris.

On another occasion, I was stuck all night at Charles de Gaulle airport during a baggage handlers' strike. All flights were cancelled, and all airport hotel rooms sold out. I discovered from the Air Canada ground staff that a British Airways captain was going to attempt a departure early the next morning before the workers came in to picket the gates. When the captain arrived, I met him in the briefing room, and he readily agreed to take me in the cockpit for what turned out to be a successful departure. I am sure that these examples of camaraderie exist in all walks of life, but are particularly common among the airline pilot community.

The second winter of my consolidation period found me, once again, as skipper of *Le Pat-Mar* in the Caribbean, operating mainly between Martinique and St Lucia. One of the games I played to amuse my visitors was to plan a departure from Martinique to arrive off the northern tip of St Lucia just before sunset. Knowing that the chances of catching a game fish in that area at that time were very high, I would casually ask my guests if they felt like having fish for dinner, then set out my troll line. Invariably, I would hook a tuna or dorado, which would be sizzling on the barbeque half an hour later, when we were anchored under the lee of Pigeon Island.

Towards the end of the winter season, I invited the boat-boys who worked at the Marigot Bay anchorage for a sailing lesson and lunch aboard *Le Pat-Mar*. I knew them well, having often frequented this spectacular anchorage during the last ten years. After the excursion, I dropped them off and singlehanded back up north to the Rodney Bay marina. As I entered the harbour, I spotted the port captain standing on the end of one of the docks waving vigorously. I immediately knew that something was very wrong because normally it would take a tropical storm to move him from his office chair. Sure enough, the news was bad: my mother had died the week before and had already been cremated. I spent a day securing *Le Pat-Mar* for the summer hiatus, phoned the owner in Montréal to inform him that his boat was safely moored and departed the next day to support my father in Wales.

Now that my mother is no longer with him, my father has lost his *raison d'être*. I stayed with him for a month, during which time we took a retrospective tour around Cornwall, where our early family life had been happiest, but he lacked enthusiasm. After our holiday, I left him in the care of my sister, while I travelled to Plymouth to deliver a boat to Paris.

The boat was a forty-five foot Princess motor yacht. Unlike sailing boats, which have displacement hulls, these fast vessels plane on top of the water and are not designed for rough seas, so I had to wait a week at the Royal Western Yacht Club in Plymouth for calm weather. When we eventually got going, it took only a few hours to cross the busy English Channel shipping lanes at twenty-five knots, and maneuver alongside in the port of Cherbourg. Since this boat's speed was five times faster than my normal cruising speed, I had to quickly rethink my relative velocity calculations when dodging the armada of ships in the English Channel. It was not a pleasant experience, and the roar of twin diesels at maximum rpm did not help. This helps to explain why those of us who normally use sails for propulsion have derogatory names for these "gin palaces." We stayed overnight in Cherbourg, where the locals have an accent similar to the *Québecois,* making me feel very much at home. The next day, we proceeded to the unprepossessing port city of Le Havre, at the mouth of the river Seine. After spending a week meandering up this picturesque waterway, visiting les Iles de la Seine, Rouen and Monet's Givernay, we locked our way into the Arsenal marina in Paris, where I had been with *Muscade* four years earlier.

As soon as we were safely alongside, I left the boat and strolled to the *Musée d'Orsay* to renew my acquaintance with the Impressionist painters. While there, I started thinking about my father's situation and decided to phone him to tell him I had arrived in Paris. There was no answer at his home, so I phoned my sister to get the latest news. I had invited the boat owners that night for a farewell dinner at one of my favourite Parisian restaurants and knew that my father would not have wanted me to cancel the evening. We toasted the memory of "the Admiral," dead at eighty-two, just three months after his beloved wife. My sister had found him in bed with his habitual, bedtime Islay single malt half finished on the night table. The dining room was set for breakfast, so he was obviously counting on living a little longer.

He had an enormous influence on my life, although there was always a healthy father/son tension between us. When I was a boy, he often quoted Kipling's line, "If you can fill the unforgiving minute with sixty seconds' worth of distance run, yours is the earth and everything that's in it, and – which is more – you'll be a man, my son."

That quote neatly sums up his life, as well as the last ten years of mine and inspires me to keep going on the same path. Of all the many happy memories of time spent with my father, one of the most gratifying is the time he came with me on a flight from Montréal to Québec City in the cockpit of my Air Canada DC9. As a former naval aviator, he was obviously thrilled to watch his son in action. The next day, when we arrived in the briefing room for the return flight, a supervisory pilot, who was planning to give me my annual flight check on the way back to Montréal, met us there. When I explained that my father would be occupying the cockpit jump seat, the check pilot agreed to postpone the test and took a seat in the first-class cabin for the return trip. After the flight, when the three of us were walking back to the pilot's lounge together, the supervisor asked my father, "Well, sir, how did he do?" My dad approved my performance, and the check flight was considered successful.

Another valuable lesson that my siblings and I learned from our father was to treat everyone as an equal. Long before I was old enough to understand what it meant, he would quote Kipling's, "If you can walk with crowds and keep your virtue, or walk with kings – nor lose the common touch." We all learned this lesson well and are little influenced by the celebrity worshipping society of today. The folk singer Joni Mitchell once said: "Celebrity worship is a mental disease." I completely agree with her and find our western culture, which puts stars from the sports and entertainment world and other celebrities at the top of the totem pole, very disturbing.

I left Paris the following day and flew to Wales to help my sister cope with our parents' affairs. I was not disappointed to have missed both my parents' funerals, preferring to remember them both fondly as they were when they were alive, discreetly living out their final chapter with dignity. All that was left to do was to scatter Dad's ashes in the Menai Straits. The Royal Anglesey Yacht Club provided their ceremonial cutter, with its brass-fittings and varnished bright work gleaming for the occasion. The Club coxswain, who knew and respected our father, motored my sister and me out into Beaumaris harbour, where we fittingly returned Dad to the sea, which had played such a prominent role in his life.

Back in Corsica for my third summer, I am thinking that it's about time to move on to Italy, Yugoslavia, Turkey, Greece and all points east. As usual, I went back to Knowlton for the months of July and August. At a meeting of the Thursday night dinner group in Montréal, one of the members tried a little match-making by inviting a friend of hers along to meet me. I will call this girl Carmen, after Bizet's fiercely independent, sultry gypsy heroine from the popular opera of the same name. There were no initial fireworks between us, but there was definitely some mutual intrigue and curiosity. We exchanged addresses and agreed to meet again. Carmen worked as a nurse practitioner on a contract basis. She had just returned from Eastern Europe, where she had been the resident nurse for a Canadian company. She was now accepting contracts to work in the far north of Québec in various First Nation communities, both Cree and Inuit. She was a huge opera fan, which was one of the few things we had in common. After her last relationship broke up, she put all her belongings into storage, and having no fixed address, stayed with different friends when between jobs. Carmen was also a passionate Québec separatist and had many friends in the upper echelons of the ruling Parti Québecois, which is planning to hold a second referendum on Québec independence.

If I am trying to find more proof that I am a coward in my affairs with women, I need look no further. Perhaps from a subconscious fear of rejection, I have always let the women in my life take the initiative in our relationships. So, even though we were quite unsuited, our relationship began to flourish when Carmen showed up at my house in Knowlton one afternoon, stayed for dinner and was still there for breakfast the next morning. Eventually, I invited her to come sailing in Corsica, and after an enjoyable month together circumnavigating Corsica aboard Muscade, she moved some of her belongings into my sparsely furnished house before flying up to James Bay for her next contract on a Cree reservation. We had embarked on a relationship of mutual convenience.

CHAPTER FIFTEEN

INDIA, JAMES BAY AND GREECE

I feel the "old enchanter" urging me to get going again. There are many more dreams to be grasped and not a lot of time left, so when I was invited to go back to India at the end of October, I leapt at the chance. For several years, my younger brother, Angus, has been "headhunted" back and forth between London department stores, including Harrods, where he began his career. He is now working as a buyer of handmade oriental carpets and fine fabrics for the Bentalls Group of stores, based in Kingston-on-Thames. His main Indian supplier has invited him, our sister Diana, and me to celebrate Diwali, the ancient Hindu festival of light, in New Delhi. Even the most upscale tour company could not possibly offer the experience of being the guests of a wealthy Indian family during such a celebration as Diwali, the most important festival in the Hindu calendar. As soon as we arrived in India, we were literally embraced by members of Vyas's family for the five days of festivities. Diwali is the celebration of the triumph of light over darkness, so there were candles and coloured lights everywhere and lots of fireworks. Feasting is very much part of the holiday. Vyas's cooks provided sumptuous spreads at every meal including many unique homemade sweets, which are only eaten at this time of the year. Part of the third day was spent praying to Lakshmi, the goddess of wealth, which, in view of my alimony payments to Debbie, seemed like a very worthwhile endeavour. Vyas and his family had their own in-house priest who conveniently orchestrated the religious parts of the occasion. We sat cross-legged around a ceremonial fire in the rooftop temple of their house listening to the priest chant prayers in Sanskrit, while throwing sandlewood chips and various herbs into the flames. I was impressed by the informality of the occasion as we all chatted and laughed amiably together, ignoring the priest, but delegating the serious religious rituals him.

I was reminded that the opera, Lakmé, by Leo Delibes, with its very beautiful "Flower Duet," is loosely based on Diwali and this same goddess. The fifth and last day of the festival marked the start of the Hindu New Year with more feasting, family visits, and fireworks in the streets.

Carmen has invited me to spend Christmas and New Year's Eve with her in Kuujjuarapik, a mixed Cree and Inuit village at the mouth of the Great Whale River on the shores of Hudson Bay, where she is working as a nurse. It didn't take me very long after my arrival there to start wondering what I was doing in that desolate, sub-Arctic community where average winter temperatures are minus twenty-five degrees centigrade, and record lows can approach minus fifty. Carmen lives in a small, pre-fabricated house provided by the government. She walks to the medical dispensary each day in this tiny village of six hundred inhabitants. Being a fitness enthusiast, she insists on taking me for long walks across the windswept, treeless, frozen tundra. My down filled coat is proving to be totally inadequate for these brisk walks, which under more moderate weather conditions, I would have relished. The rest of the time, I hunker down in her primitive pre-fab with my books, or walk around and explore the village whenever wind and weather permit. There is only one shop here, called "The Northern," which sells mostly junk food at exorbitant prices. Alcohol is discouraged, so there is an active black market, and any alcohol found in your luggage at the airport is confiscated. I managed to smuggle in some good burgundy for Christmas dinner and a bottle of champagne to toast the New Year. The nurses order their food supplies and other needs from Val d'Or, the nearest town, which is more than five hundred miles south. Their goods arrive by air, the only means of access in the wintertime. Out of respect for their commitment to the community, there is an unwritten rule that shipments to nurses are not to be inspected.

    As soon as the local residents learned that I was staying with Carmen, they welcomed me with the same consideration and appreciation they give to all their medical workers. Christmas dinner with the nursing staff was an affable affair. We feasted French-Canadian style with homemade *tourtière* (meat pie) as well as turkey. I felt a little conspicuous as the only outsider at the table. A few days later, when we were preparing to celebrate New Year's Eve, Carmen was called to the clinic for a medical emergency. After evaluating the patient, she ordered a medical evacuation flight to the hospital in Val d'Or. I accepted her offer to go along for the ride and witnessed, with awe, how real pilots and real nurses earn their living.

    The aircraft was an old DC6, with four propeller engines. The pilots had to do everything themselves, as there was no ground support at all. This meant not just flight planning and checking weather data, but also fuelling the aircraft, loading the cargo, clearing the snow and ice off the wings, and providing their own flight separation until they were able to contact Air Traffic Control for a proper clearance. These were real pilots, operating with the same spirit as their bush pilot predecessors, the men who opened up the Canadian north in the first place. What a difference from their airline pilot cousins who are spoon-fed all necessary data, fly impeccably-maintained aircraft, have a complete support team and who sit in short-sleeved white shirts nibbling lobster thermidor from the first class trolley.

Carmen and the rest of the nursing staff were equally capable, confidant, and professional. I was very impressed. An ambulance was waiting on the tarmac in Val d'Or to whisk the patient off to hospital. Carmen and I were flown back to Kuujjuarapik shortly after she had turned over her charge to the emergency workers. At some point during the ordeal, the year changed from 1994 to 1995, but nobody noticed.

I was profoundly influenced by my short sojourn in the north. Although I did not really enjoy the experience, I am glad to have been there to see things for myself. The Inuit people are still in complete limbo. When the first white man came to this area, a mere one hundred and fifty years ago, they were still living in the stone age. Since that time, they have had the impossible task of trying to catch-up as they struggle to adapt their culture to the realities of the space age. I had the rare opportunity to join the Inuit community in the village meeting hall for a pre-Christmas traditional feast of raw caribou. It was like going backwards in time. Ski-doos have replaced dog sleds, rifles have replaced harpoons and small, pre-fabricated dwellings, provided by the Federal Government, have replaced igloos, but the indigenous culture remains fragmented in a blurred whirlwind of change. In spite of all that, we southerners can certainly learn something from the Inuit people who rightly believe: "Anything one can buy has no value."

In any event, it was time for me to get going. I was no help to Carmen and I was wasting my time in her modest dwelling as a prisoner of the short days and freezing temperatures. As I have already written, Plato believed that a life of quiet contemplation was the most worthwhile, but he didn't have to contemplate living in Kuujjurapik in the wintertime, nor did he have a luxurious sailing boat waiting for him in tropical St Lucia as an alternative. As soon as my return flight landed in Montréal, I realized what I had missed most during my stay up north: Trees.

I spent two months during the winter of 1995 aboard *Le Pat-Mar* in the Caribbean. Carmen came for a holiday between finishing her contract at Kuujjurapik and starting another job in a Cree village called Waskaganish. We celebrated the carnival together in St Lucia. She was not a natural sailor, nor a good swimmer, but she was enthusiastic, blended in very well with the West Indian scene and, being an excellent chef, was a welcome hand in the galley. Shortly before Easter, I handed the boat over to Jean-Charles and flew up to northern Québec to visit her.

It is springtime in James Bay, and the black flies are thriving. Waskaganish is less primitive than Kuujjurapik. It has about two thousand inhabitants - all Cree Indians - and an interesting history going back to 1668, before it became one of the original Hudson Bay Company's trading posts. The Cree have occupied the southeastern part of James Bay for over five thousand years, making their living by hunting, fishing and trapping. It happens to be "goose break" time, the annual rite of spring when the Cree take off into the woods (yes, there are trees here). They camp in teepees, just as their ancestors have done for thousands of years, and hunt Canada geese, which have just returned from their winter-feeding grounds. I had the privilege of being invited by a family into their teepee, where a plucked and cleaned Canada goose was being roasted over an open fire in the middle of the tent. When it was cooked, I was offered first dibs on this delicious game bird. It was a meal which could only have been improved with a glass of cold Chablis. Even though this village is much further south and is definitely a vast improvement over my last experience, neither it nor Carmen can hold me here for much longer. I plan to take the next available flight south and enjoy the rest of the spring in Knowlton.

During my three summers in Corsica, I have missed the thrill of sailing into new territory and navigating *Muscade* into unknown harbours. Corsica and Sardinia have become as familiar to me as the West Indies. It is now the end of May, and today Carmen and I sailed across the Tyrrhenian Sea to the Italian island of Giglio, on the first leg of a voyage to the Ionian Islands of Greece. Even though the cruising season has not yet started, the port of Giglio was almost full when we arrived, but I managed to squeeze *Muscade* into a small space between two fishing boats.

The usual docking procedure for yachts in the Med is to put down a bow anchor, then reverse in and tie the stern of the boat to the dock. This method allows many boats to parallel park on a fairly small dock space. However, this system does not work for full-keel boats without bow thrusters like *Muscade*, which cannot be steered when going aster and are subject to the whims of wind and current. Even in perfectly calm conditions, the only way for me to reverse into a dock is to manoeuver the boat by using the rotation of the propeller. The rudder is unresponsive. There are other major disadvantages to docking stern first. The aft end of the boat is the deepest part of the hull, and the rudder and propeller are vulnerable to damage. In addition, when you are stern-to there is no privacy, as any passer-by can look directly down into the boat.

During my time in Corsica, I perfected a method of docking bow first, which works well even when I'm solo. I have a large stern anchor, permanently rigged and ready to deploy off the aft end of the boat. The chain and anchor line self-feed out of one of the cockpit lockers. I simply align the bow of the boat with the desired docking spot and steer towards it using the rudder of the self-steering vane. When I'm about one hundred feet from the dock, I slip the anchor over the stern and continue steering towards the quay, setting the anchor as I go. When close to the dock, I return to the cockpit, stop the boat, tie off the anchor rope and hop ashore with the bowline. If necessary, I can squeeze in slowly between two docked vessels by pushing them apart gently with my fenders as I approach the quay.

When we went ashore in Giglio for a hike up to the ancient citadel followed by dinner, I was pleasantly surprised to learn that Carmen spoke very passable Italian, an attribute which will be useful during our cruise down the Italian west coast. This spectacular coastline is not an ideal cruising ground for small boats, being more suited to cruise ships. There are many city and town marinas, all filled to overflowing, and some interesting offshore islands, but very few quiet, sheltered anchorages. This area is steeped in history and contains many ancient cities: Genoa, Rome, Naples, Sorrento, Pompeii, the Amalfi Coast and Sicily, but these places are best accessed and explored by land.

We were not interested in going to Rome, as we had both been there several times, so we chose to explore more remote places on our way down the coast. I am always more interested in getting the feel of a new place by walking around, stopping for coffee or a bite to eat and taking in the ambiance, rather than ticking off a check-list of must-see tourist sights. Having spent the better part of the last five years in France, I am happily renewing my acquaintance with the delights of Italian cooking, which I have always preferred to French. In Tuscany one cannot get a bad meal, a bad cup of coffee or bad glass of wine. After leaving Giglio, we sailed past Civitavecchia, Rome's port, and proceeded into the small town of Santa Marinella for the night.

The next day in the fishing port of Anzio, Carmen met a woman who recommended a restaurant known only to the locals, and succeeded in getting a reservation for dinner. We had a hard time finding the place because it had neither sign nor advertising and was tucked away on a back street. It was well worth our efforts to find it. The meal was absolutely divine with the best *fritto misto del mare* I had ever tasted. Thanks to Carmen's Italian, her curiosity and her appreciation for good food, we had hit the culinary jackpot.

Next we overnighted at the offshore island of Ponza and then sailed on to the island of Ventotene, both charming but quite crowded, so we had to share anchorages with many other boats. At Capri, there was no room at the inn, but we found a very pleasant anchorage in a cove off the south coast of the island, where we were the only boat. I remembered from studying Greek mythology that this was where Ulysses made his crew put wax in their ears to avoid the temptations of the siren's calls, then had himself lashed to the mast, so he could hear the temptress without succumbing. In spite of this threat, I took my chances, didn't bother with earplugs and slept without interruption. The next morning, we awoke early to the shrieks of seabirds fighting over scraps from a lone fishing boat. After watching the sunrise over Capri, I weighed anchor and set heading for the mainland town of Marina di Camerota, our last port of call in Italy.

Carmen has become a reliable watch keeper, so I have decided it is feasible to proceed from Camerota non-stop to the Greek island of Paxos, a three-day trip with two nights at sea. Sadly, I will have to postpone visiting the beautiful Dalmatian Coast. There is an appalling civil war going on in Yugoslavia at the moment, and the Serbian navy is shelling the historic port of Dubrovnik. The main challenge on the way to Greece will be transiting the narrow Strait of Messina with its strong currents, dense shipping traffic, and the whirlpools that Ulysses encountered, which still exist at certain states of the tide.

I timed our departure to arrive at the Strait of Messina the following afternoon, just as the current was predicted to turn in our favour. For the first day, all went according to plan and the winds were favourable. The first night, as we sailed past the

Aeolian Islands, we could clearly see the volcano on the island of Stromboli spewing flames, as it has done continuously since the beginning of recorded history three thousand years ago, making it a very reliable lighthouse. The next afternoon, when we entered the two-mile wide Strait of Messina, I could be forgiven for imagining that I was re-enacting Ulysses' Odyssey as recounted by Homer. I had avoided the siren's calls at Capri and was now actually sailing between the menacing whirlpool that represented Charybdis the sea monster, to starboard, and Scylla, the nymph that Zeus had turned into a boat-destroying beast, to port. Like Ulysses, I was heading to the Ionian Islands and was planning to visit his home island, Ithaka, where patient Penelope would be knitting by day and unpicking by night, while she waited for her sailor to return. With the help of a fresh tailwind and four knots of current, Muscade flew through the straits, dodged the armada of ferries, rounded the toe of the boot of Italy, and set heading eastwards towards Greece. Twenty-four hours later, we sailed between the islands of Paxos and Antipaxos, rounded up to the north and entered the picturesque and totally protected harbor of Gaios, where we moored bow first on the public dock. *Muscade* had finally arrived in Greece, and I had realized the dream, cherished for twenty-one years, of being there with my own boat. The only thing left to do was to hoist yet another courtesy flag from the starboard yardarm, and find a dockside taverna for a refreshing ouzo or two.

  Carmen is getting close to the end of her holiday break, so after three days of hiking around the island during the day, feasting in the tavernas of Paxos at night, and generally enjoying the pleasures of springtime in Greece, we reluctantly sailed south to the commercial port of Preveza, where I had made arrangements to haul the boat during the hot summer months. As the approach to Preveza harbour is via the Gulf of Actium, I had to abandon my impersonation of Ulysses and transform myself into the luckless Mark Anthony. We are sailing through the very battleground where in 31 BC, Mark Anthony and Cleopatra attacked the Roman Senator Octavian and were soundly defeated when fickle Cleopatra jilted her lover and retreated back to Egypt with her fleet of galleys. This defeat ended Mark Anthony's attempted coup, and solidified Octavian's grip on the Roman Empire. He was later crowned Emperor Augustus.

Other cruising sailors had recommended Preveza Marine, and I was impressed with the service. Client's boats are hauled and stored out of the water on custom-made steel cradles designed to withstand earthquakes, which are quite prevalent in this area. When I return in September to explore the Ionian Islands, the boatyard will be able to launch *Muscade* again with very little advance notice. I plan to make this marina my base for several years and cruise the Greek Islands from here each spring and autumn.

Today Carmen and I left Greece for Montréal after a perfect month aboard *Muscade*. Preveza airport is very convenient, only a five-minute cab-ride from the boatyard and offers many direct charter flights to numerous European destinations. Our taxi driver, Thomas, used to chauffeur Aristotle Onassis and his family whenever they flew into this airport *en route* to their private island of Skorpios, a few kilometres to the south. He mentioned that the Onassis family members were very tight with their money and seldom tipped him during all the years he worked for them. He would discover that, even though I have Scottish heritage and am a former airline pilot, I am a generous tipper.

The Greek Islands would be very high on a list of best sailing places in the world. Although Greece has thousands of islands, over two hundred of which are inhabited, most cruising sailors usually think of the Cyclades archipelago when planning a visit. These are the islands, oriented in a loose circle, which occupy the central part of the Aegean Sea south of Athens and include such well-known places as Mykonos and Santorini. The Cyclades have changed dramatically since I sailed around them twenty years ago. They have now been discovered by cruise ships and by ferry-hopping tourists who crowd the beaches and tavernas during the busy summer season. Another factor making the Cyclades less appealing for sailors is the strong northerly Meltemi wind, the Greek equivalent of the Mistral. To make matters worse, the Meltemi is prevalent during the optimum sailing season from May to September and often reaches gale force, making for very uncomfortable if not dangerous sailing.

For the time being, I plan to stay in the Ionian Islands, which are on the extreme western edge of Greece, due south of Yugoslavia and Albania. They are far less touristy and not affected by Meltemi winds. The main cluster of the Ionians forms a spectacular inland sea, protected from the west by the large islands of Lefkada and Kefallonia, and from the east and north by mainland Greece. Scattered around this inland sea are other islands, including Ulysses' Ithaka, many sheltered coves, some completely landlocked anchorages, and many picturesque fishing villages with protected docks. In 1953, a huge earthquake devastated this area, so most villages had to be completely rebuilt. Only the villages of Fiskardo and Spartochori were miraculously spared.

It is now the beginning of September. I returned to Greece today, invigorated by the exciting prospect of exploring the Ionians for myself during the next two months. It became apparent at the bus station in Athens that I would do well to learn the Greek alphabet if I want to get on the right bus or find a street address. When I was a navy pilot, I learned to translate the Cyrillic alphabet when keeping track of the Russian trawler fleet, poaching fish off the east coast of Canada, so grasping the Greek alphabet should not be difficult. However, I am reluctant to spend the incredible amount of time and effort it takes to master a new language, especially one spoken by less than ten million people - but I will learn enough Greek to appear respectful to the locals.

Because the main industry in Greece is tourism, most people here speak very good English.

After two days of cleaning and polishing Muscade, I asked the boatyard to put her back in the water. As soon as my first guests were settled aboard, we sailed south from Preveza, transited the small canal which separates the island of Lefkada from the mainland and entered the inland sea. Lefkada was originally part of mainland Greece until 600 BC, when the enterprising Corinthians dug the canal, making Lefkada an island and shortening their transit time from Italy to Corinth.

From many points of view, the Ionians are a sailing mecca. I decided early on that I would persuade my guests to dine ashore in the local tavernas whenever we were overnighting near a village. Greek food is one example of the healthy Mediterranean diet presently in vogue. The meals are tasty and so reasonably priced that it is hardly worth the effort of preparing dinner aboard. I have even developed a taste for the white Retsina wine, which pairs extremely well with fish. Ouzo, as an *apéritif*, is a natural progression from my *pastis* habit acquired in Corsica.

Twenty years ago when one ate in Greek tavernas, the custom was to visit the kitchen, inspect the freshness of the produce and order your meal accordingly. This is no longer the case in touristy areas, but the ritual still exists in restaurants catering exclusively to Greek clients. One of my favourite overnight spots has become Abeliki Bay on the Island of Meganisi, where I can anchor in an olive grove, swim in crystal-clear water then stroll to the village of Vathi for dinner.

The two villages untouched by the 1953 earthquake are the most picturesque, as the Italianate architecture goes back to the time of the Venetian occupation. In one of these villages, Spartochori, there is a taverna owned by Panos Konidaris, who has become a friend. His taverna has a private dock, which he lets me use whenever I am visiting this charming village. Generally speaking, the Greeks are a friendly, helpful, and accommodating people.

My last guest of the year was Carmen, who returned for some well-earned island cruising, having helped me deliver *Muscade* to Greece. For obvious reasons, our relationship is far from solid. I am living my dream life in the Greek Islands, and she is working hard for a living in northern Québec and can only join me between contracts. Culturally and literally, we are oceans apart. At the end of October, there will be another referendum on Québec separation. Carmen is a dedicated separatist, and I live in one of the most Anglophone villages in the province and will certainly cast my vote to stay in Canada, the country which has given me everything.

Carmen has come to Greece on her way to Vienna, where she has been subpoenaed to testify as an expert witness in a malpractice suit, related to her previous job in Eastern Europe. She has invited me to accompany her to Austria when our sojourn in Greece is over. With some trepidation, I have agreed to join her and lend my support during the hearing.

Though I have always enjoyed winter holidays in Austria and prefer the *après-ski* ambiance in Arlberg villages to that found in the Swiss or French Alps, Vienna has never been one of my favourite cities. It is certainly clean and beautiful with great opera houses, but I have never felt welcome there. In my early days with Air Canada, I had many layovers in Vienna at the Intercontinental Hotel, often went to performances at the State Opera or the Volks Opera and enjoyed dinners with my crew in cozy restaurants with string quartets playing waltzes in the wings, but I was always ruffled by the formality and austere nature of the burghers. My latest visit did not improve my impressions of Vienna or my relationship with Carmen. Both were unmitigated disasters.

I've never been happy tagging along on somebody else's gig. This was Carmen's show, and she was definitely calling the shots.

We managed to get tickets for *Tosca*, albeit in the nosebleed section, but that was the sole highlight of the visit. During the first intermission, we tried to move to some better seats, but were instantly ordered back to the "gods" by an officious usher who lacked any semblance of humour. After Carmen had finished her testimony, I tried to arrange Air Canada tickets back to Montréal, only to find out that the company no longer flew to Vienna, so we were obliged to take a long train ride to Frankfurt, then fly home from there. Impetuous Carmen was not amused by my nonchalance or by my incompetence. We were barely speaking.

I got back home from Vienna the day before the Québec referendum. Carmen went up to her parents' place in the Laurentians to vote, and I voted in Knowlton. On the evening of voting day, I was weary from the time change and retired early before the results started coming in. Never having owned a television, I would have missed all the drama anyway. I heard the results on CBC radio the following morning. Incredibly, at one stage in the evening, it looked as if the separatists had won, so the "yes" side went wild and started celebrating victory, but when all votes were tabulated, the initial trend was reversed and the "no" side squeaked a narrow win, leaving Canada intact. With a ninety-four per cent voter turnout, the final results were "no," 50.58% and "yes," 49.42%. I was immensely proud of the dignified way that the separatist *Québecois* handled their devastating loss. There was no rioting in the streets, no protest marches, and very little vandalism. What a wonderful example to the rest of the world of how democracy can work. However, in his concession speech, the leader of the "yes" campaign, former Québec premier, Jacques Parizeau, was less conciliatory and begrudgingly blamed the loss on "money and the ethnic vote." Carmen was traumatized by the results and soon afterwards moved her belongings out of my house and unceremoniously dumped me.

I resolved that, if I am ever fortunate enough to meet another woman and am given one more chance at establishing a stable, long lasting relationship, I will take charge of the situation and no longer follow my cowardly, line-of-least-resistance approach. Next time, it will be my turn to take the initiative and choose my companion.

CHAPTER SIXTEEN

THIRTEEN YEARS AS A VAGABOND

I am now fifty-five and in my thirteenth year as a vagabond. My contemporaries at Air Canada have a mere five years to go before they must retire. At a New Year's Eve party, I met a professor from Concordia University in Montréal who invited me to give a guest lecture this winter to his post-graduate class. He left the subject of the lecture up to me, but suggested I might lead a discussion about my alternative lifestyle. I have decided to talk to these media management students about leadership and have already started researching and composing my lecture, which I will deliver in March.

Early in January, I returned to St Lucia to prepare *Le Pat-Mar* for yet another Caribbean winter, but when I had the boat lifted out of the water for routine hull maintenance, I noticed that the rudder had become delaminated. Since it is a major job to rebuild and fit a new rudder on a boat of this size, I have abandoned my sailing plans for this winter. After coordinating the work in the boatyard, I reluctantly returned to Knowlton and winter.

One of my favourite authors is the celebrated Canadian writer, Mordecai Richler, of "*Duddy Kravitz*" fame. A teacher friend of mine, knowing that I admired Mordecai, invited me to an event in Montréal where the writer was to deliver the keynote address. The occasion was the annual convention of the Provincial Association of Protestant Teachers. When the time came for his speech, Mordecai climbed slowly to the podium, disdainfully looked down his nose over his reading glasses at his "WASPy" audience and with impeccable timing said: "Good evening fellow ethnics," which brought the house down. He was referring to the post-referendum comment by Jacques Parizeau blaming the ethnic vote for the referendum defeat.

I am in a reflective mood, once again contemplating what my long-term strategy should be to best manage my remaining years. I have calculated that, if I am lucky enough to stay healthy and miss the usual killer diseases, I have a good chance of living to be eighty-five. Given my parents' ages when they died, this estimate also makes sense genetically, so I can reasonably expect thirty more years. It sounds macabre, but it is important to calculate your life expectancy, otherwise it is difficult to plan your remaining time and finances. I have lots of options, but I'm thinking it might soon be time for another major change. I am already fully committed for this year: working for the local newspaper, preparing my guest lecture, making maple syrup with Peter, skiing in this area and out west, sailing with Jean Milette aboard *Ayacanora* in the Florida Keys, then returning to *Muscade* in Greece for the summer. Next winter will be my first opportunity for a major change.

For some time, I have been considering the idea of going to Guatemala to learn Spanish before travelling around South America for a few years. Hiking in Patagonia, getting to know the wine regions of Chile and Argentina, living in Uruguay for a winter, visiting Machu Picchu in Peru, exploring the Amazon watershed and visiting the Galapagos Islands are some of the alluring possibilities. This plan could dovetail very nicely with more summer cruising in the Mediterranean. I still have many places to explore there: Turkey, Crete, Cyprus, Malta, Yugoslavia, Venice, Tunisia and the Balearic Islands. I would be living an eternal summer with occasional breaks in Knowlton.

Change is in the air, and I am always excited by the prospect of something new. This morning, out of the blue, I woke up with the realization that I am a pilot. I hadn't given a moment's thought to flying since quitting Air Canada and had never intended piloting an aircraft again. However, today I have a strong desire to get back into the air and, more specifically, to become qualified on floatplanes. The problem is that my airline pilot's license has expired, and without many hours of study, I will not be able to pass the written exams for the most basic private pilot's license. This is because airline pilots live in a different regulatory world from private pilots, who are much more hands-on and actually use the air regulations on a daily basis. It has been over thirty years since I have manually prepared a flight plan, so I will have to relearn the basics in every respect. At least my knowledge of meteorology is still valid, and I will have no problem flying the aircraft. I am determined to pursue this idea and qualify as a floatplane pilot.

At the end of May, I went back to *Muscade* in Greece. I still can't believe how lucky I am to have my own beautiful sailing boat based there. In his book "*Lila*," Robert Persig argues that luck has to be dynamic, meaning that you have to be willing to be lucky. If you insist on clinging to static patterns in life, you won't recognize opportunities to be lucky when they arise. He argues that one should stay loose and flexible, so when there is an opportunity to be lucky, you can take full advantage of the situation.

Umberto Eco in his book, "*Foucault's Pendulum,*" elaborates on the same theme, saying that it is easy to miss opportunity, while spending your whole life looking for it. One must seize opportunity instinctively without recognizing it, as any advantage will only be apparent in retrospect. It is all very Zen. The events in this book confirm that having a wide-ranging life, being curious, and accepting as many new challenges as possible all increase your odds of being lucky. I agree with both authors and would add: The flexible will inherit the earth.

One morning, as I was rowing my way back to Muscade in my dinghy, I noticed a large motor yacht anchored in the middle of the main channel near the Ionian town of Nidri. It was an unusual place to anchor, so I stopped to see if I could be of assistance. The owner of the boat, Nikos, was the Fleet Captain for a large Greek shipping company based in New York. He was on vacation at his villa on the nearby island of Ithaka. He was accompanied on the boat by his American son-in-law and a local fisherman called Spiros. His vessel had developed serious engine problems, which, after many hours of trying, our combined expertise had still failed to fix. Nikos naturally wanted to stay aboard his disabled vessel until it was repaired. As there were no more inter-island ferries that day, I volunteered to deliver his crew back to their homes on Ithaka, a two-hour sail for *Muscade*. When we arrived at the port of Vathi, Spiros directed me to a private mooring in front of Nikos's harbour-front house where Nikos's wife and daughter were waiting on the dock to invite us into their home for a delicious dinner. The next morning, we sailed back to Nidri with spare parts and repaired the boat. Subsequently, Captain Nikos and I became friends, and Spiros never failed to give me fresh fish whenever he spotted *Muscade* sailing past his fishing grounds.

In July, while *en route* back to Knowlton, I stayed for a few days in London with my brother Angus and his family. He told me that he was tired of using his buying skills to make money for large department stores. He wants to go into business for himself. Opening some kind of retail shop in England is a possibility as is a move back to Canada where he was born during our father's posting there in the Fifties. He has always valued his Canadian citizenship and maintains a Canadian passport. Buyers for large department stores make important worldwide contacts and can become powerful agents in their own right, so management tends to mitigate this influence by moving them around to different departments. This policy means that Angus has expertise in many different retail fields.

I am not a believer in coincidences, nor do I think that some things are "meant to be." Certainly the law of averages allows events to occur that might seem like coincidences. If someone takes the New York subway to work every day while his old school friend, who now lives in Japan, occasionally uses the subway when visiting New York, there is a miniscule probability that they might bump into each other someday. If they never meet, no story will materialize, but if they do eventually spot each other, it becomes a huge event, written into their family mythologies. We tend to call such a meeting an "amazing coincidence," but it's really just the law of probabilities. For every million or so non-events, there may be one occurrence which makes for an interesting story.

In spite of the above proposition, I was astonished when I received a phone call at home from Marie Lussier, just days after my conversation with my brother about a career change. The timing was uncanny, and that is why I have a story to tell. (Marie is the former wife of André Lussier, who used to own *La Brunante)*. Marie owns a large wholesale company in Montréal, which imports textiles for home decoration. She remembered, from talking to me many years ago, that my brother was an expert in fine fabrics, and she wants to offer him a partnership in her business. She feels that she is getting too old to manage everything herself, is concerned about Québec separatist politics and is looking for someone to expand her business to Toronto. I phoned Angus right away, and several days later, he showed up in Knowlton.

After his first meeting with Marie, Angus determined that a partnership would not work. He gave her some free advice and put her in touch with some of his contacts in India, but he declined her generous offer to become a business partner. I think their age difference was a factor in his decision, and he didn't really want to move his family to Toronto. Undaunted, he scouted around to see what other potential business opportunities existed in eastern Canada. Being an expert in hand-knotted Oriental carpets, he immediately saw an opening in that field. He calculated that with his tremendous buying power and solid contacts in all the world's major carpet-making countries, he could undercut current Canadian prices by about fifty per cent and still make a reasonable profit. The next step was to bring his wife, Maria, to Canada to explore the prospects of such a radical move, and to choose a location for their new carpet shop.

On this warm August evening, Angus, Maria and I are celebrating over dinner at a terrace restaurant in Ottawa's By-Ward market. Angus has just signed a lease on an empty shop in this same historic quarter. In a few months, it will be transformed into the home of Canadian Rug Traders. Angus decided that Montréal was too big and unmanageable for his intended business and initially thought that Kingston might be a good alternative. *Feng shui* may have influenced that choice, because his family had been living happily in a town of the same name in England. However, when we visited Kingston, Ontario and looked at possible shop locations, it became obvious that it was far from ideal. The town's population was too small to have the critical mass needed for a retail carpet business, so the "Goldilocks" choice became Ottawa.

Now that Angus has signed the lease, he is concentrating all his energy on starting the new enterprise. He is obviously thrilled to be moving back to Canada, insists that the business be called Canadian Rug Traders and that the company logo should be the Canadian flag in the shape of a carpet. Angus and Maria intend to sell their house in London and move to Ottawa next January. Their two daughters are automatically Canadian citizens by virtue of their father's nationality, and Maria will apply for her citizenship. I am delighted with the prospect of having family members living in Canada and will do everything I can to facilitate their move.

During the evening, I couldn't help noticing an element of uncertainty in the conversation as Angus and Maria discussed their plans for the future. Finally, Maria raised the subject by asking me, a little tentatively, if I would consider joining them as a partner in Canadian Rug Traders. I was not entirely surprised by her offer, but was taken aback by my immediate, positive reaction. The timing could not have been better for me. After twelve years of roaming around the world, I had been looking for a change of direction. *Muscade* was safely harboured in an excellent location leaving me completely free to start a new life as a businessman. I told Angus and Maria that I would happily join them and would donate a year of my time to the new company before reassessing any future involvement. Their relief was palpable, and our evening celebration took on new meaning, now that the planning and dreaming involved all three of us. To solidify my commitment, I agreed to invest all the money I had inherited from my parents' estate in the business. We have to be completely self-financed because, in spite of our excellent business plan, no Canadian bank will lend us any startup capital. Ironically, most banks only lend money to businesses when they no longer need it.

By the end of the evening, we had formulated a plan of action. Angus and Maria will go back to London, put their house on the market and tidy up their affairs. Angus will then go to Iran, buy the carpets needed for our initial stock and ship them to Ottawa. He will resign from his job, reclaim the carpets he has out on concession with a British auction house and add them to our stock. I will return to Greece, finish off the season with my invited guests then join Angus in Turkey, where I will get my first lesson in carpet buying. After that trip, we will go to India and Pakistan together, where I will be introduced to all the players and continue my apprenticeship. In November, Angus and I will take possession of our shop, on Ottawa's Clarence Street, and complete the renovations in time for a January 1997 opening.

It wasn't until I was back aboard *Muscade*, sailing with friends in the Ionian Islands, that the full significance of my decision to move to Ottawa finally sank in. I had left that city almost forty years before to attend Naval College - with no intention of ever returning. Now destiny has brought me full circle. I am perfectly comfortable with yet another lifestyle change and am very excited about this new challenge. The prospect of contributing the sum total of my life experience to starting this family enterprise is quite compelling. There is very little overlap in the types of expertise that the three of us are bringing to Canadian Rug Traders, and this bodes well for a successful outcome. Angus is an expert retailer, accomplished buyer and is well-versed in computer technology. Maria, with her considerable experience in banking, will set up the office administration. My initial contributions will be in public relations and communications, and I will eventually become the company's buyer. My French-speaking skills will be essential, and I will be able to help smooth the transition and facilitate my family's move to Canada. Angus, my younger brother by thirteen years, will be in charge, and I will happily work under his leadership.

The "old enchanter" has offered me yet another opportunity, and I have eagerly seized it as my mantra continues to echo:

"What if the spell of a place falls upon a youthful heart, and the bright horizon calls? Many a thing will keep until the world's work is done, and youth is only a memory. When the old enchanter came to my door laden with dreams, I reached out with both hands for I knew, he would not be lured with the gold that I might later offer, when age had come upon me."

I now understand that the basic philosophy espoused by the "old enchanter," as well as other similar sentiments, lie dormant in every one of us. Socrates concluded that some version of this spirit resides in us, taking the form of our psyche, or soul, or inner voice. For some reason, thirteen years ago, I listened to that voice and implicitly trusted what it was telling me. Socrates believed that both peace of mind and altruistic behaviour come from within and that our psyche is the inner source of such altruism and contentment. My experiences, as related in this book, compel me to endorse that idea. The huge question is: How can the altruistic sentiments which lie dormant in each of our psyches, be awakened and subsequently incorporated into our every day routines, allowing happiness, peace of mind, courage, justice, decency, and moral responsibility to flourish?

Afterthoughts

JANUARY 2017

I am sitting at my desk in our Manhattan apartment reminiscing about life and trying to get my thoughts on paper. There is so much to recount. Twenty exciting years have rushed by at breakneck speed since the "old enchanter" offered me the chance to collaborate with my brother on our Persian carpet business in Ottawa. That move was certainly propitious. It changed the whole orientation of my existence and introduced me to a panoply of previously unknown and undiscovered worlds, which have added enormous depth and scope to my life and have contributed to that same mountain of new experiences, which began to take shape thirty-four years ago when I quit my airline career on a leap of faith. I am now seventy-six and, *inshallah,* have about ten more years to live. Even though neither my zest for life nor my curiosity for new adventures, have abated, I am resisting the temptation of being too greedy for more. Surely it is better to be grateful for the life I have lived, for the people I have had the privilege of meeting, for the friends I have made, and for the good fortune which has allowed me to make it this far. Whenever I get frustrated with the realization that my life cannot last forever, I recall the times that I came within a hair's breadth of being killed. Then I take a deep breath and contentedly carry on with my day with renewed enthusiasm for being alive. Although I know that it is impossible, the utopian ideal would be to lock in my present circumstances for an eternity. The realization that this cannot be done makes life even more precarious and precious.

I have concluded after a lifetime of observation that no one is ever unequivocally qualified for the job they are supposed to be doing. Robots are always able to complete a programmed task perfectly, but all mere mortals make mistakes and risk having subjective interpretations or emotional events cloud their judgment and impede their ability to perform adequately. We are really all amateurs striving to do our best while pretending to be experts in our particular field in order to maintain credibility, inspire confidence, and justify our hard-earned and well-paid positions in life, without appearing incompetent. There are very few exceptions. Furthermore, the unjust system of wealth distribution encourages us to behave as if we actually deserve our monetary compensations.

A doctor feels obliged to offer a diagnosis even if unsure of his patient's malady. A lawyer must convince his client that he can win, even though each court case has a winner and a loser. An airline pilot cannot announce to his passengers that he has no clue what is wrong with his aircraft. Politicians risk not being re-elected if they appear intransigent on policy issues. Opera singers miss notes, actors forget lines, scientists falsify research data, plumbers connect pipes backwards, judges punish innocent people, and policemen commit crimes. The more difficult the task, the greater the potential for mistakes, and the more dire the consequences. Life is a facade and so-called expertise is often nothing more than "smoke and mirrors."

However, help is on the way, as new technologies promise to reduce the incidence of the "smoke and mirrors" phenomenon.

Quantum computers, sophisticated robotics, artificial intelligence and artificial intuition are all poised to eliminate human errors and frailties. Self-driving cars and trucks will make our highways safer, precluding the need for traffic police and car insurance as well as reducing the workload for hospital emergency workers. Pilotless aircraft will soon follow, when the travelling public gets used to the concept. For the last twenty years, autopilots coupled to ground guidance systems have been landing aircraft safely in zero visibility, an impossible feat for human pilots who need to see the runway to effect a landing.

We humans come in an infinite variety of shapes and sizes. We have different intelligent quotients, skin pigmentations, hair and eye colours, sexual orientations and genetic makeups. However, we do have one common denominator: we are all mere mortals. The major differentiator, which many find hard to accept, is the accident of birth. Where we were born, the social circumstances of our parents, as well as the genes we inherit determine to a very large extent how our lives will play out. This is sometimes referred to as "the hand we are dealt," and suggests that there's not much room to manoeuver once we have left the womb, so we should not be too smug or proud of our accomplishments or successes.

When the Aryans invaded India over three thousand years ago, they introduced a caste system which established a pecking order among their conquered subjects. While this hierarchy was originally based on job description it quickly morphed into a classification by accident of birth and eventually led to the creation of hundreds of different castes. Mere mortals, like chickens, have an intrinsic desire to know where they stand in the pecking order of their societies. We strive for ways to move up the ladder although, in India, the only way to change your caste under the Aryan-imposed system was by the cycle of reincarnation.

Today, in the developed world, there is a well-defined caste system based on wealth accumulation, which has been evolving since the Industrial Revolution and the colonization of North America. It has almost completely displaced the previous aristocratic class system, which was based on feudal power and birthright. In the classification by wealth system, "old money" is considered to be more respectable than recently acquired money, because the way it was amassed is more difficult to trace. In both cases, net worth is king.

Strangely, even though we are all mere mortals, we often worship and give the largest monetary rewards to: mere mortals who excel in professional sports; mere mortals who are performers on the stage or screen; mere mortals who have inherited royal titles (a throwback to feudal systems in England, Japan, Scandinavia, Tonga et al); mere mortals who have reached the upper echelons of their religious order (popes, ayatollahs, cardinals et al); and mere mortals who have clawed their way to the top of their country's political hierarchy. In the aristocratic, feudal system, military power led to accumulated wealth. In our present system, accumulated wealth leads to political power.

Canadian Rug Traders

Twenty years ago, when we were preparing to open the shop, everyone told us that Canadian Rug Traders didn't have a hope of succeeding, a sentiment I didn't find reassuring, having invested all of my inheritance and my life savings in the business. This negativity was based on the reality that there were already two well-established carpet retailers in Ottawa. In addition, the already small critical mass of potential customers was being further diluted by travelling carpet companies which rolled into town every couple of weeks. These outfits would rent a ballroom in one of the prominent downtown hotels, where they would auction off their wares. Their sales hook, as advertised in the local newspapers, was that the carpets they were selling had been "seized by Canadian customs due to the embargo on Iranian goods." It was false advertising, as there was no such embargo in Canada. In fact, Angus and I bought and imported carpets from Iran on a regular basis. Moreover, not only was there no embargo, there was no import duty either.

Like most auctions, these sales were completely rigged against the buyer. The advertised value of each carpet was highly inflated, and bidders were told that there was no reserve (minimum price) to prevent them from getting fantastic bargains. However, the auctioneers easily dodged this policy by imbedding their own bidders in the audience to push up selling prices. These planted individuals would also make the closing bid on any carpet deemed to be selling too cheaply, effectively establishing a minimum-selling price. We would often see these same carpets back on the block at future auctions. Another of their tricks was to advertise that a carpet was made of silk, when it was actually made of mercerized cotton. It did not take us long to get to know these shady players because, whenever they were in town, they would come into our shop to browse, evaluate our prices and inspect our merchandise. Chatting away in Farsi, they seemed to realize that our low prices would force them to change their Ottawa auction strategy. The first time they visited our shop, I wished them, "goodbye and have a nice day" in their own language as they were leaving. Thinking that I understood Farsi, they were visibly shaken and always conversed in hushed tones on subsequent visits. Ironically, these auctions eventually helped our business: our customers came to realize that not only did we have far better prices, but that we fully guaranteed our products and would take our carpets back on exchange at any time. The frequency of these auctions gradually diminished and finally ceased.

Auctions take advantage of the frailty of human nature by encouraging competition between buyers, making them bid more than the item is worth or more than they had ever expected to pay in order to avoid losing face to another bidder. Sales are, by design, final and irrevocable, as the auctioneer does not want to deal with the inevitable "buyer's remorse." The fast pace of bidding and the hypnotic chatter used by auctioneers add to the drama, insinuate urgency, and destabilize bidders. Finally, there is a misconception that auctions deliver great bargains. The lesson for the consumer is to be very wary of auctions. If the deal is too good to be true, it's probably a bad deal.

Apart from the travelling shows, we had two major competitors in Ottawa: a high-end Persian company, The Sussex Rug Gallery, catering to an almost non-existent, luxury market, and a Montréal based company, Raymond and Heller, which sold more or less the same stock we did, but for much higher prices than ours. These carpet sellers treated us as an unfortunate irritation, until they realized that our low prices were going to be an existential threat. The fact that we had large, easy-to-read price tags on every carpet was a novelty in a selling environment that often determines the asking price by assessing the customers' ability to pay. Raymond and Heller was the first to go under. They neglected to match our prices, giving us a huge competitive edge. We soon convinced their manager and his brother to join our sales staff, and they were instrumental in spurring our early successes. Eventually, the other shop closed its doors and, apart from a couple of very small players, we had a virtual monopoly. Now that we had cornered the Ottawa market, our focus shifted to the rest of North America. Happily, my investment was secure.

Our business plan was to undercut the North American market by fifty percent and, at the same time, expose the ridiculous myths about hand-made carpets that have been perpetuated by dishonest dealers and used to justify outrageous prices ever since the time of Ali Baba and his forty thieves. We were able to execute this plan because Angus had established close personal ties with his suppliers in most of the countries producing hand-knotted rugs: Iran, Turkey, India, Pakistan, Nepal and Afghanistan. When he was the carpet buyer for several large London department stores, he had opened up the British market to these suppliers, helping them to make their fortunes. These individuals had subsequently become friends and had a vested interest in helping us to succeed. By purchasing our stock directly from these rug makers, we eliminated the wholesalers, both in Canada and in the countries of origin, and were able to undercut the competition and pass on the savings directly to our customers.

We were also well aware that a huge under-current of mistrust enveloped the entire Persian carpet business. In France, one of the worst insults is to call someone *un vendeur de tapis* (the equivalent of a used car salesman in North America). Our first priority was to win the trust of the community, and become recognized as fair and honest traders. Sad to say, but true nonetheless, racism played its part. The fact that Angus and I were of Celtic heritage gave us an immediate advantage over our Iranian competition in Ottawa, Montréal, and Toronto, including the bandits who ran the auctions.

Trust breeds trust, so we instituted a policy which allowed customers to take carpets home on trial before committing to buying them or returning them to our shop. Many carpet shops offer a similar service, but we imposed absolutely no obligations. No credit card information or down payment was required until the carpets were actually bought. We did not discriminate against any customer or put any restrictions on this policy. All we required was a name, phone number, and address (no official ID), before loading up the client's car with their selected carpets. This policy proved to be very popular and helped us win the confidence of the community.

We also understood that carpet shops can be somewhat intimidating, so went out of our way to make the experience of finding and buying the right carpet as easy and enjoyable as possible. We instructed our sales staff to let customers browse and not interact with them except when specifically asked a question. There was to be no "hard selling," only helpful explanations and design consultations. We paid our staff fair salaries and benefits, rather than giving them a commission on sales, so they had no incentive to harass the customers.

The high incidence of child labour in the carpet-making industry was another huge preoccupation for us and a grave concern for many customers. Fortunately, Angus had pre-empted this potential problem by joining an organization called, "Child Care and Fair." Members of this charity, founded and administered by the Baha'i faith in India and Germany, include carpet makers, wholesalers, and retailers. Members at each of these three levels forward a percentage of their sales to the charity for the benefit of the carpet workers and their families. The charity monitors its members to make sure they are not exploiting children. Apart from our purchases in Iran, where child labour is not tolerated, we bought our carpets exclusively from members of "Child Care and Fair." However, we could never give an absolute guarantee to our customers that no child labour was involved in making the carpets we were selling. There were always moral questions such as: what defines a child in the "developing world?" The entire question of moral relativity in this respect is extremely important and also encompasses the exploitation of women, but it is well beyond the scope of this book. Suffice it to say, we were always on the lookout for child workers during our buying trips and consciously avoided any unscrupulous manufacturers.

When I agreed to join Angus in his business venture, I promised him a year of my time before deciding on any future involvement. We did not pay ourselves salaries, although we did allow for reasonable expense accounts, which we used to promote the business. As I was not expecting to stay for the long haul, I rented a room in our accountant's house in nearby Gatineau, keeping my house in Knowlton as a welcome refuge on days off and reuniting with *Muscade* in the Greek Islands during longer holidays. After a slow start, during which we adjusted our stock to meet the demands of the Ottawa market, sales took off. My transition from *bohème* to "capitalist pig" had begun, as I discovered that having your own business, especially a successful one, came with a lot of perks. I was hooked by our steady progress and definitely on my way to a new career.

After three months, Angus was confident enough in my abilities to send me off alone on a buying trip to India, Pakistan and Afghanistan. What an adventure, and what a change from my former mode of travel! No more stand-by airline travel and three dollar a night guesthouses; from now on, it was first class all the way.

I was met at the airport in Delhi by a private chauffeur and whisked off to my comfortable hotel in the diplomatic compound. Everything was arranged: airline reservations, hotels and buying appointments with various suppliers. Our agent handled everything adroitly. Sold-out hotels or over-booked flights presented no problem to our man in India. He was always able to work the system to our advantage and jump the queue whenever necessary.

In the carpet-making town of Bhadohi, in northern India, I was housed in luxurious comfort at the home of our agent. Each evening, after a long and dusty day's buying, we would meet on the tranquil roof garden of his home for a delicious dinner under the stars, accompanied by interesting philosophical discussions. Even though our backgrounds could not have been more different, we had remarkably similar views on most world issues. However, I never glimpsed his wife or daughters in that strict Muslim household, nor quaffed anything stronger than a yoghurt lassi or a glass of pomegranate juice.

In Bhadohi, I would begin my daily exercise routine at six a.m. by taking a long walk through the impoverished village. At that time of the morning, families were clustered around open wood fires, cooking their *chapatis* and brewing *chai* for breakfast. Sacred cows rummaged through garbage piles looking for their first meal of the day. I felt perfectly safe and was never threatened. Without exception, I would receive a polite *Namaste* from each group as I passed by, and not one person begged. Later that day, I bought an entire collection of William Morris "Arts and Crafts" design carpets, which had been recently commissioned to commemorate the hundredth anniversary of that designer's death. These proved to be very popular in Ottawa, where the houses lent themselves to this particular style, and consequently gave us a huge surge in sales.

In the sacred city of Benares, I stayed with Hamid, our Iranian-born agent, and his family. They were Baha'i and had fled to India to escape persecution in Iran after the revolution in the late seventies. Hamid's wife was a superb cook and every evening she would treat me to a variety of delicious Persian dishes, served with handfuls of fresh herbs. I bought a large shipment of Gabbeh carpets (thick-piled, primitive tribal rugs), which were becoming very fashionable in Canada. The Swedish company, IKEA, had over-ordered from my agent, so I acquired their surplus carpets for a very good price. One morning before sunrise, Hamid arranged for a private boat to take me out on the Ganges while hundreds of Hindu pilgrims bathed in the sacred river. I felt very privileged to witness this ancient religious tradition, but felt no inclination to join them in that highly polluted water, one drop of which would probably have precipitated my demise.

Carpet making in India is mostly confined to the northern part of the country, where the Moguls introduced the art form after they invaded the region in the twelfth century. Their influence was greatest in the northern part of India, so that's where most carpets are still made today. My buying trips routinely took me to Delhi, Agra, Jaipur, Benares and Bhadohi. Kashmir is famous for its beautiful silk rugs, but these were expensive and not popular in Ottawa. Nor were traditional Persian carpets popular, the ones that graced our grandmothers' parlours with vivid coloured flowers and central medallions. We soon learned that Canadians preferred softer, vegetable dye pastels and overall patterns, and it was my job to buy what the marketplace demanded. As a buyer, I had to be very careful not to let my personal preferences influence my selections. I always tried hard to stay completely unbiased by choosing enough variety of colours and designs to please all tastes. Often, the carpets which I liked least were the first to sell in our shop.

After completing my purchases in the north of India, I returned to Delhi to have dinner at the Royal Delhi Golf Club as a guest of Vyas, who had hosted my family many years before at the Diwali festival. I was amused to observe that colonial attitudes and conventions still prevailed. Wealthy Indian club members had displaced the long departed British Raj, but treated the staff with the same pretension and disdain.

Early the next morning, I boarded a flight to Lahore in Pakistan. Even though India and Pakistan were at war over disputed territory in Kashmir, Pakistan International Airlines was allowed to operate one flight a day between the two countries. I was welcomed at the airport in Lahore by Usman, our Pakistani agent, who drove me to the Pearl Intercontinental Hotel and briefed me on our buying schedule. Usman specialized in Bokhara carpets, which we considered to be a starter rug for homeowners who were beginning to take an interest in hand-made rugs. They are easily identified by their geometric designs based on Mogul tribal symbols. There are millions of carpet-making looms in private dwellings in Pakistan, so it is a "cottage industry" in the true sense of the word. Usman had hundreds of people working for him. Typically, he would contract with a family to make a carpet of a certain size, design and colour, then provide the artisan with the exact amount of wool needed for the job. The number of knots per square inch would be specified, and the finished product carefully checked to ensure compliance. It was a cat-and-mouse game between the artisan and the agent. The artisan would try to use less wool than specified, so that any surplus wool could be secreted away and later used to make another carpet, which could then be sold on the open market. The agent would inspect the finished carpet by performing random knot counts to ensure that quality was up-to-par. I bought hundreds of these popular Bokhara carpets in all sizes and colours.

I then flew with Usman to Peshawar in search of Afghan carpets and Belouchi tribal prayer rugs. Peshawar is located at the Pakistani end of the Khyber Pass on the Afghan border and serves as a distribution point for many Afghan goods. Given the on-going war against the Taliban, most places in Afghanistan (except Kabul) were inaccessible to people like me. Usman's bother-in-law happened to be the Colonel in charge of the Khyber Rifles - the regiment guarding the pass - so we were invited to lunch in the officer's mess at the summit of the pass, before we drove down into Jalalabad in a jeep with an armed escort to buy a selection of carpets in the bazaar.

The following day, I almost caused a diplomatic incident while attempting to buy Belouchi tribal prayer rugs from an aged Haji dealer in Peshawar. A Haji is someone who has completed the obligatory pilgrimage (The Haj) to Mecca. Usman did all the bargaining in Urdu before my selection began, and didn't fully explain to me the terms of his negotiation. I later found out that the Haji was doing Usman a favour by agreeing to let me buy three hundred prayer rugs from one specific stack of about six hundred carpets. He was offering me the same low price per carpet that he charged T.J. Maxx the discount department store chain in the

United States. Usman failed to tell me that the Haji had insisted that I could only have one look at the carpets, so he was expecting me to make all my choices on the first run through the stack. As the workers started to throw down the carpets from the pile for my inspection, I casually picked the cream of the crop, unaware of any restriction. After I had seen the entire pile, I had only chosen about one hundred and fifty carpets, so blithely asked for a second look. The Haji went ballistic. He was furious because I now knew exactly what was in the pile, so he had lost his advantage. He reluctantly agreed to let me continue, and I completed my selection, getting the best three hundred carpets in the stack. After Usman explained to the Haji that I was a friend from Canada on my first buying trip, he calmed down considerably and offered us tea and sweetmeats. It was then I discovered that his English was pretty good. We parted friends.

Contrary to what one might think, there is very little price haggling between suppliers and commercial buyers like me. Carpets are traded much like any other commodity, and both sides of the trade know the current price per square foot for a given type and quality of carpet. In Pakistan, I agreed with Usman on a price per square foot for 10/20 quality (200 double knots per square inch) Bokhara carpets, then made my selection from hundreds of samples, piled high on the floor of his warehouse. It was my job to notice any faults, repairs in the weaving, or other damage and to ensure that each carpet lay completely flat on the floor before indicating my approval by giving a thumbs-up to the boys flipping the carpets. If the light in the warehouse was too dim - as it often was - I would insist on seeing the rugs outside in full daylight. When I was done, Usman simply measured the total square footage of my selected carpets and charged me the agreed amount.

When buying in the bazaar, things were a little different because the quality and style of the carpets varied from stall to stall.

Here I had to bargain, and Usman helped me to get the best price for each carpet. I was aware that even though Usman was acting as my agent, he would be getting a "kick-back" on every carpet that I purchased in the bazaar. This is the reality of doing business in this part of the world: everyone gets a piece of the action. This is yet another issue in the moral relativity discussion. One man's idea of corruption can be another man's perfectly legitimate business practice. At the very least, there was no hypocrisy. Angus had briefed me that in any bargaining situation, it was far more effective to use an emotional argument rather than a practical one, as it is more difficult to counter. I told Usman that if he noticed I was buying a flawed carpet or one that was overpriced, he should point it out to me: otherwise Angus would be furious and never forgive him. There is no practical rebuttal to that argument.

Readers may be wondering how someone as inexperienced as I could become a fairly competent carpet buyer in such a short period of time (smoke and mirrors, perhaps?). First of all, it was not a complicated or difficult learning process, and secondly, Angus had given me a very good apprenticeship. I had learned the following: A hand-knotted Persian or Oriental carpet is simply a series of individual knots assembled on the warp strings of a vertical loom. The warp threads are usually made of cotton but can also be wool or silk. When a row of knots has been completed, a weft thread is woven through the warp threads to lock the knots in place before the next row is added. The artisan follows a design, illustrated on a piece of graph paper, and inserts the knots accordingly (i.e. three red knots, two white knots, six blue knots, etc.).

The quality, and hence the price, of a carpet is determined by the following: the number of knots per square inch, the materials used (wool, silk, cotton), the type and the colourfastness of the dyes (natural or synthetic), the intricacy of design, the workmanship, the quality of the washing and finishing, and finally, the overall intrinsic "look." Anyone can easily determine the number of knots per square inch by examining the underside of a carpet, counting the number of knots in a measured inch, and squaring that number. The fact that I was buying specifically for Canadian Rug Traders made my job much easier than had I been buying for a more diverse market. The correct buying price was essential to our business plan of undercutting the North American market, so I had to leave many stunning carpets in the bazaar because, being too expensive for our clientele, they would never have sold. Before buying any carpet, I had to mentally calculate whether the selling price in Ottawa would fit our business model and still enable us to make a profit. Similarly, I only bought the designs and colours that I knew were popular with our customers.

Of course, there were always exceptions to the above rules. I had to be open-minded enough to try new designs and colours and I also bought a few more expensive carpets to offer choice and to push the sales envelope. We had to follow the latest fashion trends for interior design and not get stuck with carpets or colours that were going out of style. As our customer base expanded to other parts of North America, the buying criteria became more sophisticated. My airline and naval pilot training in rapid decision-making certainly helped me to make my selections quickly and confidently, and I was able to buy enough carpets to fill a forty-foot shipping container in under a week. Carpet buying is not for procrastinators: instinct is essential, as there is no time to deliberate over each piece.

In Iran, carpets are usually named after the city, town or village where they were made: Maschad, Isfahan, Qum, Nain, Tabriz, etc. The name does not necessarily imply quality or value. You can have a very ordinary commercial grade Tabriz worth only a few hundred dollars or a Tabriz Mahi, one with four hundred knots per square inch and silk highlights, worth thousands. Hamadan is a market town in Iran where one can buy carpets made in the surrounding villages. Even though buyers like me can tell from the design motifs the specific village of origin, these carpets are generally sold as Hamadans. Various nomadic tribes using portable horizontal looms were the original crafters of hand-knotted carpets. Carpets as well as clothing, bedding, storage bags, animal trappings and tent straps are still made by tribal women as part of their culture, usually for their own use, but also to trade in the bazaar. In Iran, the largest nomadic group that still carries on this tradition is the Qashqai tribe. Their carpets are usually sold in the market town of Shiraz and are known by that name. This area is also where the original Shiraz grape variety was cultivated. Yet another of life's ironies.

A good artisan can tie about 6000 knots a day. This means that an eight by ten foot, average quality Bokhara carpet having 200 knots per square inch would take one person three hundred and eighty days to make (2,300,000 knots). If that person was paid a fair minimum wage of fifteen dollars an hour, the labour cost alone would be $46,000, and that's just for the knotting. When the finished carpet is removed from the loom, it still has to be sheared (to make all the nap fibers the same length), washed (to bring out the luster), and finished. The finishing consists of removing all the weft knots, as it would be impossible to have one continuous weft thread for an entire carpet. Now the price of the wool has to be considered. The best wool for carpet making comes from Merino sheep, so most of the wool used in India and Pakistan comes from Australia, New Zealand or Argentina, where these sheep are bred. The raw wool fleeces are imported in bulk and are washed, carded, spun, and dyed by the carpet makers. Wool is not expensive. When I was a farmer, I got three dollars a fleece. Still, given a reasonable minimum wage, the above-mentioned carpet would cost at least $50,000 to make in the "western world." Herein lies the contradiction. Today, I can buy a similar carpet in Pakistan for $1000.

It is not difficult to see that as labour costs rise in the "developing world," products such as hand-made carpets will become unaffordable and the industry will collapse. The above example is biased towards the low side because a carpet with 200 knots per square inch is not a particularly fine carpet. 400 knots per square inch would be getting into the fine category and would cost twice as much to make. High-end silk carpets can have as many as 2500 knots per square inch. This kind of labour exploitation is by no means limited to the carpet industry. It applies in the same ratios to any hand-made item from the "developing world," and especially to anything related to clothing, shoes, towels, linens, leather goods and jewelry.

Anyone having any knowledge of how things work in most Muslim countries knows that alcohol use, although illegal, is common among the wealthier, westernized classes. Psychologists would probably confirm that the closeting and subjugation of women in these same societies tends to encourage prostitution, which is also rampant. In Pakistan, most luxury hotels permit foreign nationals to order alcohol from room service, but in the Pearl hotel in Peshawar (since destroyed by the Taliban) there was actually a public bar on the top floor. Here, guests who presented foreign passports could order beer or other alcoholic drinks, which were made in Pakistan (go figure that one out). Suppliers often came to my room for a "cold one" after a long, dusty day in the bazaar. One evening during a private dinner party at my agent's home, after I quipped that the only thing missing was an '82 Château Petrus, it wasn't long before my host produced a very drinkable Bordeaux from his cellar.

These experiences reminded me of my time spent on U.S. Navy aircraft carriers, including the *USS Intrepid*, now a museum in New York harbour. Alcohol is not permitted aboard any U.S. Navy ship, but we Canadians would joke that the only thing "dry" about their ships was the Martini. A toast to mankind's ineffable ability to defy the rules! However, drinking surreptitiously out of a paper cup in someone's cabin hardly compared with life aboard our Canadian aircraft carrier, where we dressed for dinner every night, had drinks beforehand and access to a good wine cellar.

Buyer beware! Until I got involved with Canadian Rug Traders, I was just another gullible consumer who knew none of the tricks of the retail business. Here is the inside story: The secret to any retailer's success starts with buying goods of the highest possible quality at the lowest possible price, then marking them up drastically to make huge profits. Exclusivity is a big factor, sought after and exploited by high-end retailers. If your shop is the only one selling a coveted, unique item, you have a huge sales advantage. If nobody knows what that item is really worth, that's another plus for the retailer, as customers cannot compare prices and determine value. Certain products are very difficult for the average person to evaluate and unscrupulous retailers exploit this advantage. Among the worst offenders are jewelry stores (where items are often sold for ten times their assayed value), antique shops of all description, brand-name *haute couture* fashion houses, high-end women's handbag shops, luxury watch dealers, fine art dealers, and top quality Persian carpet traders. These enterprises are some of the major exploiters of the exorbitant mark-up system.

The dilemma for consumers is their inability to determine a fair market price for an item they covet and wish to possess. Usually, the only resort is to pay the asking price. One solution to this unfair method of pricing is the barter system, which still exists in many, if not most, parts of the world. One of my Indian suppliers once asked me, "Why God created Englishmen?" and answered, "because somebody has to pay full price." That quip reminded me of my first encounter with this alternative method to fixed prices. I was in Nepal walking through a Tibetan refugee camp when I stopped to buy a couple of silver bracelets from a roadside seller. In spite of the ridiculously low price, the seller appeared to be insulted when I tried to hand over the cash without asking for a better deal. He refused my money and proceeded to give me a lesson in bartering technique.

He explained that he had the initial advantage, as he knew the fair retail value of the bracelet and how much it had cost him. I did not have the slightest idea, so it was impossible for me to determine how much the bracelet was worth. He explained that my limited advantages were twofold: I could walk away from the deal altogether, or I could limit my offer to the pre-determined maximum price that I was willing or could afford to pay. Bargaining is a serious business and must always be conducted in good faith. All verbal offers must be honoured. Any seller, unless desperate or unless supply far outweighs demand, will want to double his initial investment, so must begin by asking more than he wants in order to leave room to backtrack to that amount. Understanding this rationale gives the buyer a starting point. If an item costs ten dollars and the seller wants to get at least twenty dollars, then he has to begin by asking more than that amount. Calculating how much more is the tricky part, which the buyer must guess. But it can be an educated guess based on circumstances: How desperate does the seller appear, what does his body language suggest, what are his reactions to offers once the haggling has begun? The barter method is an acquired art for both buyer and seller, and the ideal outcome occurs when both are satisfied.

Whenever customers who were planning a holiday in Turkey, India, Iran, Morocco, etc. dropped into our shop to ask me the best way to bargain for a carpet, I would suggest that they should never pay more than half of the asking price.

At Canadian Rug Traders we did not bargain with customers, as we were confident that our prices were unbeatable anywhere in the Americas or in Europe, often being half those of our competitors. It is a fool's game to bargain in a fixed price retail environment because, if you give a discount to one customer, the word will quickly spread and everyone will ask for the same deal. Our policy did not prevent people from trying to haggle with us for a lower price, nor did we blame them or feel insulted. It seems to go with the territory when one is buying items such as antiques, used cars, artwork, or Persian carpets. Bartering is cultural, so for our customers from the Middle East or other countries where this method was the normal way of doing business, it was often seen as a loss of face to accept any asking price, no matter how inexpensive. Ironically, many retail shops, even expensive ones like Harrods, will entertain offers on large ticket items. In these cases, the bargain hunter must speak directly to the buyer, as he/she is the only one with the discretion to adjust the price.

The good news for all consumers and the bad news for unscrupulous retailers is that the Internet has become a very effective price leveler for most products. As I write, there is a revolution occurring in the way we buy goods and services in the developed world. On-line sales are increasing exponentially, while traditional retail outlets and shopping malls are facing extinction. Prices for most items, both new and used, are transparent and easily researched. On-line auction sites can sometimes lead to great bargains, but "buyer beware" still applies, as there are still some fraudulent web sites where products are extremely overpriced.

Opera Act One

As my commitment to Canadian Rug Traders became more solid, and the possibility of staying in Ottawa for an extended period became more likely, I began to think about ways I could give something back to the community. We were often solicited by various charities to donate small carpets for door prizes or auction items, and rarely refused. Angus shared my philanthropic bent, which was not entirely unselfish, as these gifts were good public relations and marketing strategies. One day, the Chairman of the

Ottawa opera company, Opera Lyra, came into the shop to ask if we would consider donating to a fundraising gala. This was the opportunity I had been waiting for and I gladly donated a room-size Persian Kashan carpet for his auction, plus smaller Gabbeh rugs as prizes for each gala table. He was surprised by my enthusiasm and came back several days later to invite Angus, Maria and me to join his table at the black-tie event. This marked the beginning of my twenty-year-long association with Opera Lyra.

At the gala auction, I purchased a supernumerary role in Opera Lyra's next opera, Tosca, which was to be performed at the National Arts Centre in Ottawa. Several weeks later, when I showed up for the first rehearsal, the stage director assigned me the role of the Cardinal of Rome, undoubtedly because I was tall, old and extinguished. The cardinal, dressed in full regalia, makes a spectacular entrance at the end of the first act, bringing up the rear of a ceremonial procession as it enters the cathedral in Rome. He is preceded by Swiss guards, priests, bishops, and a bevy of nuns. After first parading to the front of the stage, I was directed to swirl my robes around while turning my back to the audience, so I faced the entire congregation as they sang the *Te Deum* chorus for me. As the choir sang the final notes, I was to raise my hand and bless my flock. What an amazing thrill!

During the procession, the villainous chief of police Scarpia sings his aria proclaiming his lust for Tosca. The stage director asked me, as the cardinal, to throw Scarpia a disdainful blessing on my way past him. When I asked how that was done, he suggested that I visit the local Roman Catholic cathedral to perfect my blessing techniques. Dutifully, I showed up at the cathedral the next day and presented myself to the priest, who happened to be entertaining a visit from his bishop. The bishop informed me that cardinals are not usually in the habit of blessing people in the manner I had described (picky, picky), but very graciously coached me on how the benediction was done. From their warm welcome, I later surmised that the priests must have assumed that I was the star tenor instead of just a lowly extra. On opening night, Scarpia had the jitters and asked me to give him a really meaningful blessing.

Anyone who has been asked to join the board of an arts organization realizes that ones ability to raise money is the only criterion that really matters. Accordingly, it was not my brilliant performance in Tosca that prompted an invitation to join Opera Lyra's Board of Directors. Soon after becoming a board member, I was put in charge of the special events portfolio, which meant that I would be chairing the next fundraising gala and would also be responsible for liaison with the various embassies in Ottawa. Persian carpets are a magnet for ambassadors, so I had already met a number of Ottawa's one hundred and fifty foreign emissaries, which gave me a head start for my solicitations. The Ecuadorian ambassador was a good friend, and through him I had met most of the Latin American ambassadors, who incidentally were famous for giving the best diplomatic parties in town. They were also huge opera aficionados, as that art form is integral to South American culture. Just about all of the European ambassadors helped me, as did the American and Mexican delegations.

I managed to expand a program called "Dinner with the Ambassador," which became a very popular evening out for Ottawa's opera lovers. The ambassadors who hosted these lavish dinner parties found that it was a great way to meet prominent Canadians from outside diplomatic and political spheres, while their guests, who paid Opera Lyra for the privilege, got a special evening in a spectacular residence. Once an ambassador had agreed to host a dinner, I had no trouble filling the guest list.

I would often attend these dinners, and, when I did, I would usually propose the toast of thanks to the ambassador. One night at the British High Commission, I quipped during my remarks that I was going to sing an aria as a gesture of appreciation for a wonderful evening - but then demurred to a polite gasp of relief from the diners. However, the High Commissioner got the last laugh. I had not known that he was an amateur singer and that he had planned a small concert after dinner. He called my bluff by handing me the lyrics to a Gilbert and Sullivan ditty and announcing to the guests that I would be joining him for a duet. All great fun!

The first gala that I chaired was held at the rather seedy, but immensely hospitable, Italian Soccer Club. I had invited the Italian Ambassador and the Chief Justice of the Supreme Court to join my table. The RCMP went ballistic, as they had to provide security in a very insecure location. The following year provided a better venue, as I managed to secure the main lobby of the Parliament Buildings for the event. It was just after the 9/11 attack, and ours was the last public event allowed in that location before it became off-limits for private functions. At first the Master-at-Arms (a former navy man) insisted that all the gala guests be subjected to airport style security, but, when I mentioned that the Italian Ambassador had just had a farewell party in the same location without security, he relented and let everyone march in the front entrance.

All the Italian ambassadors that I met during my tenure were devoted opera lovers and very generous donors. The Italian Embassy Garden Party became a highlight of the Ottawa summer. This event for three hundred paying guests was held in the spacious gardens of the ambassador's residence and was followed by an opera concert under the stars. It was a pleasing way to raise money for the company.

After five years on the diplomatic circuit, I resigned from the Opera Lyra board to make way for new blood. I was asked to become the chairman, but my obligations to Canadian Rug Traders made that impossible.

Lisa

Readers who noticed the dedication at the front of this book will have already guessed that I did eventually meet and fall in love with the right woman - my wife, Lisa. At the tender age of sixty-two, after two false starts, I finally met my perfect other half. It happened at the French ambassador's residence during a fundraising dinner/recital by pianist Anton Kuerti. During a break in the festivities, as I was attempting to track down the ambassador to ask him to sponsor an opera event, I noticed Lisa chatting to the ambassador's wife and edged into their conversation as an interim tactic. After a few minutes, I totally forgot my opera mission and concentrated all my efforts into finding out more about this pretty, pert, and vivacious woman who had just entered my world. I knew nothing about her, had never seen her before and was unsure of her marital status. Abandoning my previous shyness, and with little hope of a positive outcome, I found the courage to ask if she was free to have lunch with me. To my utter delight, she was free to accept, and our love was able to blossom unencumbered.

The term "love at first sight" alludes to a situation where two people on first meeting discover an immediate, uninhibited, and total compatibility. In my case it was as if my entire life's experience had been a preparation for meeting Lisa. The timing, however, was absolutely critical. That is to say, if we had met any sooner, neither one of us would have been ready or able to start an exciting new life. That night, we each found an ideal partner who shared the same expectations of life, value system and cultural norms. We saw life through the same prism. No explanations were necessary. Our identities matched flawlessly. We complemented each other perfectly and were emotionally free to engage with each other. We were in love in its purest form. After our first dinner date, we both knew that we would be together for the rest of our lives.

Muscade

When Angus and I started our Ottawa business in 1997, my trusty sailing vessel, *Muscade*, was still moored in the Ionian Islands of Greece, but as my commitment to Canadian Rug Traders became more serious, and my life became more conventional, it appeared less likely that I would ever return to a sea-faring existence. In fact, it seemed far more desirable to have *Muscade* back in the Caribbean, a mere five-hour flight from Ottawa's frigid winters. I hatched the idea of sailing the boat back to the West Indies in stages. This strategy would allow me to continue my exploration of the Mediterranean on the way westwards. The plan included using the remaining time in the Med to completely refit *Muscade* so she would be as good as new for her second Atlantic crossing. Stage one was to sail from Greece to Valetta, the main harbour of the island of Malta, which I had first visited in the sixties as a navy pilot aboard the Canadian aircraft carrier, *Bonaventure*.

After spending a year in Malta, I moved the boat to Menorca, basing her there for a year before moving on to Gibraltar. The last stage was from Gibraltar to the Canary Islands - the traditional departure point for the Atlantic crossing to Barbados in the Caribbean.

One black night during the voyage from Tangiers to the Canaries, we encountered some severe weather, and I found myself up near the mast, reefing the mainsail. Hanging on for dear life as the boat tossed and the waves crashed over the bow forced me to re-evaluate my situation. I was sixty-four and the entire reason for accepting the "old enchanter's" tempting offer at age forty-two had been to embark on an adventurous life while still young enough and physically able to cope with any challenges. During the storm, I had a distinct flash of *déjà vu*. I had acted out this wild adventure many times and had always risen to the occasion. The plan to take *Muscade* back to the Caribbean was not new or exciting. It was returning to well-worn territory, and not using my remaining time to best advantage. After a consultation with Lisa, I decided to base *Muscade* in the Canary Islands for one winter, then sell her and embark upon a completely different dream, to own and cruise a vintage Dutch barge in the canals of France.

A year later, I flew to the island of La Gomera, where we had based *Muscade*, to sail her to the larger island of Tenerife and leave her in the hands of a yacht broker. While cleaning the boat and generally preparing her for the trip, I stuck a "For Sale" sign in the rigging, which almost immediately attracted the attention of a young English couple who were looking for a boat. Even though they wanted to buy a bigger boat, I invited them aboard for a drink and listened to their dreams of sailing down to the Cabo Verde Islands and across to the Caribbean. By the time we parted, I had become engrossed in their plans and suggested that they were welcome to contact me before buying their ideal boat so I could advise them about the purchase. When they found out that I was sailing to Tenerife the next day, they asked if they could come along for the ride, and I was more than happy to have their company. They lived in Los Cristianos, a town on Tenerife and had a profitable business fixing up old houses for resale.

The nostalgic six hour sail to Tenerife was to be my last aboard my faithful *Muscade*. After thirty-three years of adventuring together, two near-fatal encounters, a winter in Bermuda, eight years in the Bahamas, six years in the Caribbean, and eighteen in Europe we were bidding each other *adieu*. *Muscade*, totally refitted and as good as new, was ready to partner with another captain, a younger one ready to wind back the clock to where we had started out together all those many years ago. *Muscade* was ageless, but I was not, and it was time for me to move on to a less demanding lifestyle at a more leisurely pace. This is what the "old enchanter" meant when he said, "that he would not be lured by the gold that I might later offer when age had come upon me." Age had now come upon me, and even though I now had the gold, the "old enchanter" was no longer interested. He was too busy encouraging younger people to make the most of their lives before it was too late for them.

With fifteen knots of wind on the beam, *Muscade* gamboled happily along towards Tenerife with "Heidi" steering and my young English crew relishing every minute, while I spun them yarns about my sailing adventures and served a leisurely lunch. By the time we reached Santa Cruz, my passengers had decided that they had found their perfect boat. *Muscade* had endeared herself to her new owners and was ready to embark on a different tack. Now it was time for us to find that Dutch barge.

Friso

We found *Friso* lying quietly on her moorings in Narbonne, France. She was named after John William Friso (1687-1711), the Friesian prince and heir to the Orange-Nassau dynasty. The owners, a retired British Merchant Marine captain and his Australian wife, had lived aboard happily for many years, but now had to sell because of health problems. *Friso*, a Dutch sailing barge, was built of riveted iron in 1907 and immediately entered service as a bulk carrier on the Zuiderzee in Holland. The German occupation force commandeered her for use during World War Two, and she remained in service as a cargo-carrying, sailing barge (no engine) until 1965, when she was bought by a Dutch couple, given a Mercedes diesel engine and converted into a comfortable live-aboard vessel. She was sixty-two feet long and weighed thirty-five tons. The accommodations were superb: two double sleeping cabins, separated by a spacious bathroom, an open plan main salon/

dining area with a step-down kitchen and the *pièce de resistance*, a wheelhouse with wrap-around windows and a comfortable window seat. *Friso* met all of our expectations, so we completed the purchase arrangements without hesitation. The deal included a permanent mooring in Narbonne.

Muscade had been based in Malta when I met Lisa, so I was able to introduce her to my sailing world during many holidays in Menorca, Gibraltar and the Canaries, although she never joined me for the delivery trips between those places. While she was extremely brave and open to learning, sailing was not really her preferred activity. The barge was different. She loved it and soon became a very competent deckhand, handling the mooring lines in the locks like a seasoned deckhand.

Canal barging is the antithesis of ocean sailing. There is absolutely no stress. There are no weather problems, and no navigational worries. Mooring can be instantly accomplished by pulling over to the bank and tying up to a tree. Any mechanical problems can be solved by letting the barge drift to one bank or the other, phoning a mechanic and opening a good bottle of wine. There is unlimited fresh water available, and provisioning in France is a dream. A typical day would start by cycling to the *boulangerie* for croissants, getting underway mid-morning, pulling over to the bank for lunch and finding a charming village with a good restaurant for the overnight stay. Good wine was completely taken for granted.

Friso had all the comforts of home, and we spared no expense with the furnishings, including some custom-made oriental carpets courtesy of my suppliers in Pakistan. I knew that she was to be my last boat, so we made the very best of our time aboard. Typically we would cruise for six weeks every May/June and six weeks every September/October. It was an idyllic lifestyle, which we shared with many friends and family members. After eight years of cruising, we sold *Friso* to an Australian couple, who are, at this writing, still happily cruising all over Europe during the Aussie winter.

Opera Act Two

Five years after resigning from the Board of Opera Lyra, I was asked to re-join as the chairman. I had started to wind down my involvement with Canadian Rug Traders, working only during my brother's holiday breaks and doing occasional buying trips. After consulting with Lisa, I somewhat reluctantly agreed to accept yet another invitation. It was an excellent example of my "smoke and mirrors" theory, as I had no idea what I was getting into or what was expected of me. Certainly, I could chair a board meeting, make a speech and work the room at various events, but that was the limit of my experience. I also privately wondered, "why me?" but was reassured that the nominating committee had unanimously agreed on my appointment. I knew that I would be inheriting some accumulated debt, about ten per cent of the annual budget, which seemed manageable. I rushed out to get a copy of *Opera Management for Dummies,*" but the bookstore was sold out - an ominous sign.

The list of my board members read like a copy of the "Who's Who in Canada." Former Canadian ambassadors, heads of crown corporations, assistant deputy ministers, prominent lawyers, the C.E.O. of the National Arts Centre, titans of industry, journalists, university professors, and former military bigwigs. The opera company's patron was the Chief Justice of the Supreme Court, and my advisory council included the Prime Minister's wife and a generous hi-tech millionaire. Impressive as the Board was on paper, I soon discovered that only a few members were pulling their weight. As is often the case with volunteer boards, some members were actually taking more in benefits than they were giving in contributions, while a few had insinuated their way onto the Board solely to enhance their social standing in the community.

The first "red flag" went up when my predecessor refused to meet me for a turnover briefing. I invited him and his wife to dinner, offering them open dates over a two-week period, but they declined all invitations. Then he resigned from the Board shortly after I took over, even though, as past chairman, he was supposed to be on my Executive Committee. The rats were starting to leave the sinking ship: I had no idea why, but I knew that I had to find out quickly where it was leaking.

One of my first unpleasant tasks was to write letters to several board members who had not paid their annual dues to the company. Even though these amounts were paltry compared to other opera companies, my Finance Committee's attempt to raise them was voted down by the Board, and several members threatened to resign if their dues were increased. The Board with over twenty-five members, was clearly too cumbersome. To make matters worse, most members had been automatically re-appointed many times after their three-year term limit had been waived, so many of them had been serving for a very long time indeed. However, as bad as the situation was, there seemed no pressing need to rebuild the Board. Clearly, managing the staff, overseeing the daily operations of the company, reducing the debt and producing first rate opera had to be my first priority.

After becoming Chairman, I insisted on attending the weekly staff meetings and I interviewed all my staff members individually. It was obvious that there were personality conflicts, leadership problems and financial woes, as well as general incompetence and low morale in the office. The Artistic Director was the only staff member doing his job properly, but he had a disdainful and distant working relationship with the General Director. The General Director appeared to be completely out of her depth, and I judged that she should never have been appointed to that position, in the first place. The Board had promoted her from her previous position as company bookkeeper when the Artistic Director wanted more time off to further his conducting career. Until that change, he had been doing both jobs quite successfully. In promoting her, the Board took the line-of-least-resistance instead of conducting a proper search for a qualified person. Now I was left to pick up the pieces and deal with the consequences of that bad decision. One of my board members, a respected human resources expert, agreed to assess the problems in the office, and after her investigation she confirmed my suspicions that things were even worse than I thought.

All this was unfolding during rehearsals for our next opera, Macbeth. This opera's name is believed by theatre insiders to be jinxed, so is often alluded to as simply the "Scottish opera," a superstition which apparently helps mitigate the curse. For Opera Lyra, Macbeth was indeed cursed at the box office, so even though the production was excellent, we lost more money than expected.

Most North American opera companies can count on roughly three per cent of their city's population attending opera performances - but not in Canada's capital city where the number was less than one per cent. Due to poor box-office sales, Macbeth simply added to the company's growing accumulated debt. Because ticket sales cover only a small percentage of overall costs, all operas lose money on each performance even with a full house. The short-fall has to be made up by grants, donations and fundraising events.

A little light came into my life when a prospective board member offered to donate a very large gift to the company. He wanted to make sure that he was not throwing good money after bad, so I met with my General Director to get a briefing on our actual cash position. She assured me that, apart from our accumulated debt, everything was rosy, and there were no out-standing bills to pay. Later that same evening, I received a personal phone call at home from the General Director of the San Francisco Opera, whom I knew. He asked me when we intended to pay the money we owed for the set of Magic Flute, which had been rented from his company two years previously. I was furious. My General Director was falsifying the truth to hide her incompetence. She had not committed fraud, but was lying to hide the fact that she was unable and unqualified to do her job. My Finance Committee members and I had been stupidly naïve and far too trusting.

As the General Director was leaving on a two-week vacation, I told her that I would take over her job in her absence, which did not please her. On my first day at her desk, I uncovered an unmitigated disaster, far worse than anyone could have suspected and completely hidden from the Board's supposed oversight. We were six months in arrears on our office rent. The phone lines were scheduled to be cut off at the end of the week. A cheque for the set rental of our next opera - scheduled to open in a month - had bounced, as had a cheque to the transport company which was delivering it. The bank account was overdrawn to the maximum credit limit, and there was a full payroll to be met at the end of the week. In addition, I found a stack of cheques issued by our accountant, but not mailed out by the General Director because she knew that there was not enough money in the bank to cover them. One of the cheques was to the Ottawa Convention Centre for the catering of our last gala. I also found several of the General Director's un-cashed salary cheques in this bundle. We were in serious financial trouble.

I summoned our account manager from the bank the next day and asked him to bring all the monthly statements for the last two years. The statements revealed that one of my board members had illegally co-signed a large margin of credit to help out her friend, the General Director, without telling the Board or the Finance Committee. The bank should never have authorized this credit extension. I also found out that the current financial statements, as presented to the Annual General Meeting, had been falsified, and had not been properly audited. I was in full crisis mode and immediately ordered a moratorium on all bill payments. Lisa and I personally covered the Friday payroll.

At an emergency board meeting, we appointed an interim General Director, a man who came out of retirement, agreeing to work for a nominal sum to help the company get back on its feet. He had been the vice president of operations for one of Canada's largest crown corporations, and was an extremely competent administrator. When the General Director came back from her holiday, I relieved her of her duties, but kept her on staff temporarily, as I needed her knowledge to ensure a smooth transition. She had been a one-person show, and all the company's documents were stored on her personal computer. It was absolutely essential that I access that data and down-load it into the company's records. The office files were non-existent, meaning that there was not enough data available for an accounting firm to do a proper audit.

It was too late to cancel the opera Pagliacci already in rehearsal. The title - the Italian word for clowns - pretty well described the staff and board members I was trying to save from ruin. I made an appearance on stage before each performance to appeal for money from the audience, with limited results. The production was artistically acclaimed, but, once again, we lost more money than expected on each of the four performances. The final sentence in the libretto uttered by the crazed and cuckolded killer clown, Canio, is "La commedia è finita," which proved to be more prophetic than I could ever have imagined.

After Pagliacci, my interim General Director and I went into full recovery mode. First, we cancelled the entire up-coming season, while managing to persuade most subscribers to donate their ticket money back to the company in return for a tax receipt. My Artistic Director negotiated favourable terms with the singers we had under contract for future operas, some of whom generously waived their contracts without any compensation. We worked with the National Arts Centre and with the arts funding agencies of all three levels of government to refill the coffers. The National Arts Centre was our biggest creditor, so they had a vested interest in our survival and insisted that we engage a skilled arts administrator to help our interim General Director. Because we were on the verge of financial ruin, they hired and paid the salary for a performing arts expert, who was able to concentrate on rebuilding the company artistically, while my General Director and I worked on the finances. After six months, we were ready to start thinking about producing opera once again, but not before we had consulted bankruptcy lawyers as a contingency, in case our best efforts failed.

Several of my board members came to the rescue during the crisis by making generous donations to keep the company going. Others, concerned that they were liable for the company's failure - as indeed they were - resigned from the Board, saving me considerable trouble later. Now was the time to recruit a new Board, trim the numbers to a maximum of ten and impose obligatory three-year term limits. The new term limits disqualified most of my Board members and automatically helped to clear the decks. I managed to recruit an extremely qualified board member who eventually took over from me as chairman when my three-year term was completed. He had been an assistant deputy minister for a Canadian government department, C.E.O. of the Museum of Civilization, loved opera and knew exactly how to handle Ottawa's political machinations. Between us, we put together an excellent, competent Board and initiated a worldwide search for a new General Director. As there was no budget for this search, the National Arts Centre agreed to let us put the costs on our tab, which was now approaching a gigantic sum.

Alas, like most operas librettos, this saga eventually came to an unhappy ending - although nobody died. My search committee found and hired an excellent General Director from the United States who picked up the pieces and began an admirable job of running the company. My successor as chairman and his Board - perhaps the most qualified in the company's history - took the helm and got the lumbering ship sailing again. Unfortunately during the crisis, and unknown to anyone, the potential opera audience in Ottawa had dwindled to staggeringly low numbers, and after three years of valiant efforts by all concerned, Opera Lyra failed. The last opera, the popular Marriage of Figaro, attracted a dismal one-quarter of one per cent of the population. Ottawa, the capital of a G-8 nation could no longer support an opera company (or a ballet company for that matter). The situation was scandalous and a pathetic commentary on the cultural landscape of Canada's capital.

When I first took over Opera Lyra, I tried to solicit the support of a wealthy philanthropist who loved opera. After assessing the situation, he concluded that any contribution he made would not help the company because there was no critical mass of support for live opera in Ottawa. Unfortunately, he proved to be absolutely correct.

Opera Lyra's demise begs the question about the future prospects for opera companies worldwide. In the past few years, due to dwindling audiences, at least ten cities in North America have lost their opera companies, including Baltimore, Cleveland, Spokane and the New York City Opera. Under Peter Gelb's management, the Metropolitan Opera initiated a program to screen their operas live in participating movie theatres throughout the world. In Ottawa these broadcasts are very popular, but ironically, were also detrimental to Opera Lyra, as it was much easier for opera aficionados to drive to a big box movie complex with free parking and cheap popcorn to hear the best voices in the world than it was to get dressed up and drive to the National Arts Centre to see live opera. One can hardly blame them. Soon after the Met initiative to screen live opera, La Scala in Milan and Covent Garden in London followed suit. Ironically, these initiatives seem to be increasing the general popularity of opera while simultaneously forcing small companies out of business.

Unfortunately, when small opera companies fail, the entire support system for the larger companies also crumbles because the seedbed for singers, conductors and directors withers. In most European countries, opera is subsidized by the state, but these grants are constantly being cut back. Opera audiences worldwide - at live performances and in the cinemas - are represented by a grey haired demographic. Even in Italy, young people have little interest in opera. This sad situation is not surprising when one considers the costly infrastructure and logistical support needed to produce opera: a large opera house, a full symphony orchestra, elaborate sets and costumes, virtuoso singers, a qualified opera conductor, a creative stage director, sophisticated lighting and often an elaborate chorus and dance troupe. Attempts have been made to stage minimalist productions, but these rarely meet with success. It seems that live opera is bound to eventually disappear from our culture, although the music will surely endure.

High Spirits

Even though I am not superstitious and think that anything occult is nonsense and have no faith in anyone's God, I have encountered an inexplicable spiritual presence on two separate occasions.

The first time was in Sun Valley, Idaho, when we were visiting Lisa's ageing aunt, who was living out her final years in a small granny flat attached to her son's house. When I answered a knock on her bedroom door, I found myself face to face with the Dalai Lama. As I shook his outstretched hand, looked into his smiling face and mumbled something about, "meeting your holiness," I definitely felt a higher spiritual presence. The Dalai Lama was a friend of Lisa's cousin and had been invited to Sun Valley to convene a seminar on compassion.

The second experience was in Rome at the Vatican. I had been invited to attend the investiture of an archbishop whom I had befriended when he was serving as an assistant to the Papal Nuncio in Ottawa. The ceremony was Roman Catholic theatre at its impressive best, with superb choir music and pageantry. The candidate spent most of the ceremony lying face down on a Persian carpet in front of the altar. When he eventually did get to his feet, he proceeded down the aisle to bless the congregation. I was sitting on the aisle and got the full force of his delivery, which proved to be a second spiritual experience. He knew that I was a non-believer, which may have been one reason I had been invited.

At the champagne cocktail party and formal dinner in the Vatican after the event, I got the distinct impression that the numerous cardinals, archbishops and bishops involved as Vatican administrators were far more concerned about their career paths than about religious doctrine, which seemed a secondary consideration. At any rate, I got a peek into an affluent world of impeccably dressed intellectuals with expensive tastes and wondered about their millions of dirt-poor followers.

Of the two experiences, the one with the Dalai Lama was by far the most intense and most spiritual and I will cherish that amazing encounter for a long time.

Last Hurrah

If I were invited to give a speech to a university graduating class anywhere in the developed world, I would tell the students: Congratulations, after winning the lottery of birth you have now leveraged that birthright with study and hard work into a university degree. Life is a grand game of chance and adventure with very few rules, the principal one being: do no harm. The game becomes easier to negotiate once you realize that you are actually walking backwards through life, so you can never see where you are going and have no idea what lies in your path or where that path will lead. To complicate matters, looking back on the road already travelled will not give you a clear perspective of the recent past. It takes several years before a realistic analysis of where you have been comes into focus and becomes useful data. Thus, patience becomes crucial to understanding life.

For example, if at the age of thirty, you cast back and remember what you thought about yourself at twenty, you will realize that you were doubly wrong: wrong about your relevance to the world at that time, and wrong about where you thought you would be today. Expect these same misconceptions to replay in similar fashion through all your iterations until the end of the game. Your younger-age analysis of life will always be incorrect in retrospect. Understanding and accepting these realities makes the game easier to play, because you will perceive that life is less serious than you were led to believe. Accepting that you can never predict the future will encourage you to live for the moment, stress the importance of flexibility, emphasize the role of serendipity and ease disappointments when things don't work out as planned.

There are no tangible prizes for winning this game: none for longevity, none for wealth accumulation, none for being a "celebrity" because any fame or other legacy will soon fade into obscurity. The game can last until you are very old or be terminated at any time. The real prizes for winning are self-esteem, peace of mind, serenity and self-confidence induced by knowledge. Having no regrets, fear or envy gives you bonus points.

I would add that it is essential to have realistic dreams, avoid mediocrity at all costs and not be overly concerned about tomorrow. Never be afraid to make mistakes. Make plans, but be flexible even as you make firm commitments to put them into action. Never refuse or defer invitations or chances to embark on something new and different. Draw strength from the arts, music, poetry, literature and the fidelity of nature, Above all, always keep an eye out for "old enchanter." Follow his advice, and don't disappoint him if he comes to call.

Printed and bound by PG in the USA